A Matter of Taste

The Junior League of Morristown, Inc.
Morristown, New Jersey

The Junior League of Morristown, Inc.
Morristown, New Jersey

The Junior League of Morristown, Inc. is an organization of women committed to promoting voluntarism, to developing the potential of women, and to improving communities through the effective action and leadership of trained volunteers. Its purpose is exclusively educational and charitable.

The proceeds realized from the sale of *A MATTER OF TASTE* will be returned to the community through the projects of The Junior League of Morristown, Inc.

Additional copies may be obtained by addressing:

A MATTER OF TASTE
The Junior League of Morristown, Inc.
7 King Place
Morristown, New Jersey 07960

For your convenience, order forms are included in the back of the book.

The Junior League of Morristown, Inc. wishes to thank all those who have contributed their time and expertise to A MATTER OF TASTE:

Wine Suggestions:	Henry Nunez, The Chatham Wine Shop
	James M. Teegan, Wine Cellars of Barnardsville
Cover Artwork:	Kean College Design Production Studio
Cover Artwork:	Kean College Design Production Studio
Interior Artwork:	Kean College Art Department
	Ed Terantino
Manuscript Computer Input:	Jennifer Hiser
Endpaper Artwork:	Adaptation of Haviland & Co.
	pattern, Imperatrice Eugenie

First Printing, June, 1989
Second Printing, April, 1990
Third Printing, February 1998

A Tradition of Training Woman to Build a Stronger Community

cookbook resources

541 Doubletree Drive
Highland Village TX 75067
(972) 317-0245

Table of Contents

Introduction

Taste, as we refer to it in this cookbook, cannot be explained by mere physiology. It is as individual as temperament, and just as hard to define.

From infancy, a child begins to express preferences and dislikes in food. These evolve throughout our lives, affected by scent and vision, circumstance and memory. We make associations with food that include far more than its flavor. The wonderful smell of a holiday meal, the dark gleaming bronze of the turkey are linked in our minds with family, tradition, and congeniality. It is this memory, as well as our taste buds that brings us pleasure from a meal.

That most renowned of food essayists, M.F.K. Fisher, recalls a time when she was about 10 years old and her father drove her and her little sister, Anne, back to Los Angeles from Great Aunt Maggie's ranch. They had left her mother behind to help with the canning, which gave the girls some private time alone with their father. They stopped beside a stream, bought some water to drink, and ate the supper which the cook had packed for them. Mrs. Fisher does not remember now what they ate except for a peach pie, still warm from the oven, with lots of thick, cold cream. Her father cut the pie into three pieces for them to share, and with the sharing of this meal came her realization that food was something more than a daily necessity. All three, in later years remembered that simple meal as one of the most delicious they have ever experienced.

Whether you prefer relatively simple recipes or ones that are more complex, the variety of unique selections in A MATTER OF TASTE will enable you to serve many memorable meals. It is up to you to provide the ambiance. To help you make these culinary works unforgetable, we have included serving and garnishing suggestions with many of the recipes, as well as sample menus for creating that perfect, special event.

We believe we have achieved a balance of ease and elegance in these recipes, and have also included a few which may be considered challenging. All, we assure you, will work. Over the past two years we collected and triple tested over 2,000 recipes from our members. From these we have selected the best 300 or so. This was not an easy task. There was such diversity of opinion in choosing among the final outstanding recipes that in some cases a fourth test was required — which just proves our point: it's all "A Matter Of Taste!"

The Cookbook Committee

Overview

The Junior League of Morristown, Inc. (JLM) is an organization of women committed to promoting voluntarism, to developing the potential of women, and to improving communities through the effective action and leadership of trained volunteers. Its purpose is exclusively educational and charitable. JLM is one of 8 Junior Leagues in New Jersey and one of 290 Leagues in the United States, England, Canada, and Mexico. JLM was established in 1936 and since that time JLM has initiated a wide range of community volunteer projects benefitting women, children, the elderly, and the arts. These projects are developed by JLM's volunteers after a lengthy research process to identify community needs. To facilitate project startup, JLM provides short-term financial and volunteer assistance. Once this is done, a project will be turned over to another community organization for long-term management, if it is appropriate.

JLM's projects have ranged from *Children's Theater*, where JLM volunteers helped children learn about the arts, to *Chemocare* where volunteers provided support to women dealing with cancer, to the *Nursing Home Guide* which helped people find nursing homes for loved ones to *Born to Read*, a program which reinforces with new mothers the importance of reading to their children. JLM also helped found enduring organizations, including the *Jersey Battered Women's Shelter*, the *Arts Council of the Morris Area*, and *Volunteers for Morris County*, all which have significantly impacted the lives of others.

During the 1996-97 year JLM undertook five new community projects: helping to found a *Christmas in April* chapter in Morris County to rehabilitate homes of the elderly and disabled; a *Rainbows Program*, a discussion group to help elementary school children dealing with death and divorce; a *Story Circle* reading program for children at the Jersey Battered Women's Shelter; with the *Deirdre O'Brien Child Advocacy Center* in Morristown. These projects join the *League's Marrow Donor Typing Program*, a *Nearly New Thrift Shop*, a *Scholarship* program recognizing high school seniors with excellence in voluntarism and a *Community Grants* program.

JLM has an active membership of 150 women from Morris and Somerset Counties. Women join the Junior League for many reasons including the opportunity to help others through the services and projects sponsored by JLM; for the opportunity to learn new skills available through training programs sponsored by the Junior League; and for the opportunity to make new friends.

With a worldwide membership of 193,000 women, the Junior League is today one of the leading volunteer organizations for women. It is an organization which welcomes women from all walks of life, growing and changing to better meet the needs of a multicultural, highly diverse membership of single and married women, working at home and outside the home. Founded in 1901 by Mary Harriman from New York to meet the needs of the poor and disadvantaged, the Junior League has a rich history of community service and voluntarism. Women who join the Junior League of Morristown, Inc. join this worldwide volunteer organization.

For questions on JLM's community projects or membership, please call
the JLM office at 973-539-2266

Fishawack Barbecue

In 1926, hundreds of people, dozens of horses, oxen and other livestock participated in a "Three Towns Pagent", a collaboration of residents of Chatham, Madison and Summit. Chathamites protrayed the Lene Lenape Indians and the "Crossing of the Fishawack" (now the Passaic River). Now, the town of Chatham hosts a Fishawack Festival every other year, featuring artists, craftsmen, and a gigantic barbecue in front of the town firehouse.

Marinated Barbecued Shrimp
Salad Soup
Cheddar Crisps

Peas, Please
New Potato Salad
Barbecued Butterflied Leg of Lamb
Naked Apple Pie

Whatney's English Ale
Iced Tea

Princeton Tailgate Party

The first college football game was played on November 6, 1869 in New Brunswick, New Jersey. Rutgers defeated the College of New Jersey (now Princeton University) 6 to 4. A tradition of tailgating followed.

Vegetable Pizazz

Cold Spinach Soup

Picnic Hamper Salad
Medieval Parsley Bread
Cold Steak Salad
Wine: Kendall Jackson Sauvignon Blanc

Date Bars and Back-to-Basic Brownies

Après Ski Buffet

Vernon Valley Great Gorge is New Jersey's own answer to the exhilarating sport of skiing. The wonderful rural village of Vernon offers three great mountains and features more than 25 miles of interconnecting skiable terrain.

Camembert Sauté with Bradens Hunter's Mustard

Almost Ceasar Salad
Savory Wheat French Bread
Veal Marengo
Wine: Joseph Drougin Laforet Pinot Noir

Very Vanilla Ice Cream with Jamocha Rum Sauce
Coffee

After-Theater Supper

The New Jersey Shakespeare Festival was founded in 1963 in Cape May, New Jersey. Currently located at Drew University in Madison, the Actors' Equity company presents five plays annually; drawing from the works of Shakespeare, as well as classic and contemporary works. By the early 1990's the repertory company expects to become one of only a dozen theatres around the world to have presented the entire Shakespearean canon.

Tuscany Toast

Romaine and Endive Salad
Pasta and Prawns
Wine: Jordan Winery Chardonnay

Chocolate Fleck Cream Cake
Coffee and Tea

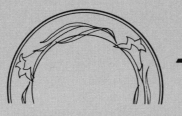

Menus

A Black Tie Evening at Drumthwacket

This historical treasure is the official residence of the Governor of New Jersey. Drumthwacket, derived from two old Celtic words meaning "wooded hills", was built in 1835 by Charles Olden, the 28th Governor of New Jersey. The mansion has been the site for many State affairs and charitable events.

Steamed Artichokes Verde
Wine: Robert Mondavi Pinot Noir

Crêpes Coquilles
Wine: Bridgehampton Chardonnay

Blueberry Sorbert

Carrots a la Champagne
Parsley Potatoes
Lobster Stuffed Tenderloin
Wine: Louis Latour Mersault

Salad with Warm Brie Dressing
Sterling Rolls

Charlotte Russe Supreme
Sparkling Ruby

Mocha Truffles
Demi Tasse

Pre-Concert Luncheon at Waterloo Village

This quaint, 18th century village lies along the banks of the Morris Canal. Guides in period costume lead tours through the apothecary, gristmill and furnished homes. Enjoy lunch with friends before one of the summer concerts held there.

Welcome Wafers
Wine: Sanderman Character Sherry

Mushroom Chive Bisque

Three Vegetable Pâté
Frenchtown Bread
Chicken Salad Suprème
Wine: Schramsberg Crémant Champagne

Lime'n Gin Fizz
Snowballs
Coffee and Tea

Victorian Tea at Cape May

As the nation's oldest seaside resort, this Victorian town is noted for its gingerbread architecture, gaslights and tree lined avenues. Many of its lovely Victorian homes offer Bed and Breakfast accomodations to visitors.

Victorian Lace Cookies
Sugar Cakes
Mini Pecan Tarts
Watercress Tea Sandwiches
Hot Mushroom Turnovers
Fudge Cake with Chocolate Silk Frosting
Creme Quadroon

Earl Grey Tea and Orange Spice Tea

A Gathering before Apple Picking at Fosterfields

In 1976, Fosterfields was designated as the first living historical farm in New Jersey. This 200 acre facility offers the public an opporunity to learn about turn-of-the-century farming techniques and to experience New Jersey's agricultural heritage.

Somerset Cider
Proper Brown Bread with Cream Cheese
Pineapple Puff
Vintage Ham with Grapes
Cranberry Crown Cake
Coffee and Tea

Gourmet Dinner after the Hunt

An annual Autumn festivity in New Jersey is the Far Hills Race Meet. This tent and tailgating event has been a mid-October tradition at Moorlands Farms in Somerset County since 1920. Friends gather to watch the horses race, celebrate the seasonal change and enjoy good food among friends.

Fresh Salmon Mousse with Two Sauces
Wine: Alsatian Trimbach Pinot Blanc

Tomatoes Brookhollow
Grilled Potatoes
Veal Chops with Pesto
Wine: Jordan Winery Cabernet Sauvignon

Endive and Edible Flower Salad
White Chocolate Mousse with Raspberry Sauce
Wine: Schramsberg Cuvee De Pinol

APPETIZERS
and
BEVERAGES

Appetizers and Beverages

Appetizers

Bradens Hunter's Mustard, 20
Brie en Croûte, 18
Camembert Sauté, 20
Cheddar Crisps, 29
Cheese and Wine Mold, 18
Chicken Pillows, 22
Country Pâté, 27
Escargot Pâté, 24
Fresh Salmon Mousse with
   Two Sauces, 19
Hot Mushroom Turnovers, 21
Layered Brie and Pesto, 17
Marinated Barbecued Shrimp, 23
Morristown Mushrooms, 26
Sea Girt Shrimp Spectacular, 26
Sesame Chicken with
   Honey Dip, 23
Superbowl Sausage Puff, 25
Tuscany Toast, 28
Vegetable Pizzaz, 28
Welcome Wafers, 24

Beverages

Apricot Delight, 35
Banana Frost, 32
Breakfast Berry Blizzard, 30
Citrus Cup, 35
Orange Julius, 30
Peach Blossom, 33
Somerset Cider, 31
Sparkling Ruby, 34
Strawberry Bowl, 31
Strawberry Rum Snow, 34
Tequila Snowcones, 32
Whiskey Tea 'n Sea, 33

Layered Brie and Pesto

A wonderful collage of flavors, perfect for a party buffet

1 cup firmly packed, chopped fresh basil
³/4 cup grated Parmesan cheese
¹/2 cup firmly packed, chopped fresh
    parsley
¹/4 cup pine nuts or walnuts
2 cloves garlic, quartered
¹/3 cup olive oil

1 (8 ounce) package cream cheese,
    softened
4¹/2 ounces Brie cheese, rind removed,
    softened
¹/2 cup whipping cream

Yield: 4 cup mold

- Use a blender or food processor to combine fresh basil, Parmesan cheese, fresh parsley, pine nuts, and garlic.

- Cover and process with several on/off turns until a paste forms. Stop machine several times to scrape down sides. With machine running, slowly add olive oil and process to the consistency of soft butter.

- Beat cheeses together in a small bowl until almost smooth.

- In another bowl, whip cream until soft peaks form.

- Fold whipped cream into cheese mixture.

- Line a 4 cup bowl or mold with several layers of plastic wrap. Spread ¹/4 of the cheese mixture in mold. Spread ¹/3 of the pesto filling over cheese mixture. Repeat layers twice. Spread remaining cheese mixture on top. Cover and chill overnight.

- Unmold and peel off plastic wrap. Garnish with fresh sprigs of basil and parsley, making a green wreath at the base. Serve with unsalted crackers.

Brie en Croûte

Flaky and golden on the outside, luscious and sensual on the inside

1   (12 ounce) jar apricot preserves
1   (1 pound) round Brie
1   (17½ ounce) package frozen puff
       pastry
1   egg
1   teaspoon water

Yield: 8 servings

- Preheat oven to 400°.

- Spread apricot preserves on top of Brie.

- Defrost pastry and lightly roll. Set Brie on one sheet of pastry and cut to fit so that pastry reaches up and around sides of Brie, even with top. Cut second piece of pastry to fit the top. Seal top to bottom and decoratively flute seam.

- Cut out leaves and flowers from pastry scraps. Beat together egg and water to make an egg wash. Affix pastry leaves and flowers to top with egg wash and then brush over entire pastry surface.

- Bake for 25 minutes at 400°.

- Baked Brie should sit for 45 minutes to 1 hour before cutting.

- Serve with apples, grapes, strawberries, or crackers.

Cheese and Wine Mold

A vintage delight . . . imagine it served on a wintry eve in front of a crackling fire.

2½   cups grated sharp cheddar cheese
⅛   teaspoon nutmeg
⅛   teaspoon white pepper
¼   cup dry white wine, such as French
       Blanc de Blanc
4   tablespoons butter, softened

Yield: 2 cup mold

- Combine cheese, nutmeg, and pepper in a small bowl.

- Heat wine just to boiling and pour over cheese. Beat for 10 minutes with mixer.

- Add butter and pour into oiled 2 cup mold. Chill over night. Unmold. Let stand at room temperature for one hour before serving.

- Serve with apple and pear wedges.

Fresh Salmon Mousse with Two Sauces

An elegant, refreshing, and attractive first course.

Salmon Mousse:
1   envelope unflavored gelatin
1/4   cup cold water
1/2   cup boiling water
1/2   cup mayonnaise
1   tablespoon lemon juice
1   tablespoon grated onion
1/2   teaspoon Tabasco
1/4   teaspoon paprika
1   teaspoon salt
2   cups cooked fresh salmon
1   tablespoon chopped capers
1/2   cup heavy cream

Sour Cream Dill Sauce:
1   egg
1   teaspoon salt
pinch fresh ground black pepper
pinch sugar
4   teaspoons lemon juice
1   teaspoon grated onion
2   tablespoons finely chopped fresh dill
1 1/2   cups sour cream

Sauce Verde:
1/2   cup mayonnaise
1/2   cup sour cream
5   sprigs watercress
5   sprigs parsley
1   green onion, minced
1/2   teaspoon salt
1/4   teaspoon dried dill weed

Garnish:
lemon slices
salmon roe
watercress

Yield: 3 cup mold

The Salmon Mousse:
- Soften gelatin in cold water. Add boiling water and stir until gelatin is dissolved. Cool.

- To the dissolved gelatin, add mayonnaise, lemon juice, onion, Tabasco, paprika, and salt. Mix well and chill to consistency of unbeaten egg whites.

- In a food processor, finely chop salmon. Add chilled gelatin and process to form a purée.

- By hand, stir in capers.

- Whip cream until thick and fold in salmon purée.

- Turn into an oiled 3 cup mold and chill until set.

The Dill Sauce:
- Beat egg until fluffy and lemon colored.

- Add salt, pepper, sugar, lemon juice, onion, and dill. Mix well. Blend in sour cream and chill.

The Sauce Verde:
- Put all ingredients in a blender. Cover and whirl on high until smooth. Chill.

Note: The salmon mousse can be made in a fish mold with sauces served on the side for presentation. To serve as a first course, the mousse can be made in a round or loaf mold with slices served on individual plates and sauces decoratively poured over top. Garnish with lemon slices, salmon roe, and watercress.

Camembert Sauté

Excellent served with Bradens Hunter's Mustard.

Cheese:
1   (6″ round) Camembert cheese, medium soft, rind removed
1   egg, beaten
1   cup bread crumbs
4   tablespoons unsalted butter
$^1/_2$ cup chopped green onion tops

Garnish:
seedless grapes

Yield: 12 servings

- Dip the cheese in the egg and then coat both sides with bread crumbs.

- Heat 2 tablespoons butter in a skillet until it starts to brown. Over high heat, brown the cheese round on both sides. The outside of the cheese should be crispy. Remove to a heated serving platter and keep warm.

- Add the remaining butter to the skillet. When foamy, sauté the onions for 2 minutes. Pour over cheese and serve immediately.

- Serve with stoneground wheat crackers. Garnish with small clusters of seedless grapes.

Bradens Hunter's Mustard

A hot and spicy condiment to serve with cheese, ham, sausage, or cold sliced meat.

$^1/_2$ cup distilled white vinegar
1   cup Coleman's dry mustard
1   egg
$^3/_4$ cup brown sugar
$^1/_2$ cup sugar
$1^1/_2$ teaspoons curry powder
$1^1/_2$ teaspoons oregano
$1^1/_2$ teaspoons dill weed
2   teaspoons parsley flakes

Yield: 2 cups

- Stir together vinegar and mustard. Let sit at room temperature overnight.

- Beat egg slightly and combine with sugars. Stir into mustard mixture. Add spices and mix well.

- Turn mustard into the top of double boiler and cook until mixture thickens. Remove from heat and cool.

- Spoon into a jar or container that can be sealed. Chill.

Note: The mustard will keep indefinitely in the refrigerator.

Hot Mushroom Turnovers

Be prepared for the compliments; these always get rave reviews!

Dough:

3   (3 ounce) packages cream cheese, softened
1/2 cup butter, softened
1 1/2 cups flour, sifted

Mushroom Filling:

1/2 pound mushrooms, sliced
1   large onion, minced
3   tablespoons butter
1   teaspoon salt
1/4 teaspoon thyme
2   tablespoons flour
1/4 cup sour cream
1   egg, beaten

Yield: 4 dozen

The Dough:
- With an electric mixer, beat together the cream cheese, butter, and flour until a soft dough forms. Wrap dough in wax paper and refrigerate for 1 1/2 hours.

The Mushroom Filling:
- Over medium heat cook mushrooms and onions in butter until tender.

- Stir in salt, thyme, and flour. Stir in sour cream. Cool filling.

The Turnovers:
- Preheat oven to 450°. Grease 2 cookie sheets.

- On a well floured surface, using a floured rolling pin, roll out half the dough. Keep the rest of the dough refrigerated. Roll dough 1/4" thickness and cut into rounds with a 2 3/4" or 3" diameter cookie cutter.

- On each round place 1 teaspoon of filling. Brush edges with beaten egg. Fold round in half and press edges together with a fork to seal. Prick the top of the turnover with a fork so steam can escape during the baking. Repeat with remaining dough and filling. Can be frozen at this point.

- Place turnovers on prepared cookie sheets and brush with beaten egg.

- Bake at 450° for 12 – 15 minutes or until golden brown.

- Serve hot.

Chicken Pillows

Everyone wants just one more of these flaky, tender bites . . . they're irresistible.

2   whole chicken breasts, skinned,
       boned, and halved (about 1 pound)
3   tablespoons lemon juice
2   tablespoons olive or vegetable oil
1   teaspoon finely chopped garlic
1   teaspoon oregano
1/2 cup butter
1/2 pound phyllo or strudel leaves

Yield: 2 dozen

- Cut the chicken into 1" cubes. Combine lemon juice, oil, garlic, and oregano in a small bowl. Mix well. Add chicken and turn to coat with marinade. Cover and refrigerate overnight.

- Preheat oven to 400°.

- Melt butter over low heat. Unwrap phyllo or strudel leaves and place on a sheet of wax paper. (Keep phyllo covered with another sheet of wax paper or a slightly damp tea towel at all times to prevent drying out.) Cut leaves in half, lengthwise, with scissors. You will have two sets of long strips, about 6" wide. Take one strip, fold in half crosswise and brush with melted butter.

- Place two pieces of chicken at short end and roll up in pastry to midpoint. Fold edges of pastry in, like a package, and continue rolling.

- Brush all over with butter and place on a cookie sheet. Repeat with remaining chicken and strips. (Pastries may be frozen at this point.)

- Bake at 400° for 15 minutes or until golden. (Bake at 400° for 20 minutes if frozen.)

- Serve hot.

Sesame Chicken with Honey Dip

Served by popular request each year at an annual tailgate party.

Chicken:
1/2   cup mayonnaise
1 1/2 teaspoons dry mustard
2   teaspoons instant minced onion
1   cup fine dry bread crumbs
1/2   cup sesame seeds
2   cups uncooked cubed chicken

Honey Dip:
1   cup mayonnaise
2   tablespoons honey

Yield: 2 dozen

The Chicken:
- Preheat oven to 400°.

- Mix mayonnaise, mustard, and minced onion in a shallow dish or pie pan, set aside.

- Mix crumbs and sesame seeds.

- Toss chicken in mayonnaise mixture, then roll in crumb mixture. Place on baking sheet.

- Bake at 400° for 12 – 15 minutes, or until lightly browned.

The Honey Dip:
- Combine honey with mayonnaise.

- Serve hot or at room temperature with dip.

Marinated Barbecued Shrimp

Beware of party crashers lured by the tempting aroma from your grill!

1   pound peeled and cleaned shrimp, medium or large
1/4   cup olive oil
1   tablespoon chopped parsley
3/4   teaspoon basil
1/2   teaspoon oregano
2   cloves garlic, minced
3/4   teaspoon salt
2   teaspoons coarsely ground black pepper
2   tablespoons lemon juice

Yield: 4 servings

- Place shrimp in a large bowl. Combine all other ingredients and pour over the shrimp. Mix well. Refrigerate for at least one hour.

- Put shrimp on skewers and cook over hot coals for three minutes on each side. Use extra marinade to baste shrimp while it cooks.

Escargot Pâté

A unique blend of flavors that creates a masterpiece.

1	(4¹/₂ ounce) can escargot, about 24
¹/₂	cup cold butter
3	cloves garlic, crushed
1	tablespoon dry white wine, such as French Blanc de Blanc
4	ounces cream cheese
2	green onions, cleaned, trimmed and chopped into 1″ pieces
¹/₄	cup chopped fresh parsley

pinch white pepper

Yield: 1¹/₄ cups

- Rinse the escargot under cold running water.

- Heat ¹/₄ cup butter in small frying pan and add garlic, wine, and escargot. Cover and simmer 5 minutes, stirring often. Reduce heat.

- Cut remaining butter and cream cheese into cubes. In a food processor, combine the butter and cream cheese cubes, onion, parsley, and pepper. Add the hot escargot mixture, scraping the pan to get all of the butter sauce. Process the mixture until smooth.

- Pour into a shallow serving bowl, cover the bowl and refrigerate until firm, at least 2 hours.

- Serve with thin slices of fresh French baguette bread and sweet gherkin pickles.

Welcome Wafers

Wonderful with a glass of sherry before an elegant meal.

³/₄	cup butter
¹/₂	cup grated cheddar cheese
¹/₃	cup crumbled bleu cheese
¹/₂	clove garlic, minced
1	teaspoon parsley
1	teaspoon chives
2	cups flour, sifted

Garnish:
herb blossoms
herb leaves

Yield: 6 dozen

- Preheat oven to 350°.

- In a food processor, cream together butter, cheddar cheese, and bleu cheese. Add garlic, parsley, chives, and flour. Process until dough is formed. Shape into 1¹/₂″ diameter rolls. Cover with plastic wrap and chill 2 hours.

- Slice roll at ¹/₄″ intervals. Place slices on an ungreased cookie sheet and bake 8–10 minutes.

- Serve on a plate garnished with herb blossoms and leaves.

Superbowl Sausage Puff

When the Giants were competing in the Superbowl, our New Jersey team was cheered on with state spirit and pride. Superbowl parties were in evidence across the state.

Sausage Puff:

1   (17½ ounce) package frozen puff pastry sheets
1   pound hot and spicy sausage, casing removed
1   pound mild sausage, casing removed
1   cup grated Swiss cheese
1   tablespoon grated Parmesan cheese
1   teaspoon tarragon
⅛   teaspoon garlic powder
1   tablespoon summer savory
½   cup chopped fresh parsley
1   teaspoon basil
3   eggs, beaten (set aside 2 tablespoons of beaten egg)
2   tablespoons water

Mustard Dip:

½   cup Dijon mustard
¼   cup honey
1   teaspoon crushed tarragon

Garnish:
fresh parsley

Yield: 15–20 servings

The Puff:

- Preheat oven to 350°.

- Brown sausage slowly over medium heat, drain and let cool. Mix sausage, cheeses, tarragon, garlic powder, summer savory, parsley, basil, and eggs.

- Roll out each pastry sheet.

- Place half of sausage mixture lengthwise on one pastry sheet, roll up and pinch ends to seal. Repeat process with second sheet. Place rolls on cookie sheet and turn each roll into a semi-circle.

- Mix together the reserved 2 tablespoons of beaten egg with water to make an egg wash. Brush pastry rolls with egg wash.

- Bake at 350° for 35 – 40 minutes.

The Dip:

- Blend mustard, honey, and tarragon.

- Serve pastry on a round platter with a small bowl of the mustard dip in the middle. Slice as desired. Garnish with fresh parsley.

Morristown Mushrooms

Use as a spread on crackers or a filling for crêpes or croissants.

4   slices bacon
$^1/_2$ cup chopped onion
1   (8 ounce) package cream cheese
$^1/_2$ pound mushrooms, chopped
$^1/_2$ cup sour cream
white pepper

Garnish:
fresh dill sprigs

Yield: 8" pie

- Preheat oven to 325°.

- Fry bacon, crumble, and set aside. Reserve drippings. Sauté onions in bacon drippings. Drain. Add cream cheese to onions. Heat and stir until cheese is melted. Add mushrooms and heat thoroughly. Stir in sour cream, bacon, and a pinch of white pepper.

- Spoon mixture into an 8" pie plate and bake at 325° for 30 minutes.

- After baking, transfer into a serving bowl, garnish with fresh dill sprigs and serve hot with firm hearty crackers.

Sea Girt Shrimp Spectacular

An easy, make ahead appetizer that can be frozen.

4   ounces unsalted butter, softened
1   (8 ounce) package cream cheese
4   tablespoons mayonnaise
2   tablespoons fresh lemon juice
2   tablespoons grated onion
2   (4$^1/_2$ ounce) cans tiny shrimp, drained
red food coloring

Garnish:
lemon round
parsley

Yield: 2 cups

- Cream together butter, cream cheese, and mayonnaise in food processor.

- Add lemon juice, onion, and shrimp.

- Cream everything together with a few drops of red food coloring. Refrigerate for 24 hours. (Can be frozen at this point).

- Serve in a crock garnished with lemon round and parsley. Spread on celery sticks or bland crackers.

Country Pâté

A palate pleaser at a reasonable price, prepared with minimum effort.

Pâté:

4	slices bacon
1	pound boneless pork
8	ounces boneless veal
4	ounces ham
1/3	cup flour
8	ounces chicken livers, halved
1/4	cup butter
2	eggs
1/2	cup brandy
1	large onion, chopped
1	medium carrot, chopped
4	cloves garlic
1	tablespoon paprika
1	teaspoon salt
1	teaspoon dried crushed rosemary
1/2	teaspoon pepper
2	bay leaves

Garnish:
cherry tomatoes
small gherkin pickles
olives

Yield: 20 servings

- Preheat oven to 350°.

- Partially cook bacon, place on paper towels and set aside. Grind pork, veal, and ham together using a food processor (one half of the meat at a time). Place meat in a bowl and stir in flour.

- Cook chicken livers in butter until pink.

- In food processor, combine the livers and all remaining ingredients except the bacon and bay leaves. Process until smooth. Stir into the meat mixture.

- Place the bacon in the bottom of a 9 × 5 × 3″ loaf pan. Spoon the pâté mixture in carefully and top with bay leaves.

- Cover pan with foil and place on cookie sheet.

- Bake at 350° for 1½ hours.

- Remove foil and pour off fat, do not remove pâté from pan. Place pan on rack and weight the pâté. (To weight it, place heavy foil on top of the pâté surface and use a second loaf pan into which you have placed two 15½ ounce unopened vegetable cans.) Cool to room temperature and refrigerate overnight with the weight in place.

- To serve, remove the bay leaves and unmold the pâté onto a serving platter. Garnish with the bay leaves, cherry tomatoes, small gherkin pickles, and olives. Slice thinly and serve on party size bread or whole wheat and stone ground wheat crackers.

Vegetable Pizzaz

A beautiful party dish that can vary with the vegetables in season.

2 packages refrigerator crescent dinner
    roll dough, large size
2 (8 ounce) packages cream cheese,
    softened
1 cup mayonnaise
1 package Italian salad dressing mix
1 large carrot, diced
1/3 cup chopped red bell pepper
1/3 cup chopped green beans
1/3 cup sliced mushrooms
1 pint cherry tomatoes, cut in half
1 cup small broccoli flowerets
1/3 cup grated Monterey Jack cheese
1/3 cup grated cheddar cheese

Yield: 6 dozen

- Preheat oven to 350°.

- Spread rolled dough on a cookie sheet, pressing together, and making a slightly raised edge. Bake at 350° for 10 minutes. Cool.

- Mix cream cheese, mayonnaise, and Italian dressing mix and spread on the crust.

- Decorate the top with an assortment of the raw vegetables. Gently press the vegetables into the cream cheese mixture. Sprinkle the grated cheeses on top. Cut into 1 1/2″ squares. Serve chilled.

Note: *Your choice of seasonal vegetables can be arranged to make interesting geometric designs.*

Tuscany Toast

In Tuscany, picnickers slice the bread, top it with the tomato mixture, and leave it on a rock in the sun to warm and intensify the flavor.

2 large, firm, ripe tomatoes, chopped
1 cup loosely packed, chopped fresh
    basil
1/4 cup chopped endive
1/4 cup virgin olive oil
salt
freshly ground black pepper
1 loaf Italian bread

Yield: 2 dozen

- Mix chopped tomatoes, basil, endive, and olive oil and let sit at room temperature. Add salt and pepper to taste.

- Slice bread and cut into appetizer size pieces. Toast bread pieces.

- Top with tomato mixture and serve immediately.

Cheddar Crisps

These are crispy crackers that stand on their own.

1³/4 cups flour
¹/2 cup cornmeal
¹/2 teaspoon sugar
¹/2 teaspoon salt
¹/2 cup butter
6 ounces sharp cheddar cheese, shredded
2 tablespoons white wine vinegar
¹/2 cup water
coarsely ground black pepper

Yield: 32 crisps

- In a large mixing bowl, mix flour, cornmeal, sugar, and salt. With a pastry blender or two knives, used scissor fashion, cut in butter until mixture is the texture of coarse crumbs.

- Using a fork, stir in cheese, white wine vinegar, and water just until the mixture forms a soft dough. Shape into a large ball. Cover with plastic wrap and refrigerate for 1 hour (or until firm enough to handle).

- Preheat oven to 375°. Grease 2 cookie sheets.

- Take ¹/4 of the dough from the refrigerator and on a lightly floured surface, with a floured rolling pin, roll dough to an approximate 13″ diameter circle. The dough should be paper thin. Cut the round into 8 equal wedges.

- Place on large, greased cookie sheet and sprinkle the wedges with pepper. Press pepper into the dough.

- Bake for 12 – 15 minutes or until crisp.

- Repeat with last three portions of dough.

- Store cheddar crisps in an airtight container.

Breakfast Berry Blizzard

A smooth and creamy, complete and filling breakfast

2	tablespoons yogurt
2	teaspoons bran
6	whole frozen strawberries
2	tablespoons frozen orange juice concentrate
1/2	banana
6	ice cubes

Yield: 1 serving

- Put all ingredients in blender and whirl at high speed until well blended and smooth.

- Serve immediately.

Orange Julius

A light, refreshing citrus afternoon pick-me-up

1	(6 ounce) can frozen orange juice concentrate
1	cup water
1	cup milk
1	teaspoon vanilla extract
2	tablespoons honey
1	egg
10	ice cubes

Yield: 4 servings

- Put all ingredients, except ice cubes, into blender and whirl at high speed. While blender is running, add ice cubes one at a time until cubes have been crushed and the mixture is thick.

- Pour into old fashioned glasses and serve immediately.

Somerset Cider

Spice up your next meeting with this.

2	quarts cider
1½	quarts cranberry juice
½	cup brown sugar
½	teaspoon salt
4	cinnamon sticks
1½	teaspoons whole cloves
1	teaspoon whole allspice
1	small orange, quartered

Yield: 3½ quarts

- Pour juices into an automatic coffee percolator (30 cup capacity). Place remaining ingredients in the basket and perk as usual.

- Serve piping hot in coffee cups.

Strawberry Bowl

Begin a brunch beverage tradition with this special wine cooler.

4	cups sliced fresh strawberries
½	cup sugar
3	tablespoons freshly squeezed lemon juice
4	cups white Zinfandel wine
4	ice cubes
1	cup seltzer water

Yield: 2 quarts

- Put berries in the bottom of a pitcher. Sprinkle with sugar and lemon juice. Let stand for 30 minutes at room temperature.

- Pour wine over the berries and add ice cubes. Chill for 2 hours.

- Strain berries, reserving the wine. Purée the berries. Sieve and strain purée, reserving the juice and discarding the seeds and pulp.

- Pour reserved wine, berry juice, and seltzer water in a glass pitcher. Stir with a wooden spoon. Pour into chilled wine goblets and serve immediately.

Tequila Snowcones

Poolside perfect . . . just drink it slowly as it packs a punch!

4   lime slices
coarse (kosher) salt
5   cups ice cubes
1   (6 ounce) can frozen limeade
3   ounces white Tequila
3   ounces Triple Sec

Yield: 4 servings

- Rub the rim (inside and outside) of four old fashioned glasses, using one lime slice per glass. Discard the lime slice. Pour the salt into a deep saucer and twirl the rim of each glass in the salt so that a thin layer of salt adheres to the moistened rim.

- Fill blender with ice cubes. Pour limeade concentrate, Tequila, and Triple Sec over the ice and whirl in blender on high speed until no large chunks of ice remain.

- Pour into prepared glasses and serve immediately. Any leftover beverage can be stored in the freezer.

Banana Frost

Creamy, rich, and refreshing

1   small banana
1   ounce white rum
1/2   cup milk
1/8   teaspoon vanilla extract
1   dash bitters
1   cup crushed ice

Garnish:
sprig of mint

Yield: 1 serving

- Place banana in blender and whirl on high speed until smooth.

- Add rum, milk, vanilla, bitters, and ice. Whirl on medium speed until well combined.

- Pour into chilled collins glass, garnish with sprig of mint and serve immediately.

Peach Blossom

A change of pace from rum-based fruit drinks for your next patio gathering

3   cups sliced canned peaches, drained
1   (6 ounce) can frozen lemonade
        concentrate
6   ounces vodka
2   cups ice cubes

Garnish:
6   perfect strawberries with leaves and
        stems

Yield: 6 servings

- Place peaches, lemonade concentrate, and vodka in blender. Fill blender to the top with ice cubes and whirl on high speed until smooth.
- In each strawberry make one vertical cut going three-quarters of the way through the berry, leaving the leaves and stem intact.
- Pour peach mixture into chilled old fashioned glasses and garnish each glass with a strawberry on the rim. Serve immediately.

Whiskey Tea 'n Sea

Perfect on a midsummer's eve

1   (12 ounce) can frozen lemonade
        concentrate
1   (6 ounce) can frozen orange juice
        concentrate
1½ cups blended whiskey
6   cups water
2   cups iced tea
1   cup sugar

Garnish:
julienne strips of orange zest
julienne strips of lemon zest

Yield: 10 servings

- In a plastic container large enough to allow for expansion, add all ingredients and stir well. Cover and freeze for at least 6 hours.
- At serving time, scoop frozen mixture into old fashioned glasses. Garnish with julienne strips of orange and lemon zest and serve with a demitasse spoon.

Strawberry Rum Snow

Begin your evening with this and who knows what it could lead to . . .

1	(6 ounce) can frozen lemonade concentrate
1	(6 ounce) can frozen limeade concentrate
1	(10 ounce) package frozen strawberries
¾	cup golden rum
3	cups water

Garnish:
lime wedges

Yield: 8 servings

- Place lemonade concentrate, limeade concentrate, and strawberries in blender and whirl on high speed until smooth.

- Pour strawberry mixture into a plastic container large enough to allow for expansion. Add water and rum, stir until well combined. Cover and freeze 12 hours or overnight.

- To serve, scrape the top of the frozen mixture with a spoon to form a snow. Spoon snow into chilled old fashioned glasses. Garnish with a lime wedge and serve with a short straw.

Sparkling Ruby

An elegant drink to be served with dessert.

1	(10 ounce) package frozen raspberries, defrosted
3	ounces Bauchant (orange liqueur)
1	bottle brut champagne, chilled

Garnish:
6   fresh violet blossoms

Yield: 6 servings

- Purée raspberries. Sieve and strain purée, reserving the juice and discarding the seeds and pulp. Chill the raspberry juice.

- Combine raspberry juice, liqueur, and champagne in a pitcher. Stir well with a wooden spoon.

- Pour into chilled tulip champagne glasses. Float one violet blossom in each glass and serve immediately.

Apricot Delight

Truly delightful on a hot summer night, served after dinner instead of dessert.

3/4 cup sugar
1 (6 ounce) can frozen lemonade
  concentrate, defrosted
1 (6 ounce) can frozen orange juice
  concentrate, defrosted
4^1/2 cups water
1 cup apricot brandy
1^1/2 cups Seven-up

Garnish:
orange slices

Yield: 6 servings

- Whirl sugar with lemonade concentrate and orange juice concentrate in blender.

- In a plastic container that is large enough to allow for expansion and can be tightly covered, pour in concentrate mixture, water, and apricot brandy. Mix well. Cover and freeze 12 hours or overnight.

- At serving time, scoop out 3/4 of a cup of the frozen mixture and put into a chilled long stemmed goblet. Over this pour 1/4 cup of Seven-up. Garnish each goblet with an orange slice and serve with a demitasse spoon.

Citrus Cup

Take a sip, close your eyes, and you are in a tropical paradise.

1/2 cup golden rum
1/2 cup white rum
1/2 cup Triple Sec
1^1/2 cups fresh sqeezed orange juice
1/2 cup fresh squeezed grapefruit juice
1/2 cup Rose's sweetened lime juice
1 cup seltzer water

Garnish:
orange slices
lime slices

Yield: 5 cups

- In a glass pitcher, combine golden and white rums, Triple Sec, orange juice, grapefruit juice, and Rose's lime juice. Stir well with a wooden spoon. Chill thoroughly until ready to serve.

- Just before serving, stir in seltzer water. Garnish pitcher with orange and lime slices.

- To serve, pour into wine goblets half filled with crushed ice.

BREADS

Breads

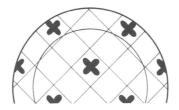

Savory Wheat French Bread

A substantial, robust bread, hearty with cheese and herbs

3 cups whole wheat flour
1 cup grated Parmesan cheese
2 teaspoons salt
3 teaspoons oregano leaves
1 teaspoon garlic powder
2 (¹/₄ ounce) packages active dry yeast
3¹/₄ cups water
2 tablespoons honey
5 – 5¹/₂ cups unbleached flour
cornmeal
1 egg, beaten

Yield: 4 loaves

- In a large bowl, using an electric mixer at medium speed, combine wheat flour, Parmesan, salt, oregano leaves, garlic powder, and yeast.

- In a small saucepan, heat together water and honey until very warm (120° – 130°).

- Add warm liquid to flour mixture. Blend at low speed until moistened. Beat for 3 minutes at medium speed.

- By hand, stir in flour to form a stiff dough.

- On a floured surface, knead in 1 – 1¹/₂ cups flour, to form a smooth elastic dough. Knead about 8 minutes.

- Grease the inside of a large bowl, place dough in bowl and loosely cover with plastic wrap. Place bowl in a warm (80° – 85°) place and let dough rise until double in size (approximately 1 hour).

- Grease two cookie sheets and generously sprinkle with corn meal. Punch down and divide dough into 4 equal pieces. Form into 12″ long loaves with tapering ends. Place on prepared cookie sheets and cut diagonal slits on top of loaves.

- Loosely cover cookie sheets with plastic wrap and let loaves rise until double in size (approximately 45 minutes).

- Preheat oven to 375°.

- Brush loaves with beaten egg and bake at 375° for 20 minutes. Remove from oven and brush with cold water. Return to oven and bake for 10 – 15 minutes or until hollow sounding when tapped.

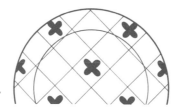

Pinwheel Loaves

Each delicious slice is a pinwheel swirl.

2   cups milk, scalded
$^1/_2$ cup solid all-vegetable shortening, at
      room temperature
$^1/_2$ cup sugar
2   tablespoons salt
1   cup cold water
2   ($^1/_4$ ounce) packages active dry yeast
1   cup lukewarm water
$7^1/_2 - 8$ cups all purpose flour, sifted
$^1/_4$ cup molasses
$2^1/_2$ cups whole wheat flour
$2 - 2^1/_2$ cups enriched flour, sifted

Yield: 3 loaves

- Blend shortening, sugar, and salt into hot scalded milk. Add cold water and cool mixture to lukewarm.

- In a large bowl, dissolve yeast in lukewarm water. Stir in milk mixture. Add 4 cups of the all purpose flour and beat until smooth.

- Cover bowl with a clean cloth, set it in a warm place, and let dough rise until double in size (approximately 1 hour).

- Punch down and divide dough into two equal parts. Place each part in a separate large bowl.

- Working with the first part, blend in $3^1/_2 - 4$ cups all purpose flour to form a stiff dough.

- Working with the second part, stir in molasses. Blend in whole wheat flour and as much of the enriched flour as necessary to form a dough that doesn't stick to your fingers.

- Grease two large bowls.

- Knead white and whole wheat doughs separately on a well floured surface until each is smooth and elastic (5 – 7 minutes). Place doughs in prepared separate bowls, turn each dough over once to grease the entire surface.

Continued on next page

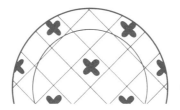

- Cover bowls with clean cloths and set each in a warm, draft-free place and let rise until double in size (approximately 1½ hours). If the whole wheat dough has not risen sufficiently in 1½ hours, allow it to rise a little longer and proceed to shape the white dough.

- Grease three 9″ × 5″ × 3″ loaf pans.

- Divide each dough into three equal parts. On a lightly floured surface, roll out each piece to an 8″ × 12″ rectangle. Place a whole wheat rectangle on top of a white rectangle. Press doughs together firmly. Roll up tightly beginning with the 8″ side. Tuck ends under the roll and place in a prepared loaf pan. Repeat procedure twice.

- Cover each loaf pan with a cloth and let rise in a warm, draft-free place until double in size (approximately 1 hour).

- Preheat oven to 375°. Bake for 45–50 minutes. (After cooling loaves, they can be wrapped and frozen.)

Note: This makes wonderful bread for Orangery French Toast (page 131).

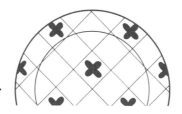

Bakers' Bread

Mix it up in the evening and bake it in the morning.

2	*(¹/4 ounce) packages active dry yeast*
2	*teaspoons salt*
¹/3	*cup vegetable oil*
¹/3	*cup sugar*
2	*eggs*
2	*cups warm water*
²/3	*cup powdered milk*
1	*cup wheat germ*

6¹/2 – 7 cups flour
vegetable oil

Yield: 2 loaves

- Grease two 9″ × 5″ × 3″ loaf pans with vegetable oil.

- Have all ingredients at room temperature or slightly warmer.

- In a large mixing bowl, stir together yeast, salt, oil, sugar, eggs, water, powdered milk, and wheat germ. Add 3 cups flour and beat with an electric mixer at medium speed for 8 minutes.

- Add another 2 cups flour and stir by hand. (No need to make dough smooth.)

- Sprinkle 1 cup of flour in a 10″ diameter circle on the kneading surface. Turn dough onto the floured circle.

- Rub your hands with vegetable oil and knead dough until it stiffens. Knead another 8 – 10 minutes to make dough smooth and elastic. Add remaining flour if necessary.

- Cover dough with plastic and a doubled towel. Let dough rest for 20 minutes. Knead down dough and divide into two equal halves.

- On a lightly oiled surface, roll out one half of the dough to an 8″ × 12″ rectangle. Roll up dough, jelly roll fashion, beginning with the 8″ side. Tuck ends under the roll and place in a prepared loaf pan. Repeat with remaining half of dough.

- Cover with plastic wrap and refrigerate for 2 hours or up to 24 hours.

Continued on next page

- Preheat oven to 350°.

- Remove bread from the refrigerator and uncover 10 minutes before baking. Brush the top of each loaf with vegetable oil.

- Bake at 350° for 40–50 minutes. (After cooling, loaves can be wrapped and frozen.)

Cheese Bread

The wonderful aroma of this bread wafting through the house can warm body and soul.

2   (*¹/4 ounce) packages active dry yeast*
¹/2   cup lukewarm water
1   *cup milk, scalded and cooled*
¹/4   cup sugar
2   *teaspoons salt*
5   *cups flour, sifted*
2   *cups finely grated sharp cheddar
     cheese*

Yield: 2 loaves

- In a large bowl, dissolve yeast in water.

- Stir together milk, sugar, and salt. Pour into yeast mixture.

- Stir in one half of the flour, then add the cheese. Mix thoroughly and add remaining flour.

- Knead dough on a floured surface for about 10 minutes or until dough becomes elastic.

- Grease the inside of a large bowl, place dough in bowl and cover with a damp towel. Let rise until double in size.

- Punch down and let rise again.

- Grease two 9″ × 5″ × 3″ loaf pans.

- Knead down and divide dough in half. Form each half into a loaf and place in prepared pans. Cover with damp towels and let rise again.

- Preheat oven at 375° and bake for 40–45 minutes or until hollow sounding when tapped.

Note: This bread is particularly good toasted. Also try toasting one or two slices and then cutting them up into cubes for use as croutons on soup or salad.

Cinnamon Twists

Melt-in-your-mouth mini Danish pastry twists.

Twists:

3/4	cup milk
3	tablespoons sugar
2	tablespoons solid all-vegetable shortening
1/4	teaspoon salt
1	cake yeast
1/4	cup warm water
1	egg
3	cups flour
1/2	cup margarine, at room temperature
1/2	cup sugar
2	teaspoons cinnamon
1/4	cup very finely chopped or ground pecans

Nut Icing:

1 1/2	cups confectioners sugar
2	tablespoons milk
1	teaspoon almond extract
1/2	cup very finely chopped or ground pecans

Yield: 3 dozen

The Twists:

- Grease two cookie sheets.

- In a medium size saucepan, heat milk until little bubbles form. Add 3 tablespoons sugar, shortening, and salt. Cool to lukewarm.

- Dissolve yeast in warm water.

- Beat dissolved yeast and egg into milk mixture. Stir in flour.

- On a floured surface, knead dough until well mixed. With a floured rolling pin, roll dough into a rectangle about 1/3" thick.

- Divide the stick of margarine into thirds. Dot the upper two thirds of dough with one third of the margarine.

- Mix together 1/2 cup sugar, cinnamon, and pecans. Sprinkle evenly over dough.

- Fold the lower one third of the dough up and the top one third down. Roll out dough to approximately the same size rectangle and about 1/3" thick. Dot the upper two thirds of dough with one third of the margarine. Fold as before.

- Repeat entire process using the last third of margarine. Fold as before.

- Roll out dough once more into a rectangle about 1/3" thick. Cut dough lengthwise into 1" strips and then into 3" long pieces. Twist and place on prepared cookie sheets.

Continued on next page

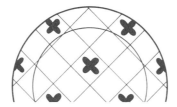

- Cover with a clean cloth and let rise until double in size (approximately 1 – 1 1/2 hours).

- Preheat oven to 450° and bake for 6 – 8 minutes.

The Icing:
- In a small bowl mix together confectioners sugar, milk, and almond extract until smooth. Mix in pecans.

- While twists are still hot, brush with icing.

Sterling Rolls

An heirloom recipe, passed from one generation to the next.

2   *(1/4 ounce) packages active dry yeast*
1 1/2 *cups warm water*
1/3   *cup margarine, at room temperature*
1   *egg*
1/4   *cup sugar*
1 1/2 *teaspoons salt*
4   *cups flour*

Yield: 2 dozen

- In a large bowl, stir together yeast and water to dissolve.

- Add margarine, egg, sugar, salt, and 2 cups of the flour. Beat with a whisk until smooth.

- Add the remaining 2 cups flour. Stir with a wooden spoon until smooth (approximately 30 seconds).

- Cover and let rise until double in size.

- Preheat oven to 400°. Grease muffin pans.

- Divide dough into 24 equal parts and place each piece in a muffin cup. (Can be made early in the day to this point, and baked just before serving.)

- Bake at 400° for 12 – 15 minutes or until golden brown.

- Rolls can be frozen after baking.

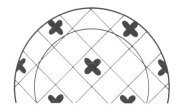

Frenchtown Bread

A simplified version of the classic French baguette.

2   (¹/4 ounce) packages active dry yeast
2   cups lukewarm water
¹/4   cup solid all-vegetable shortening, at
        room temperature
1³/4 tablespoons sugar
1   tablespoon salt
8   cups bread flour
cornmeal
1   egg white
1   tablespoon cold water

Yield: 2 loaves

- Stir yeast and water together in a large bowl. Let stand 10 minutes.

- Add shortening, sugar, and salt. Beat in flour.

- On a floured surface, knead dough until it is smooth and satiny. (Add extra flour if necessary.)

- Form into a ball. Cover with a clean cloth and let rise until double in size (approximately 2 hours).

- Punch down and let dough rest 30 minutes.

- Preheat oven to 400°. Grease a cookie sheet and generously sprinkle with cornmeal.

- On a floured surface, using a rolling pin, roll out dough into a large rectangle. Cut rectangle in half. Roll each half *very tightly* into bread loaves. Place loaves on prepared cookie sheet.

- Beat together egg white and water. Brush the top and sides of loaves with the egg wash.

- Cut diagonal slits on top of loaves. Bake at 400° for 30 minutes, then reduce heat to 375° and bake an additional 15 minutes.

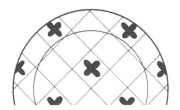

Dilly Bread

Nothing is colder than a seaside Nor'easter. So bundle up, light a fire in the fireplace and warm your insides with a bowl of Stone Harbor Chowder (page 72) and a wedge of Dilly Bread.

1	(¹/4 ounce) package active dry yeast
¹/4	teaspoon baking soda
2	tablespoons sugar
1	teaspoon salt
2	teaspoons grated onion
1	tablespoon dill weed
1	teaspoon dill seed
2¹/2	cups flour, sifted
¹/4	cup water
2	tablespoons butter
1	cup large curd cottage cheese
1	egg
melted butter	

Yield: 1 large loaf

- In a large bowl, using an electric mixer at medium speed, combine yeast, baking soda, sugar, salt, onion, dill weed, dill seed, and ¹/4 cup flour.

- In a small saucepan, heat water until very warm (120° – 130°) and melt butter in it.

- Add warm liquid to yeast mixture and beat at medium speed, occasionally scraping the bowl.

- Add cottage cheese, egg, and ¹/2 cup flour and beat at high speed for 2 minutes.

- By hand, beat in remaining 2 cups flour to make a stiff dough.

- Cover with a clean cloth and let rise until doubled in size (approximately 1¹/2 hours).

- Grease a 2 quart soufflé or casserole dish.

- Stir down and place dough in prepared dish. Cover and let rise until double in size (approximately 45 minutes).

- Preheat oven to 350°.

- Brush dough with melted butter and bake for 35 – 40 minutes.

- Serve immediately after baking.

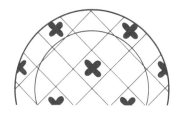

Medieval Parsley Bread

A real sandwich bread, to serve toasted or plain with slices of cheese and cold roasted meats.

2   tablespoons active dry yeast
2   cups warm water
6   tablespoons honey
6–7 cups unbleached flour
1²/₃ tablespoons coarse salt (kosher or sea salt)
¹/₄ cup melted butter
4   eggs
1   teaspoon dried rosemary
1   teaspoon dried basil
¹/₂ cup chopped fresh parsley
¹/₄ teaspoon cinnamon

Yield: 2 loaves

- In a large bowl, sprinkle yeast over ¹/₂ cup of warm water. Stir in honey. Let stand 5 minutes.

- Add remaining water and 3 cups of flour. Beat with a wooden spoon, about 200 strokes. Cover with a damp cloth and set in a warm place. Let rise until double in size (approximately 30–45 minutes).

- Punch down dough, beat in the salt, butter, and 3 eggs.

- Crush the rosemary and basil in a mortar. Add parsley and make a paste. Add the cinnamon and blend. Add the herb and spice mixture to the dough.

- With a wooden spoon, beat in 3 cups of flour. The dough should have a delicate green color. Knead with your hands until dough comes away from the sides of the bowl. Turn the dough onto a lightly floured board or marble slab and knead until smooth, shiny, and elastic (approximately 10–12 minutes). Add small amounts of flour if the dough is too sticky.

- Grease the inside of a large mixing bowl, place dough in the bowl, cover with a damp cloth, and let rise until double in size (approximately 50 minutes).

- Punch down dough, cover and let rise again until double in size (approximately 30 minutes).

- Punch down dough and turn onto a lightly floured surface and let stand for 5 minutes.

Continued on next page

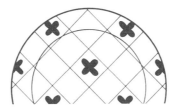

- Butter 1 large cookie sheet or 3 (8″) metal pie pans.

- Divide dough into three equal pieces. Shape each piece into a turban-like mound. Place on prepared cookie sheet. Cover with a clean dry cloth and let rise in a warm place until double in size (approximately 25 minutes).

- Preheat oven to 375°.

- Lightly beat remaining egg. Brush tops and sides of loaves with the beaten egg.

- Bake loaves at 375° for 40–50 minutes or until nicely browned. A loaf should sound hollow when tapped on top. Remove from oven and let cool on racks. (After cooling, loaves can be wrapped and frozen.)

Poppy Seed Loaf

Richer than a bread, but not as sweet as a cake.

1	cup sugar
2	eggs
3/4	cup vegetable oil
1	teaspoon vanilla extract
1/4	cup poppy seeds
1	teaspoon salt
2	teaspoons baking powder
2	cups flour
1	cup evaporated milk

Yield: 1 loaf

- Preheat oven to 350°. Grease and flour a 9″ × 5″ × 3″ loaf pan.

- Stir together sugar, eggs, oil, vanilla, and poppy seeds.

- Combine salt, baking powder, and flour. Alternately add flour mixture and milk in small amounts to sugar mixture, beating after each addition.

- Pour into prepared pan and bake at 350° for 50 minutes or until center springs back when lightly touched.

- Cool 15 minutes on a rack. Remove from pan, slice and serve warm or at room temperature with butter and marmalade.

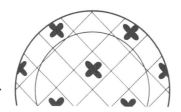

Pumpkin Spice Bread

An autumn harvest of flavor, one loaf to keep and one to share.

3½   cups flour
1½   teaspoons salt
1   teaspoon nutmeg
1   teaspoon cinnamon
½   teaspoon pumpkin spice
¼   teaspoon ground cloves
¼   teaspoon ground ginger
2   teaspoons baking soda
3   cups sugar
1   cup vegetable oil
4   eggs
⅔   cup water
2   cups canned pumpkin
½   cup golden raisins
½   cup chopped walnuts

Yield: 2 loaves

- Preheat oven to 350°. Grease two 9″ × 5″ × 3″ loaf pans.

- Mix together dry ingredients.

- Add oil, eggs, water, and pumpkin and beat for 2 minutes.

- Stir in raisins and walnuts.

- Pour into prepared pans and bake at 350° for 1 hour.

Iron Skillet Corn Bread

If you like a moist, full flavored cornbread with a light crumbly texture, give this one a try.

1   cup cornmeal
½   cup flour
1   tablespoon wheat germ
3   tablespoons sugar
1   teaspoon baking powder
1   teaspoon baking soda
½   teaspoon salt
1   cup non-fat yogurt
¼   cup vegetable oil
2   large eggs, slightly beaten

Yield: 1 loaf

- Preheat oven to 400°.

- Wipe the inside of a 9″ iron skillet with a small amount of vegetable oil and place in oven for 5 minutes.

- Stir together dry ingredients.

- Beat in yogurt, oil, and eggs into dry ingredients using a wooden spoon. Beat well.

- Pour batter into hot skillet and bake 20 – 25 minutes or until golden brown. Serve hot with butter.

Note: To vary flavor, stir in ½ cup grated sharp cheddar cheese or ½ cup coarsely chopped onion after beating in eggs.

Lemon Tea Bread

A hot cup of freshly brewed tea and a slice of Lemon Tea Bread can warm and cheer up even the coldest, grayest winter day.

Bread:

6	tablespoons butter, at room temperature
1	cup sugar
1	tablespoon grated lemon peel
2	eggs
1/2	cup milk
1 1/2	cups flour
1/2	teaspoon salt
1	teaspoon baking powder
1/2	cup finely chopped pecans

Glaze:

1/4	cup sugar
3	tablespoons lemon juice

Yield: 1 loaf

The Bread:

- Preheat oven to 325°. Grease a 9″ × 5″ × 3″ loaf pan.

- Cream together butter and sugar with an electric mixer.

- Add lemon peel, eggs, and milk. Beat well.

- Stir together flour, salt, and baking powder. Add dry ingredients to beaten mixture and beat together at low speed just until smooth.

- Fold in pecans.

- Turn batter into prepared loaf pan and bake at 325° for 45–50 minutes. When done, remove from oven and set on a wire rack. Cool for 10 minutes.

The Glaze:

- In a small saucepan combine sugar and lemon juice. Heat until sugar dissolves.

- Spoon warm glaze over bread while bread is still hot.

- Cool completely on a wire rack before slicing and serving.

Note: Orange Tea Bread can be made by substituting orange peel and juice.

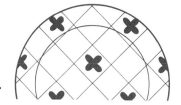

Coconut Quick Bread

While on vacation at a famous shore resort, one of our members was served this delectable bread. Hope you enjoy it as much as she did.

1¼ cups shredded coconut
2⅔ cups flour
1 cup sugar
4 teaspoons baking powder
1 teaspoon salt
1½ cups milk
1 egg, slightly beaten
2 tablespoons peanut oil
1 teaspoon coconut extract

Yield: 1 loaf

- Preheat oven to 325°.

- Scatter shredded coconut on an ungreased cookie sheet. Bake for 10 minutes. While baking, open the oven two or three times and shake the cookie sheet or stir the coconut with a wooden spoon so that it is evenly toasted. Remove from oven and cool.

- Turn oven temperature up to 350°. Lightly coat the inside of a 9″×5″×3″ loaf pan with vegetable spray.

- Sift flour, sugar, baking powder, and salt into a medium size bowl. Stir in coconut.

- Combine milk, egg, peanut oil, and coconut extract in another bowl. Mix well. Add to dry ingredients all at once. Stir until just blended. *Do not over mix.*

- Turn batter into prepared loaf pan and bake at 350° for 1 hour. Cool.

- Slice when cool and serve with Strawberry Butter (page 56).

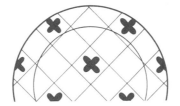

Sugar Loaf Orange Biscuits

Seldom do you get so much for such little effort. A surprise ingredient produces a magical result.

2 cups flour
3 teaspoons baking powder
1/2 teaspoon salt
1/4 cup butter, softened
1 tablespoon grated orange peel
1 orange, squeezed for juice
milk
30 cubes of sugar
1/4 cup Grand Marnier (orange liqueur)

Yield: 2 1/2 dozen

- Preheat oven to 450°.

- Sift together flour, baking powder, and salt.

- With a pastry blender or two knives, used scissor fashion, cut in butter until the mixture is the consistency of coarse cornmeal.

- Stir in orange peel.

- Combine the juice of 1 orange and enough milk to make 3/4 cup liquid.

- Make a well in the center of the crumb mixture and add the liquid all at once. Beat by hand 1/2 minute.

- Turn the dough onto a lightly floured board and knead quickly and gently 1/2 minute.

- Roll out to 1/2″ thickness and cut with a (2″ diameter) round cookie cutter. Place rounds on ungreased teflon cookie sheets.

- Dip each sugar cube in Grand Marnier and then place on a round.

- Bake at 450° for 12 – 15 minutes or until lightly browned.

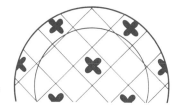

Crusty Brown Wheat Bread

When soup is for supper round out the meal with this hearty bread, good wine, and cheese.

cornmeal
3 cups whole wheat flour
¼ cup quick oats
1 tablespoon wheat germ
1 teaspoon salt
¼ teaspoon baking soda
1 teaspoon baking powder
1¼ cups whole milk
¼ cup distilled white vinegar

Yield: 1 loaf

- Preheat oven to 425°.

- Sprinkle cornmeal generously over the bottom of an 8″ iron skillet or metal pie pan.

- In a large bowl stir together dry ingredients.

- Pour milk into a small bowl. Pour vinegar into milk. *Do not stir.* Let stand for 2 minutes.

- Pour liquid combination into dry ingredients and mix together with a wooden spoon. When well combined, form into a ball. Place ball in the center of the prepared skillet and flatten ball to a 7″ round.

- Using a sharp knife cut a deep cross from side to side in the top of the dough.

- Bake at 425° for approximately 40 minutes. Bread should be brown and hollow sounding when tapped. Remove from oven and cool slightly before cutting into wedges and serving.

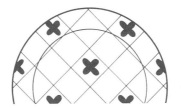

Proper Brown Bread

A return to those golden days of yesteryear . . .

1	cup whole milk
1	teaspoon distilled white vinegar
1/2	cup cornmeal
1/2	cup rye flour
1/2	cup whole wheat flour
1	teaspoon salt
3/4	teaspoon baking soda
1/4	cup molasses
1/3	cup raisins
1	pound coffee can

Yield: 1 loaf

- Grease the coffee can with butter.

- Pour milk into a small bowl. Add vinegar to milk. *Do not stir.* Let stand for 2 minutes.

- Stir together dry ingredients.

- Pour liquid combination into a large bowl and stir in molasses and raisins. Add dry ingredients in several portions, beating well after each addition.

- Turn dough into prepared coffee can. Cover with a layer of buttered wax paper and then a layer of aluminum foil. Arrange cover layers so that they are puffed up (to allow for expansion) and sealed air tight.

- Set the coffee can on a rack in a large pot. Add water to a level three quarters of the way up the sides of the coffee can. Cover pot and bring the water to a boil. Turn heat down and let water simmer for 2 hours. Check the level of the water every half hour and add water if necessary.

- Remove can from pot and cool completely.

- Remove bottom of the can with a can opener. Remove cover layers and push bread out of the can.

- Slice and serve with butter or cream cheese.

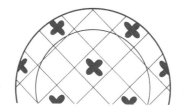

Pear Bread

Pear perfection for breakfast or brunch, or topped with preserves

1/2	cup margarine, at room temperature
1	cup sugar
2	eggs
1	teaspoon vanilla extract
2	cups flour
1/2	teaspoon salt
1/2	teaspoon baking soda
1	teaspoon baking powder
1/8	teaspoon nutmeg
1/4	cup plain yogurt
1	cup peeled, cored, and coarsely chopped pears

Yield: 1 loaf

- Preheat oven to 350°. Grease a 9″ × 5″ × 3″ loaf pan.
- Cream together margarine and sugar. Beat in eggs and vanilla.
- Stir together flour, salt, baking soda, baking powder, and nutmeg.
- Add the flour mixture, alternately with the yogurt, to the egg mixture.
- Stir in the pears.
- Turn batter into prepared loaf pan and bake at 350° for 1 hour.

Strawberry Butter

A simple touch that adds so much to fresh biscuits, muffins, and breads.

1	(10 ounce) package frozen strawberries, defrosted
1	cup unsalted butter, softened
1	cup confectioners sugar

Garnish:
1	large strawberry
1	mint sprig

Yield: 2 1/2 cups

- Put all ingredients into a food processor and process until well combined. Turn off, scrape down the sides and process until smooth.
- Place in a serving bowl. Chill.
- To serve, place strawberry in the center of the butter and garnish with leaves from the mint sprig.

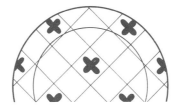

Citrus Hot Cross Buns

A Sunday tradition, filled with fruit and memories

The Buns:

1	cup freshly squeezed orange juice
1/2	cup butter, softened
1/2	cup sugar
1	teaspoon cinnamon
1/4	teaspoon nutmeg
1/2	teaspoon salt
2	(1/4 ounce) packages active dry yeast
1/4	cup lemon juice
3	eggs
1	cup golden raisins
1	tablespoon grated lemon peel
1	tablespoon grated orange peel
4	tablespoons bitter orange marmalade
1/2	cup finely chopped pecans
5 1/2	cups flour
1	egg yolk
2	tablespoons cold water

Citrus Icing:

1	cup confectioners sugar
1	tablespoon fresh squeezed orange juice
1/2	teaspoon lemon extract

Yield: 32 buns

The Buns:

- Heat 3/4 cup orange juice to simmer. Pour juice over butter, sugar, cinnamon, nutmeg, and salt.

- Dissolve yeast in a combination of lemon juice and 1/4 cup reserved orange juice. When dissolved, add to orange juice and spice mixture.

- Beat in eggs. Stir in raisins, lemon peel, orange peel, marmalade, and pecans.

- Gradually add flour to make a soft dough.

- Turn dough onto a well floured surface and knead until smooth.

- Grease the inside of a large bowl, place dough in bowl and cover with a clean cloth. Let rise until double in size (approximately 2 hours).

- Preheat oven to 375°. Grease 2 cookie sheets thoroughly.

- Punch down and turn dough out onto a well floured surface. Divide dough in half. Cut each half into sixteen pieces. Shape each piece into a smooth ball and place 2″ apart on prepared cookie sheets.

- Using scissors cut a cross in the top of each ball.

- Beat together the egg yolk and cold water. Brush the top and sides of each ball with the egg wash.

- Bake at 375° for 20 minutes or until golden brown. Remove from oven and cool. (Buns can be frozen at this point.)

The Icing:

- Mix together confectioners sugar, orange juice, and lemon extract to form a smooth thick icing. Before serving, top each cooled bun with a dab of icing.

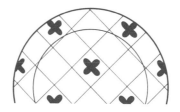

Jersey Blueberry Bran Muffins

Freshly picked, big, luscious New Jersey blueberries make this a special breakfast treat.

1   cup boiling water
1   cup 100% Bran cereal
1/2   cup margarine, at room temperature
1 1/2   cups sugar
2   eggs
2   cups buttermilk
2   cups All Bran cereal
2 1/2   cups flour
2 1/2   teaspoons baking soda
2   tablespoons wheat germ
pinch of salt
1 1/2   cups fresh blueberries

Yield: 2 dozen

- Preheat oven to 350°. Grease muffin pans or line with fluted paper cups.

- Pour boiling water over 100% Bran and let it steep.

- Cream together margarine and sugar. Beat in eggs and buttermilk. Mix in the steeped bran, (liquid and all).

- Stir together All Bran, flour, baking soda, wheat germ, and salt. Add to buttermilk mixture and combine well. (This mixture may be made ahead and kept in a tightly sealed container in the refrigerator for up to 7 weeks.)

- Just before baking, stir in fresh blueberries.

- Fill prepared muffin cups two thirds full with batter. Bake at 350° for 20-25 minutes. Serve immediately.

Banana Nut Breakfast Cupcakes

Cupcakes for breakfast? Your child will think he's still dreaming.

1 1/2   cups flour
1 1/2   cups sugar
1   teaspoon baking soda
1/2   teaspoon salt
2   eggs
1/2   cup melted butter (no substitutes)
3   very ripe bananas
1/2   cup sour cream
1/2   cup chopped walnuts

Yield: 1 1/2 dozen

- Preheat oven to 375°. Set fluted paper baking cups in muffin pans.

- Place all ingredients, except nuts, in a food processor. Process until well blended.

- Add nuts and pulse until they are combined.

- Fill baking cups half full with batter.

- Bake at 375° for 20-25 minutes or until a cake tester comes out clean.

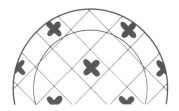

Coffee Spice Cake

Rich, full-bodied flavor for a country kitchen breakfast

2 cups brown sugar
2 cups flour
$1/2$ cup butter, at room temperature
2 tablespoons freeze dried coffee
  granules
$1/2$ teaspoon salt
1 tablespoon cinnamon
$1/4$ teaspoon nutmeg
1 teaspoon baking soda
1 cup sour cream
1 egg
$1/2$ cup chopped walnuts or pecans

Yield: 8 servings

- Preheat oven to 350°. Butter a 9″ square baking pan.
- Place sugar, flour, butter, coffee granules, salt, cinnamon, and nutmeg in a food processor. Pulse on and off until crumbly and completely blended. *Do not over process.*
- Spoon half the crumb mixture into the prepared baking pan.
- Stir baking soda into sour cream and add to the remaining crumbs. Add the egg and pulse the food processor on and off to blend.
- Pour batter over crumbs in the baking pan. Sprinkle nuts over the batter. Bake at 350° for 40–45 minutes.

Sour Cream Coffee Cake

A homemade treasure, perfect for welcoming new neighbors.

1 cup butter, at room temperature
1 cup sugar
2 eggs
2 cups sifted flour
1 teaspoon baking powder
1 teaspoon baking soda
$1/2$ teaspoon salt
1 cup sour cream
1 teaspoon vanilla extract

Filling:
$1/3$ cup brown sugar
$1/4$ cup sugar
2 teaspoons cinnamon
1 cup ground walnuts (optional)

Yield: 10–12 servings

- Preheat oven to 350°. Grease and flour a bundt pan.
- Cream butter and sugar in a food processor or blender. Add all other ingredients and process until smooth and fluffy.
- Pour one half of the batter into the prepared bundt pan.
- Stir together all filling ingredients.
- Sprinkle on top of poured batter. Pour remaining batter evenly over filling.
- Bake at 350° for 1 hour. (Cake can be frozen after it cools.)

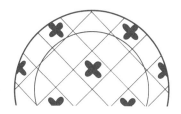

Butter Pecan Snack Cake

A butter rich cake with a crunchy nut topping

Cake:
2	eggs
1	teaspoon vanilla extract
1	cup sugar
1	cup plus 1 tablespoon flour
1½	teaspoons baking powder
¼	teaspoon salt
½	cup heavy cream
½	cup butter, melted

Nut Topping:
3	tablespoons sugar
¼	cup butter
½	cup chopped pecans

Yield: 8 servings

The Cake:
- Preheat oven to 325°. Grease and flour a 9″ glass pie pan.

- Mix together eggs, vanilla, and sugar. In a separate bowl, stir together flour, baking powder, and salt. Add to egg mixture. Stir in cream and melted butter.

- Pour batter into prepared pan and bake at 325° for 30 minutes.

The Topping:
- Combine all ingredients in a small saucepan and heat until butter is melted. Spoon topping on cake. Return to oven.

- Turn oven temperature up to 375° and bake an additional 10 minutes. (Cake will not appear completely set until it cools).

- When cake cools, cut into wedges and serve.

Morning Celebration

An old world recipe to cherish and pass along.

1/4   cup lukewarm water
2   (1/4 ounce) packages active dry yeast
1   cup milk, scalded
1/4   cup butter, at room temperature
2   eggs, beaten
4³/4 cups flour
1/2   cup sugar
1   teaspoon salt
1/4   cup melted butter
1   egg, beaten

Fruit and Nut Filling:
2¹/2 cups very finely ground walnuts
1   cup sugar
2   tablespoons cinnamon
3/4   cup seedless golden raisins (optional)

Yield: 4 loaves

- Dissolve yeast in water.

- Add butter to scalded milk. Cool.

- Add eggs and yeast to milk mixture.

- In a large bowl combine 4 cups flour, sugar, and salt. Add milk mixture. Mix well with floured hands. Add some or all of remaining 3/4 cup flour, if dough is sticky. Knead dough in the bowl and form into a ball.

- Grease the inside of a second large bowl, place dough in the bowl and set in a warm place to rise until double in size.

- Punch down and let rise again for 1 hour.

- Preheat oven to 325°. Grease two cookie sheets.

- Stir together filling ingredients.

- Divide dough into four equal pieces. Form each piece into a ball. Working with 1 ball at a time, roll out on a well floured surface to a 12″ diameter circle. The dough should be paper thin.

- Brush with some of the melted butter and sprinkle with one quarter of the filling. Roll tightly, jelly roll fashion, and shape roll into a horseshoe. Place on baking sheet (two horseshoes per sheet).

- Repeat process for remaining dough balls. Brush each horseshoe with beaten egg.

- Bake at 325° for 20–25 minutes or until golden brown. (After cooling, the cakes can be wrapped and frozen.)

Note: To roll the very elastic dough paper thin, keep turning it over.

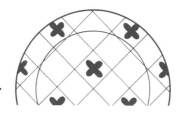

Cinnamon Sugar Balls

Delectable miniature muffins . . . bet you can't eat just one.

1/3 cup margarine, softened
1/2 cup sugar
1 egg
1 1/2 cups flour
1 1/2 teaspoons baking powder
1/4 teaspoon salt
1/4 teaspoon nutmeg
1/2 cup milk

Topping:
2 teaspoons cinnamon
2/3 cup sugar
1/2 cup margarine, melted

Yield: 2 dozen

- Preheat oven to 350°. Grease miniature muffin pans.

- In a food processor mix together margarine, sugar, and egg.

- Sift together dry ingredients.

- Alternately add dry ingredients and milk to food processor, processing well after each addition.

- Fill prepared muffin cups two thirds full with batter. Bake at 350° for 20-25 minutes or until golden.

- Remove muffin pans from oven and individual muffins from cups.

- Mix together cinnamon and sugar.

- Roll hot muffins in melted margarine and then roll in the cinnamon sugar mixture. Serve immediately.

Orange Cream Butter

A trick from the restaurant trade: serve waffles, biscuits, muffins, and breads with flavored butter spreads.

1 (8 ounce) package cream cheese, softened
1/4 cup butter, softened
1/4 teaspoon cinnamon
1 teaspoon vanilla extract
1 tablespoon finely grated orange peel
confectioners sugar

Garnish:
1 orange peel spiral

Yield: 1 1/4 cups

- Cream together cream cheese, butter, cinnamon, vanilla, and orange peel. Taste.

- If you want to sweeten spread, add confectioners sugar, 1 teaspoon at a time until desired sweetness is reached.

- Place in a serving bowl. Chill for 24 hours.

- Before serving, return to room temperature and garnish with orange spiral.

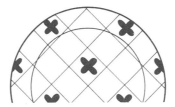

Cranberry Crown Cake

No holiday is complete without a festive beginning, a breakfast cake rich in eggs, sweet with sugar, and laden with fruit and nuts.

Cake:

¹/₂	cup unsalted butter
1	cup sugar
2	eggs
2	cups flour
1	teaspoon baking powder
1	teaspoon baking soda
1	cup sour cream or plain yogurt
1	teaspoon almond extract
1	(16 ounce) can whole berry cranberry sauce
³/₄	cup ground almonds

Sugar Glaze:

³/₄	cup confectioners sugar
1–2	teaspoons water
1	teaspoon almond extract

Yield: 8–10 servings

The Cake:

- Preheat oven to 350°. Grease and flour a 10″ bundt or tube pan.

- Cream together butter and sugar with an electric mixer. Beat in eggs one at a time.

- Sift together flour, baking powder, and baking soda. Alternately add small amounts of sour cream and flour mixture to creamed mixture. Stir in almond extract.

- Spoon one half of the batter into the prepared pan. Spread one half of the cranberry sauce over the batter and sprinkle with one half of the nuts. Repeat layers with remaining ingredients.

- With a long knife, cut through and swirl batter and layers.

- Bake at 350° for 50–60 minutes.

- Cool on a rack for 20 minutes before removing cake from pan.

The Glaze:

- Beat together all ingredients with a whisk or fork until smooth. Drizzle on cooled cake.

SOUPS
and
SANDWICHES

Soups and Sandwiches

Mushroom Chive Bisque

For a romantic tryst, begin with a bisque.

1   pound mushrooms, sliced
³/₄   cup butter
6   tablespoons flour
³/₈   teaspoon dry mustard
1   teaspoon salt
3   cups chicken broth
2   cups half and half
¹/₄   cup dry sherry
¹/₄   cup finely chopped chives

Garnish:
whipped cream
lavender chive blossoms

Yield: 5–6 servings

- In a large saucepan, sauté mushrooms in butter until limp.

- Add flour, mustard, and salt. Cook for an additional minute.

- Pour in the chicken broth and cook over low to medium heat until the soup thickens.

- Add the half and half, sherry, and chives and heat to serving temperature. Let the soup stand over low heat until ready to serve.

- *To serve the soup cold*: after adding the half and half, sherry, and chives, put mixture in a food processor, blend and chill.

- Garnish with whipped cream topped with a chive blossom.

Corn Silk Chowder

Use New Jersey corn, golden yellow and fresh from the fields.

2 slices bacon
1 small onion, chopped
2 medium potatoes, peeled and diced
2 cups fresh corn
1/2 cup chopped celery
2 cups chicken broth
1/4 teaspoon garlic powder
1/2 teaspoon seasoned salt
1/4 teaspoon pepper
2 tablespoons flour
2 cups buttermilk
parsley

Yield: 6 servings

- In a large saucepan, cook the bacon until crisp. Drain on paper towels and crumble.

- Cook the onion in the bacon drippings until they are limp.

- Add potatoes, corn, celery, 1 1/2 cups chicken broth, garlic powder, salt, and pepper. Bring to a boil, reduce heat, and simmer for 15 minutes.

- In a small bowl, blend the flour and remaining chicken broth. Add to simmering soup. Cook and stir until thick.

- Lower the heat and stir in the buttermilk. Heat through but do not boil.

- Top with crumbled bacon and chopped parsley.

- Serve with Cheese Bread (page 43).

Satin Pea Soup

A delicately flavored, pale, satin green soup

1   (10 ounce) package frozen peas,
       defrosted and drained
1/2   cup chopped leeks
10   spinach leaves
12   large lettuce leaves
1 1/2 cups chicken broth
1/2   teaspoon dried chervil
1/8   teaspoon white pepper
3/4   cup light cream
2   tablespoons butter

Garnish:
spinach leaves

Yield: *4 servings*

- In a large saucepan, simmer together the peas, leeks, spinach, lettuce, chicken broth, chervil, and pepper.

- Simmer with the lid on for 20 minutes.

- Pour the mixture into a food processor and process until smooth.

- Pour the soup through a sieve back into the saucepan. Add the light cream and butter. Simmer another 20 minutes.

- Serve in bowls garnished with a few finely cut ribbons of spinach floating on top.

Red Pepper Soup

This soup delights the eye and excites the sophisticated palate.

1   tablespoon olive oil
4   tablespoons unsalted butter
7 – 8 sweet red bell peppers, julienned
1   carrot, thinly sliced
3   shallots, sliced
1   clove garlic, minced
1   pear, peeled, quartered, and seeded
4   cups chicken broth
2   dashes Tabasco
1   teaspoon sugar
salt
freshly ground black pepper

Garnish:
sour cream
chopped chives

Yield: *8 cups*

- Heat the oil and butter in a large sauté pan. Sauté the peppers, carrot, shallots, garlic, and pear over medium heat for 8 – 10 minutes, or until tender.

- Add the chicken broth, Tabasco, and sugar. Bring to a boil, reduce heat and simmer, covered, for 25 – 30 minutes.

- Purée everything in a food processor. Add salt and pepper to taste.

- Serve hot or cold, garnished with sour cream and chives.

The Ultimate Cheddar Cheese Soup

The aroma of garlic, the crunch of vegetables, the velvety smoothness of cheese . . . truly a sensory experience.

1   clove garlic, minced
1   cup finely chopped onion
2   tablespoons butter
1   cup sliced mushrooms
1   red bell pepper, diced
1   pound extra sharp cheddar cheese,
            grated
2   tablespoons cornstarch
2   cups chicken broth
6   ounces ham, diced
1   teaspoon Worcestershire sauce
2   cups half and half
1   cup small broccoli pieces, cooked
3/4   cup diced and cooked carrots
salt
freshly ground black pepper

Garnish:
watercress sprigs

Yield: 6–8 servings

- In a skillet, sauté the garlic and onion in butter until limp, over low to medium heat.

- Add the mushrooms and red bell pepper. Cook and stir a few minutes longer.

- Mix together the cheese and cornstarch.

- In a large saucepan, bring the chicken broth to a boil. Reduce the heat and add the cheese and cornstarch mixture a little at a time. Stir until smooth.

- Add the ham, Worcestershire, half and half, onion mixture, broccoli, and carrots. Heat over low heat until hot, adding salt and pepper to taste.

- Serve in a white ironstone tureen garnished with watercress sprigs.

Mushroom and Artichoke Soup

An imaginative pairing of distinctively different flavors

3	tablespoons butter
2	tablespoons finely chopped onion
3/4	cup thinly sliced mushrooms
2	tablespoons flour
1½	cups chicken broth
2½	cups half and half
1	(13 ounce) can artichoke hearts, drained and diced

salt
cayenne pepper
Beau Monde seasoning

Garnish:
fresh mushroom slices
whole scallions

Yield: 4–6 servings

- In a large saucepan, melt the butter and sauté the onions and mushrooms for approximately 5 minutes or until golden brown.

- Stir in the flour and cook slowly for 2 minutes.

- Slowly add the chicken broth and half and half. Stir over low heat until the mixture thickens.

- Stir in the artichokes and add the seasonings to taste.

- Serve in brightly colored bowls garnished with a scallion swizzle stick and a few slices of mushrooms floating on top.

Onion Soup au Gratin

Perfect on a cold blustery night or après skiing or skating

6	medium onions, thinly sliced
3	tablespoons butter
3	tablespoons vegetable oil
1	tablespoon sugar
1	teaspoon salt

dash of nutmeg

7	cups strong beef bouillon, hot
1/4	cup dry sherry
6	slices French bread, toasted

grated Swiss cheese
grated Parmesan cheese

Yield: 6 servings

- Preheat oven to 300°.

- Sauté onions in butter and oil until soft. Add sugar, salt, and nutmeg and toss well. Cook down slightly, until the onions are golden brown.

- Add hot bouillon and bring to a boil. Simmer 10 minutes.

- Add the sherry. Season to taste.

- Ladle soup into 6 ovenproof soup bowls. Top each with a slice of French bread. Place approximately 2 tablespoons Swiss cheese on top of bread. Cook in a 300° oven for 10 minutes or until cheese melts and bubbles.

- Serve with Parmesan cheese.

Stone Harbor Chowder

Succulent beds of clams abound along the Jersey Shore.

3   *dozen hard shell clams or 2 (8 ounce) cans minced clams plus 1 bottle clam juice*
4   *slices lean bacon*
³/₄   *cup chopped onions*
³/₄   *cup sliced celery*
4   *cups peeled and diced potatoes*
2   *cups milk*
1   *cup half and half*

Garnish:
butter pats
chopped fresh parsley

Yield: 6–8 servings

- If you choose to buy or gather the clams, steam open in about 2 cups of water in a pot with a lid. This takes about 10 minutes. Discard any that fail to open. Save the cooking liquid as you drain the clams. Remove shells and chop clams coarsely.

- In a large saucepan, brown the bacon, drain on a paper towel, and crumble. Sauté the onion and celery in the bacon fat until the onion is limp.

- Add potatoes and 2 cups of the clam liquid. Cover and simmer until potatoes are tender.

- Take 1 cup of the cooked potatoes out of the pot and purée in a blender or food processor with the milk and the half and half. Return this purée to the saucepan and let the soup thicken.

- Add the clams and the crumbled bacon.

- Heat gently. *Be careful not to boil, as this would toughen the clams.*

- A dot of butter and a sprinkling of parsley in the serving bowl is traditional.

Oyster Stew

Year in, year out, oyster stew is an Atlantic shore specialty.

1/3	cup butter
1	tablespoon Worcestershire sauce
1/2	teaspoon salt
1/2	teaspoon pepper
1	teaspoon paprika
3	cups clam juice
1	pint shelled oysters
2	cups milk
1	cup cream

Garnish:
fresh chopped parsley or
     fresh chopped watercress

Yield: 5–6 small servings

- In a saucepan, heat together the butter, worcestershire, salt, pepper, and paprika.
- Stir in the clam juice and add the oysters. Cook only until the edges of the oysters curl.
- At this point, add the milk and cream veryslowly, stirring constantly. Heat almost to a boil and serve.
- Garnish with fresh chopped parsley or watercress and serve with oyster crackers.

Classic Chowder

Not chic or trendy, just an all American classic

1/2	cup finely chopped onion
1/2	cup butter
1/4	cup flour
2	teaspoons salt
1/2	teaspoon white pepper
1/4	teaspoon mace
4	cups light cream
1/2	pound small shrimp, shelled and deveined
1	(7 ounce) package frozen crabmeat, defrosted and drained
1/4	cup dry sherry

Yield: 6 servings

- In the top of a double boiler, over direct heat, sauté the onion in butter until the onions are soft but not brown.
- Remove from heat and add flour, salt, pepper, and mace. Stir until smooth and well blended.
- Stir in the light cream and cook the mixture over direct heat, stirring until thickened.
- Add the shrimp and place the saucepan over hot, not boiling water. Cook uncovered for 15–20 minutes until the shrimp are completely cooked.
- Add the crabmeat 5 minutes before the end of the cooking time.
- Just before serving, stir in the dry sherry.

Note: Serve with Watercress and Spinach Salad (page 100) and Dilly Bread (page 47).

Cream of Broccoli Soup

Your choice . . . serve steaming hot or refreshingly cold.

3	tablespoons butter
1	small onion, diced
1	large apple, diced
4	cups chicken broth
2	pounds fresh broccoli, chopped
¾	teaspoon coriander
½	teaspoon salt
½	cup heavy cream
½	cup sour cream

Garnish:
lemon slices

Yield: 4 servings

- In a large saucepan, heat the butter and add the onion and apple. Sauté for 2–3 minutes or until tender. Add the chicken broth and broccoli. Heat to boiling, reduce heat, and simmer for 8 minutes, or until broccoli is tender.

- Purée the entire mixture in a food processor. Season with coriander and salt.

- In a separate bowl whip the heavy cream until stiff peaks form. Fold in the sour cream and set aside.

- Reheat puréed mixture to serving temperature.

- Mix in cream combination just before serving and garnish with lemon slices.

- *To serve cold:* mix in cream combination and refrigerate until serving time.

Tofu Soup

A light soup with a hearty oriental flavor

1   pound tofu
1   cup watercress
2   small green onions, diced
1/2   cup ground pork
3   teaspoons light soy sauce
1/2   teaspoon dry sherry
1   tablespoon plus 2 teaspoons vegetable
       oil
8   cups water
2 1/2 teaspoons salt
1/4   teaspoon sugar
2 1/2 tablespoons cornstarch
1/2   teaspoon hot sesame oil (optional)

Yield: 6–8 servings

- Wash the tofu and cut it into 1/2" squares that are 1/4" thick.

- Cut the watercress, leaves and stems, into pieces about 2" long.

- Place the ground pork in a small bowl. Add 1 teaspoon soy sauce and the dry sherry to the meat. Mix well.

- In a large saucepan, heat 1 tablespoon of oil until it starts to smoke. Turn the heat down slightly and add the watercress. Stir well to cook evenly. This should only take 15 seconds. Remove and set aside.

- Place 2 teaspoons of vegetable oil in the saucepan and heat again until the oil is hot and begins to smoke. Turn the heat down and add the ground pork. Stir until the meat is almost cooked. Add the tofu to the meat and stir several times. *Do not break the tofu.*

- Add 8 cups of water and heat until it boils. Add 2 teaspoons soy sauce, salt, and sugar. Mix well, being careful not to break the tofu.

- In a small bowl mix the cornstarch with a small amount of cold water. Stir this into the soup and bring to a boil.

- Add the cooked watercress. If spicy flavor is desired, add hot sesame oil. Serve immediately.

Note: Ground beef can be used instead of ground pork for a different flavor.

Salad Soup

Different than a gazpacho, this soup is one of a kind.

1	clove garlic
2	large tomatoes, seeded and chopped
2	cucumbers, peeled, seeded, and chopped
1	onion, chopped
1	green bell pepper, seeded and chopped
1	cup tomato juice
1/4	cup wine vinegar
1/4	cup olive oil
1	tablespoon tarragon
1/4	teaspoon Tabasco
2	teaspoons sugar
1	teaspoon salt
1	(10 1/2 ounce) can condensed beef consommé

freshly ground black pepper

Yield: 6 servings

- Cut garlic in half and rub the inside of a large glass or pottery bowl. Add chopped vegetables to bowl.

- Combine liquids and spices. Pour over vegetables. Chill for several hours or overnight.

- Serve ice cold in small bowls.

Note: This is delicious as is, or you may offer small bowls of croutons, sliced radishes, chopped hard boiled eggs, and sour cream so that your guests may add their own garnishes.

Chilled Cranberry Cream

Pretty 'n Pink — a beautiful beginning to a holiday meal.

1	pound fresh cranberries
	cinnamon stick
1	cup sugar
2	cups heavy cream
	salt
	freshly ground black pepper

Garnish:
sour cream
nutmeg

Yield: 4 servings

- Place the cranberries and cinnamon stick in a saucepan and cover with water plus 1/2" of additional water. (The cranberries are buoyant, so measure the water carefully.)
- Boil gently until cranberries are very tender and fall apart. Remove the cinnamon stick and add sugar to taste.
- Purée the cranberries in a food processor and strain well.
- Add the cream and reheat until just simmering. *Do not boil.* Add salt and pepper to taste. Chill.
- Serve in glass bowls and garnish with a dollop of sour cream and a dash of nutmeg.

Off-Beet Borscht

A hearty, thick, zesty soup that can be served as an informal first course before dinner.

4	cups chicken broth
32	ounces cooked beets
2	tablespoons dill weed
2	teaspoons seasoned salt
	juice of 2 lemons
1	teaspoon freshly ground black pepper
2	tablespoons low sodium soy sauce
2	tablespoons sugar
1	pint sour cream

Garnish:
lemon slices
dill weed

Yield: 4–6 servings

- Combine the chicken broth and beets in a food processor. (Due to the amount, you will probably have to do this in two batches.) Process for about 10 seconds.
- Add the dill weed, seasoned salt, lemon juice, pepper, soy sauce, and sugar.
- Place all of the ingredients in a saucepan and simmer for 15 minutes.
- If you plan to serve this cold, cool a bit and then refrigerate in a covered container.
- Just before serving, stir in sour cream. Garnish each serving with a lemon slice and a sprinkle of dill weed.

Garden Soup

A potpourri of exquisite garden ingredients

2   tablespoons butter
1/4   cup chopped onion
2   cups unpeeled, seeded, and chopped cucumber
1   cup watercress leaves
1/2   cup peeled and finely diced potatoes
2   cups chicken broth
2   sprigs parsley
1/2   teaspoon salt
1/4   teaspoon pepper
1/4   teaspoon mustard
1   cup heavy cream

Garnish:
chopped radish
snipped chives
diced cucumber

Yield: 4–6 servings

- In a large saucepan, cook the onions in the butter until they are limp.

- Add the cucumber, watercress leaves, potatoes, chicken broth, parsley, salt, pepper, and mustard. Simmer 15 minutes or until the potatoes are tender.

- Purée the mixture in a food processor.

- Add the cream to the puréed mixture.

- The soup may be served hot or cold, garnished with a sprinkling of radishes, chives, and cucumber.

Cold Spinach Soup

An epicurean delight, for a picnic, barbecue, or hot summer night

2   (10 ounce) packages frozen chopped
       spinach, defrosted
2   tablespoons vegetable oil
1   medium onion, finely chopped
3   cups chicken broth
1   lightly packed cup fresh basil
1   cup light cream
¹/₂   cup plain yogurt
salt
freshly ground black pepper

Garnish:
¹/₄   cup minced pimento

Yield: *6 servings*

- Drain the spinach in a large sieve, pressing with the back of a wooden spoon to eliminate as much water as possible.

- Heat the oil in a large skillet, add onion and sauté until soft and translucent.

- Stir in spinach and cook for 2–3 minutes, stirring constantly.

- In a large saucepan, bring chicken broth to a boil. Add the spinach mixture and basil.

- Purée the soup in 2–3 batches in a blender. Pour the soup into a serving bowl and stir in the cream. Cover loosely and let cool.

- When soup reaches room temperature, stir in the yogurt. Add salt and pepper to taste. Cover and chill.

- At serving time, garnish with minced pimento.

Rainbow Pitas

A colorful garden rainbow packed in a pita

3	cups shredded red cabbage
2	cups sliced celery
2	cups shredded carrots
1/3	cup sunflower seeds
alfalfa sprouts	
8	mini pitas
1	cup mayonnaise
1	teaspoon curry powder

Yield: 8 servings

- In a large bowl, combine the red cabbage, celery, and carrots.

- Blend together mayonnaise and curry. Fold into rainbow mixture and combine well.

- Toss in sunflower seeds.

- Cut the mini pitas in half. Open each half like a pocket and fill with rainbow mixture. At serving time, top each pita with a teaspoon or more of alfalfa sprouts.

Note: Vegetable shredding is quick and easy with a food processor.

Watercress Tea Sandwiches

An easy to prepare luncheon or tea time delight

1	small bunch watercress
5	hard boiled eggs, peeled
5	tablespoons mayonnaise
2 1/2	tablespoons Dijon mustard
1/4	teaspoon salt
1	(1 pound) loaf thinly sliced white bread

Yield: 25 sandwiches

- Trim 1/2 the watercress of stems. Wash and drain leaves. Pat dry with paper towels. Coarsely chop the leaves. Save the rest for garnish.

- In a food processor, coarsely chop the eggs. Add the mayonnaise, mustard, and salt. Process until smooth. Fold in the chopped watercress and chill.

- Spread the mixture on a slice of bread, topping with another slice. Trim the crusts and cut into finger sandwiches.

- Garnish with additional sprigs of watercress.

Note: For an attractive presentation, use a combination of white, whole wheat, and pumpernickel breads.

Lord Sterling Crab

A sandwich spectacular for your local royalty

1   pound crabmeat, thoroughly cleaned
        and shredded
2   tablespoons minced green bell pepper
3/4 cup finely chopped celery
2   tablespoons minced onion
1   cup mayonnaise
1   cup cubed cheddar cheese
dash Worcestershire sauce
dash Tabasco
salt
freshly ground black pepper
dash lemon juice
8   fresh buns or croissants, split in half
grated Parmesan cheese

Garnish:
shredded lettuce
paprika

Yield: *8 servings*

- In a large bowl, mix all sandwich ingredients thoroughly. Adjust seasoning to taste.

- Lightly brown the buns or croissants under the broiler.

- Remove from heat and spread crabmeat mixture on top of the buns or croissants.

- Sprinkle with Parmesan cheese and broil until lightly browned and bubbly.

- Serve at once, garnished with shredded lettuce and a sprinkling of paprika.

SALADS
and
DRESSINGS

Salads and Dressings

Fajita Salad

Here is a great new twist to the fajita fad.

Dressing:
1/2	cup olive oil
1/4	cup lemon juice
1/4	cup chopped fresh cilantro
3	green onions, chopped
1	teaspoon minced garlic
3/4	teaspoon salt
3/4	teaspoon pepper

Salad:
1	(15 1/2 ounce) can pinto beans, drained and rinsed
1	avocado, diced
3	medium tomatoes, seeded and diced
1	head lettuce, shredded
1	head radicchio, shredded or 2 bunches watercress

Fajitas:
1	pound beef (sirloin or flank steak)
1/2	teaspoon seasoned salt
1/2	teaspoon pepper
1/2	teaspoon olive oil
6	flour tortillas

Yield: 4–6 servings

The Dressing:
- Combine all ingredients in a container with a tight fitting lid. Shake well until thoroughly combined.

The Salad:
- Pour 3 tablespoons of dressing over pinto beans. Toss well.

- In another container, toss 3 tablespoons dressing with avocado and tomato chunks.

- In a large bowl, toss lettuce and radicchio or watercress with remaining dressing.

The Meat:
- Sprinkle meat with salt and pepper. Brush a cast iron skillet with oil and heat over high heat until it begins to smoke. Sear meat for about 2 minutes on each side, or until rare or medium rare.

- Slice very thin across the grain.

Assemble and Serve:
- Preheat oven to 200°. Warm flour tortillas in oven for a few minutes.

- Line a large platter with greens. Arrange sliced steak in center of greens; place beans on one side of meat, avocados and tomatoes on the other.

- Serve salad with a dish of warm tortillas. Guests roll their own tortillas filled with salad ingredients.

Optional:
- Serve with side dishes of Mexican salsa, sour cream, black olives, etc.

Chicken Salad Suprème

This salad makes a beautiful impression when served with cold asparagus vinaigrette.

2 cups diced cooked chicken
1½ cups strawberries, sliced in half
1½ cups fresh pineapple chunks
1 cup seedless green grapes
1 cup diagonally sliced celery
2 cups mayonnaise
½ teaspoon salt
freshly ground black pepper
½–1 teaspoon ground ginger
½ cup blanched and slivered almonds
1 tablespoon butter
leafy greens
10 whole strawberries

Yield: 4–6 servings

- Combine chicken, fruit, and celery in a bowl. Toss to mix.

- In a small bowl, combine the mayonnaise, salt, pepper, and ginger. Mix thoroughly.

- In a small frying pan, sauté the almonds in the butter until golden brown. Remove from pan and chill.

- Arrange leafy greens on a serving platter. Gently combine the chicken mixture with enough dressing to moisten. Mound chicken salad in the center of the greens. Top with almonds and whole strawberries. Serve immediately with remaining dressing on the side.

Wine: *California Extra Dry Champagne*

Cold Steak Salad

A meal in itself when served with Frenchtown Bread (page 46).

Dressing:
1/4   cup vegetable oil
1/3   cup white wine vinegar
2   tablespoons Dijon mustard
2   cloves garlic, minced
1   teaspoon soy sauce
1/2   teaspoon worcestershire sauce
1   teaspoon onion salt
freshly ground black pepper

Salad:
2   pounds grilled or broiled steak, chilled
2   (8 ounce) cans artichoke hearts,
     drained and quartered
1   pint cherry tomatoes
1   pound mushrooms, sliced
3/4   cup diced celery
2   tablespoons chopped fresh chives
3   tablespoons chopped fresh parsley

Yield: 8 servings

The Dressing:
- In a container with a tight fitting lid, combine dressing ingredients. Shake well until thoroughly mixed.

The Salad:
- Thinly slice steak and cut into bite size pieces.

- Combine steak with remaining salad ingredients.

- Toss salad with dressing. Chill for 6 or more hours. Stir and serve.

Note: Cold leftover steak, London Broil, or roast beef can be used.

Ham and Turkey Salad

An eclectic mix of flavors and textures

1 1/2   cups mayonnaise
1 1/2   teaspoons curry powder
2   teaspoons soy sauce
4   cups diced cooked turkey
2   cups diced cooked ham
1   cup slivered almonds
1   cup seedless grapes, halved
lettuce leaves

Garnish:
seedless grapes

Yield: 8 servings

- Blend mayonnaise, curry powder, and soy sauce until well combined.

- Combine turkey, ham, almonds, and grapes in a large container. Add mayonnaise mixture and toss until well coated.

- Cover and chill for several hours or overnight.

- Serve on a bed of lettuce leaves and garnish with additional seedless grapes.

Chicken Collage Salad

This salad is a feast for the eyes as well as the palate.

Dressing:

1/3	cup vegetable oil
1/4	cup red wine vinegar
1/4	cup lemon juice
1	tablespoon sugar
1	teaspoon salt
1/2	teaspoon pepper
1/4	teaspoon minced fresh garlic

Salad:

1	cup ripe olives, sliced in wedges
1/2	green bell pepper, cut into strips
1/4	cup finely chopped red onion
2	tablespoons thinly sliced pimento
4	cups shredded lettuce
1	avocado, cut into crescents
1 1/2	cups boned cooked chicken, cut into strips

Yield: *4 servings*

The Dressing:

- Combine all ingredients in a container with a tight fitting lid. Shake well until thoroughly combined. Refrigerate for at least 30 minutes.

The Salad:

- Just before serving, combine all salad ingredients except for avocado and chicken. Toss salad ingredients with enough dressing to lightly coat.

- Arrange salad on a platter and place chicken strips and avocado slices on top of salad. Serve with remaining dressing on the side.

Tangy Pasta Wheels

The sweet and sour sauce definitely gives this pasta salad a new twist.

Dressing:
1/4	*cup extra virgin olive oil*
1	*tablespoon white wine vinegar*
1	*teaspoon sugar*
1/4	*cup mayonnaise*
1/4	*cup sour cream*
1	*teaspoon salt*

freshly ground black pepper

Salad:
2	*cups pasta wheels (rotelle)*
1/2	*medium red onion, finely chopped*
1/4	*cup finely chopped red or green bell pepper*
1	*stalk celery, finely chopped*
1	*small carrot, diced*
2	*tablespoons finely chopped fresh chives*
1	*tablespoon finely chopped fresh parsley*

Garnish:
red or green bell pepper strips
fresh parsley

Yield: 4 servings

The Dressing:
- In a bowl, combine the dressing ingredients. Beat vigorously with a wire whisk until very creamy and smooth.

The Salad:
- Bring a large quantity of salted water to a boil in a large pot. Add pasta and cook for 5–6 minutes or until "al denté." Drain well.

- Transfer the pasta to a large bowl and add the onion, red or green pepper, celery, carrot, chives, and parsley.

- Pour dressing over pasta mixture and toss until well coated. Cover and refrigerate for several hours to blend flavors.

- Remove the salad from the refrigerator 30 minutes before serving. Garnish with red and green pepper strips and fresh parsley.

Bow Tie Salad

An "antipasto" in a salad bowl . . . perfect for a picnic

Dressing:
1 1/4 cups mayonnaise
1/3 cup freshly grated Parmesan cheese
1/3 cup chopped fresh parsley
1/4 teaspoon oregano
1/4 teaspoon basil
1 small clove garlic, minced

Salad:
4 ounces bow tie pasta, cooked and
    drained
4 ounces salami, cut into 1/2" cubes
1 (8 ounce) can artichoke hearts,
    drained and quartered
1 cup sliced mushrooms
1 cup thinly sliced zucchini
1 cup broccoli flowerets
1/2 cup diced red and green bell pepper

Yield: 6 servings

The Dressing:
- In a large bowl, stir together dressing ingredients until smooth.

The Salad:
- Add pasta and other salad ingredients to bowl with dressing. Toss well to coat thoroughly.

- Cover and refrigerate for at least 2 hours to let the flavors blend.

Chutney Chicken Salad

An international collage of ingredients in perfect harmony

Dressing:
2 cups mayonnaise
5 ounces Chut-Nut
1 teaspoon curry powder

Salad:
4 whole chicken breasts, boned,
    skinned, and cooked
1 (12 ounce) can peanuts
1 (7 ounce) package flaked coconut
1 cup raisins

Yield: 12 servings

The Dressing:
- Combine all ingredients. Stir until curry is thoroughly blended.

The Salad:
- Cut chicken in chunks. Combine with peanuts, coconut and raisins.

- Toss salad ingredients with dressing. Refrigerate until ready to serve.

Mandarin Shrimp Salad

A rainbow of colors and flavors that is delightful to behold.

Dressing:

3/4	cup sugar
1/3	cup white wine vinegar
1	teaspoon salt
1	teaspoon dry mustard
1	cup oil
1	tablespoon celery seed

Salad:

2	cups cooked shrimp (approximately 1 pound)
1	cup diced celery
1/2	cup diced red onion
1/4	cup diced green bell pepper
4	cups lettuce, torn into bite size pieces
1	(11 ounce) can mandarin oranges, drained
1	cup canned pineapple chunks, drained
1/4	cup flaked coconut
1	(8 ounce) can water chestnuts, chopped
1/3	cup almonds or cashews

Yield: 8–10 servings

The Dressing:

- Combine all dressing ingredients in a container with a tight fitting lid. Shake well until thoroughly combined.

The Salad:

- Cut shrimp into halves or thirds. Toss shrimp with celery, onion, green pepper, and lettuce. Add enough dressing to moisten and toss until thoroughly coated. Mound on serving plattter.

- Arrange oranges, pineapple, coconut, water chestnuts, and nuts on top. Serve with remaining dressing on the side.

Pasta with Fresh Tomato and Basil Sauce

Balsamic vinegar gives this salad its special flavor.

2	pounds fresh ripe tomatoes
1	cup coarsely chopped fresh basil
3	tablespoons balsamic vinegar
1	(3¾ ounce) jar capers, drained and rinsed

salt
freshly ground black pepper

1	pound small pasta shells

¾–1 cup extra virgin olive oil

Yield: 6 servings

- Peel, seed, and chop tomatoes. Combine tomatoes with basil and marinate at room temperature for 1–2 hours, or overnight in the refrigerator.

- Blend vinegar and capers, add salt and pepper to taste. Pour over tomato mixture and toss until combined.

- Bring a large amount of salted water to a boil. Cook pasta until "al denté" and drain well.

- Transfer pasta to a platter, pour olive oil over and toss until well coated. Mix in the marinated tomatoes. Let stand at least 30 minutes.

- Serve at room temperature or refrigerate several hours and serve cold.

New Potato Salad

A tribute to the past that is "right on" for today.

5	pounds red, new potatoes
1	pound bacon, diced
¼	cup Dijon mustard
2	tablespoons lemon juice
1	teaspoon salt
1	teaspoon white pepper
1	teaspoon freshly ground black pepper
3	tablespoons chopped fresh parsley
3	tablespoons chopped fresh basil
1	medium red onion, diced
½	red bell pepper, diced
2	celery stalks, diced
2	cups mayonnaise

Garnish:
finely sliced Spanish olives

Yield: 8–10 servings

- Boil potatoes until tender. Let cool and slice. Skins may be left on or peeled.

- Sauté bacon until crisp, sprinkle over potatoes with drippings. Toss until potatoes are coated.

- Add remaining ingredients, except mayonnaise, and toss gently.

- Mix in mayonnaise until desired consistency is reached.

- Chill for at least 2 hours before serving. Serve garnished with Spanish olives.

Jersey Reds with Herb Dressing

Our New Jersey Beefsteak Tomatoes are nationally famous, but any red, ripe, luscious tomato will be complimented by this dressing.

Dressing:
2/3	cup vegetable oil
1/3	cup tarragon vinegar
2	tablespoons sour cream
1	teaspoon Dijon mustard
1	clove garlic, crushed
2	tablespoons chopped fresh parsley
2	tablespoons chopped fresh basil or fresh mint

Salad:
4	ripe tomatoes, thinly sliced
2	shallots, chopped

Garnish:
basil or mint leaves
edible flowers

Yield: 4–6 servings

The Dressing:
- Combine dressing ingredients in a container with a tight fitting lid. Shake until well blended. Refrigerate until ready to serve.

The Salad:
- Arrange sliced tomatoes on serving platter. Pour dressing over tomatoes. Sprinkle with shallots.
- Garnish with basil or mint leaves and edible flowers, such as pansies, nasturtiums, snapdragons, azaleas, or freesias.

Orange–Onion Salad with Celery Seed Dressing

Contrasting flavors combine for a refreshingly different taste.

Salad:
1/2	cup sliced almonds
3–4	cups dark salad greens, torn (Romaine, escarole, watercress, etc.)
1	(11 ounce) can mandarin oranges, drained
1	small red onion, sliced thin and separated into rings

Dressing:
1/4	cup vegetable oil
1/2	teaspoon salt
2	tablespoons cider vinegar
1/4	cup honey
1/2	teaspoon celery seed

Yield: 6–8 servings

The Salad:
- Spread almonds on a baking sheet and bake at 300° for approximately 10 minutes until golden. Watch carefully, so they do not burn. Let cool.
- Combine lettuce, oranges, and onion in salad bowl. Add toasted almonds.

The Dressing:
- Combine dressing ingredients in a blender and whirl until well blended. Toss with salad mixture until thoroughly coated.

Picnic Hamper Salad

The hearty flavor of this salad makes it perfect for a fall tailgate picnic buffet.

1	head cauliflower, cleaned and broken into flowerets
1	cup shredded sharp cheddar cheese
1	small onion, diced (about ⅓ cup)
1	(10 ounce) package frozen green peas, defrosted and uncooked
1	(3 ounce) jar real bacon bits
1	tablespoon salad herbs
1	teaspoon celery salt
2	cups (or less) mayonnaise

Yield: 6–8 servings

- Combine all ingredients. Toss until thoroughly mixed.
- Refrigerate several hours or overnight.

Cabbage Patch Salad

This is true to the saying, "Fresh is best."

Dressing:
1	cup white wine vinegar
1	teaspoon dry mustard
¾	cup vegetable oil
1	teaspoon celery seed

Salad:
1	medium cabbage, shredded
2–3	carrots, shredded
1	medium onion, coarsely chopped
1	green bell pepper, coarsely chopped
1	large cucumber, peeled and thinly sliced
½	cup sugar
salt	

Yield: 10–12 servings

The Dressing:
- Combine dressing ingredients in a small pan and bring to a boil, stirring occasionally. Cool.

The Salad:
- Place shredded cabbage in a large container with a cover. Add carrots, onion, and green pepper in a layer over cabbage. Place cucumber in a layer over the top. Sprinkle with sugar and a little salt.
- Pour dressing over the vegetables, cover and chill for at least 24 hours before serving. (Tastes much better the next day.)
- Before serving, stir well to mix thoroughly. (Keeps well for 4–5 days.)

Peas, Please

Never in or out of season . . . always just right.

2   (10 ounce) packages frozen green
       peas, defrosted and uncooked
2   cups sliced celery
1   cup coarsely chopped radishes
1/2   cup thinly sliced green onions
1 1/2 cups sour cream
2   tablespoons vegetable oil
1/2   teaspoon Dijon mustard
1   teaspoon salt
freshly ground black pepper
1   head lettuce, shredded

Yield: 8 servings

- Combine vegetables in a large bowl.
- Stir together sour cream, oil, mustard, salt, and pepper. Fold gently but thoroughly into vegetables. Cover and chill several hours or overnight.
- To serve, line a platter with shredded lettuce. Spoon pea salad on top.

Oriental Slaw

This is definitely not cole slaw! These unusual ingredients merge for a remarkable taste.

Dressing:
1/2   cup vegetable oil
beef flavor packet from oriental noodles
2   teaspoons vinegar
2   tablespoons sugar
1/4   teaspoon salt
1/2   teaspoon pepper

Salad:
1   (3 ounce) package oriental noodles,
       beef flavor
3   tablespoons sunflower seeds
1/2   cup sliced almonds, toasted
1   head cabbage, shredded
1   medium red onion, thinly sliced

Yield: 12–15 servings

The Dressing:
- Combine ingredients in a food processor and process until thoroughly mixed.

The Salad:
- Preheat oven to 350°.
- Break up oriental noodles into a food processor and process with a few short bursts of power until coarsely crushed.
- Spread crushed noodles, almonds, and sunflower seeds on a cookie sheet and toast at 350° for 6–8 minutes, or until golden. Set aside.
- Pour dressing over cabbage and onion and toss until well combined. Refrigerate for 2 or more hours. Just before serving, add noodles, almonds, and sunflower seeds. Toss gently.

Fiesta Aspic

A League member living in Mexico adapted her classic tomato aspic recipe to reflect the spicy cuisine of that country. This is the happy result.

1	cup tomato sauce
2	cups V-8 juice
1	tablespoon chopped onion
4	peppercorns
8	whole cloves
1	tablespoon oregano
1/4	teaspoon cayenne pepper
1	teaspoon thyme
1	teaspoon salt
2 1/2	tablespoons unflavored gelatin
1/2	cup water
2	tablespoons lemon juice
6	tablespoons vinegar
1/2	cup chopped olives
1/2	cup peeled, seeded, and chopped cucumber
1/2	cup chopped celery
lettuce	

Yield: *4 cup mold*

- In a saucepan, combine the tomato sauce, V-8, onion, all the spices, and salt. Heat until simmering, and continue to simmer, covered, for 15 minutes. Strain.

- Sprinkle gelatin over water and let soften for 5 minutes.

- Add lemon juice and vinegar to strained tomato mixture. Mix in softened gelatin until well combined. Refrigerate until mixture begins to thicken.

- Add olives, cucumber, and celery to thickened mixture.

- Rinse a 4 cup mold with cold water. Pour aspic into mold and chill until firm. Unmold onto lettuce lined platter and serve.

Artichoke–Asparagus Salad

This elegant salad looks even lovelier when garnished with edible flowers.

Salad:
1	teaspoon sesame seeds
1/2	pound fresh asparagus spears
1	(6 ounce) jar marinated artichoke hearts
1/2	cup sliced fresh mushrooms
1/4	cup sliced green onions
1	tablespoon vinegar
1	teaspoon sugar
1/4	teaspoon salt

Tabasco
1   head lettuce, shredded

Garnish:
assorted edible flowers: nasturtiums, pansies, snapdragons, azaleas, or freesias

Yield: 4–6 servings

- Place sesame seeds on a baking sheet and bake at 300° until golden. Watch carefully to avoid burning.

- Steam asparagus for 10 minutes, or until crisp-tender. Place cooked spears in a 10″ × 6″ × 2″ baking dish.

- Drain artichoke hearts and reserve marinade. Slice any large artichokes in half.

- Add artichokes, mushrooms, and green onions to asparagus.

- Combine reserved marinade, vinegar, sugar, sesame seeds, salt, and several dashes of Tabasco. Pour marinade over vegetables. Cover and refrigerate for several hours.

- Arrange shredded lettuce on serving platter. Remove vegetables from marinade with slotted spoon and place on top of shredded lettuce. Garnish with edible flowers.

Romaine and Endive Salad

Perfection from the garden of earthly delights

1   medium head Romaine lettuce
¹/₃ – ¹/₂ pound endive
2   cloves garlic
¹/₄   teaspoon salt
1   rounded teaspoon Dijon mustard
3   tablespoons white wine vinegar
¹/₂   cup extra virgin olive oil
freshly ground black pepper
¹/₄   cup freshly grated Parmesan cheese
¹/₄   cup pine nuts, lightly toasted

Yield: 6–8 servings

- Wash, dry, and thinly slice the Romaine and endive.

- Boil the garlic in a small saucepan of boiling water for 10 minutes. Drain well.

- In a large salad bowl, mash the garlic to a paste with the salt. Whisk in the mustard and vinegar. Continue whisking as you add the oil in a fine stream until well blended.

- Add the endive and Romaine. Toss to combine well and season with pepper. Sprinkle with Parmesan and pine nuts.

Three Leaf Salad

The hearty flavor of this salad goes well with grilled beef or lamb.

Dressing:
1   cup extra virgin olive oil
¹/₄   cup lemon juice
1   teaspoon salt
2   cloves garlic, pressed
1   cup grated Swiss cheese

Salad:
3   large heads soft lettuce (Boston, Ruby, Butter Crunch, or Salad Bowl)
2   tablespoons sesame seeds, toasted
6   strips bacon (fried, drained, and crumbled)

Yield: 8 servings

The Dressing:
- Combine all ingredients except cheese in a blender. Whirl at high speed for 30 seconds. Just before serving, put very cold cheese in blender and whirl again.

The Salad:
- Wash and dry lettuce. Tear into bite size pieces.

- Pour dressing over lettuce and toss until lettuce is thoroughly coated.

- Sprinkle bacon and sesame seeds on top. Toss lightly and serve.

Note: Swiss cheese must be thoroughly chilled. Best if stored in coldest part of refrigerator.

Salad with Warm Brie Dressing

The dressing tastes best when made with a young Brie, not quite ripe, with the rind snowy white.

Croutons:
5	slices whole wheat or multi-grain bread
3	tablespoons butter
1	clove garlic

Salad:
1	head Romaine lettuce
1	bunch watercress

Warm Brie Dressing:
1/2	cup vegetable oil
4	tablespoons chopped onion
1	tablespoon chopped garlic
1/3	cup tarragon vinegar
1	tablespoon lemon juice
3	teaspoons Dijon mustard
7	ounces Brie cheese

Yield: 6 servings

The Croutons:
- Remove crusts from bread and cut into cubes.

- Melt butter in a heavy skillet. Put garlic through a garlic press and add to butter. Stir. Fry bread cubes in garlic butter until golden.

- Remove from skillet and drain on paper towels.

The Salad:
- Wash and dry Romaine. Slice vertically through the center spine of each leaf. Then slice each piece horizontally into 1½″ strips.

- Wash, dry, and remove tough stems from watercress. Toss with Romaine and arrange on individual plates.

The Dressing:
- Heat oil in a heavy skillet and fry onion and garlic until limp and slightly golden. Turn heat to warm.

- Add vinegar, lemon juice, and mustard. Combine well.

- Remove the thin layer of the rind from the Brie. Discard the rind. Cut the cheese into chunks.

- Turn up the heat under the skillet. Add the Brie and stir with a wooden spoon until melted.

- Pour dressing over greens and top with croutons. Serve immediately while still warm.

Watercress–Spinach Salad

The vivid green of this salad is lovely when served in a glass salad bowl.

Salad:
2   bunches watercress
4   cups loosely packed spinach leaves
6   strips bacon, cooked crisp, drained, and crumbled

Dressing:
1/2   cup vegetable oil
2   tablespoons tarragon vinegar
2   teaspoons olive oil
1   egg
1/2   teaspoon sugar
1/2   teaspoon dry mustard
1   heaping teaspoon Dijon mustard
salt
freshly ground black pepper
1   clove garlic, pressed

Yield: 6 servings

The Salad:
• Wash greens and remove large stems. Dry thoroughly and tear into bite size pieces. Place greens in large bowl and sprinkle with bacon.

The Dressing:
• Combine all ingredients except garlic and mix thoroughly.

• Just before serving, add garlic, mix well, and toss dressing with greens.

Romaine Toss

The tangy dressing is prepared right in the serving bowl, so it is a snap.

Dressing:
6   tablespoons olive oil
1   large clove garlic, crushed
1   tablespoon prepared dark mustard
1   tablespoon worcestershire sauce
1   teaspoon prepared horseradish
1   egg
3–4 tablespoons fresh lemon juice
3   tablespoons grated Parmesan cheese

Salad:
1   large head Romaine lettuce
1/2–1 cup croutons
freshly ground black pepper

Yield: 4–6 servings

The Dressing:
• Pour olive oil into a large wooden salad bowl. Add garlic. While beating with a fork, gradually add mustard, worcestershire, horseradish, egg, and lemon juice. Keep beating until you have a frothy uniform dressing.

• Mix in Parmesan cheese.

The Salad:
• Wash and thoroughly drain Romaine. Tear into bite size pieces.

• Toss lettuce in dressing until thoroughly coated. Add croutons and a generous amount of freshly ground black pepper.

Endive and Edible Flower Salad

Surprise your guests with the latest trend . . . edible flowers.

Dressing:

1/2	teaspoon curry powder
1/4	cup white wine vinegar or fresh lemon juice
1	tablespoon sugar
1	teaspoon salt
1/4	teaspoon freshly ground black pepper
3/4	cup olive oil or vegetable oil

Salad:

1	head Belgian endive
1/2	pound spinach leaves
1	large head Bibb lettuce
1	head red leaf lettuce
1	small carrot, pared and julienned
1	small stalk celery, julienned
1/4	pound green beans, julienned

assorted edible flowers: pansies, nasturtiums, snapdragons, azaleas, or freesias

Yield: 8 servings

The Dressing:

- In a medium saucepan, over medium-high heat, cook curry powder 2–3 minutes, stirring constantly. Remove saucepan from heat, stir in vinegar, sugar, salt, and pepper.

- Whisk in oil, a few drops at a time, until dressing is completely combined. Set aside while arranging salads.

The Salad:

- Wash and crisp salad greens. Remove tough stems from spinach. Tear all into bite size pieces.

- Rinse flowers and place on paper towels in refrigerator until ready to serve.

- On each of eight salad plates, arrange a portion of each salad green. Arrange carrot, celery, and green bean strips over lettuce. Place 4–8 blossoms on each salad.

- Spoon about 2 tablespoons dressing over each salad. Serve immediately.

Note: At some grocers, you can buy an assortment of wild young greens and edible flowers called "mesclun."

Almost Caesar Salad

An inspired preparation of a classic

Croutons:
1   loaf French or Italian bread
1½   tablespoons vegetable oil

Dressing:
3   teaspoons finely chopped garlic
2   eggs
⅛   teaspoon salt
4   tablespoons lemon juice
6–8   flat anchovies
2   teaspoons Dijon mustard
1   teaspoon worcestershire sauce
4   tablespoons olive oil
freshly ground black pepper

Salad:
2   medium heads Romaine lettuce, torn
        into bite size pieces
1   cup freshly grated Parmesan cheese

Yield: 8 servings

The Croutons:
- Cut a loaf of French or Italian bread into 1½″ slices. Cut slices into cubes.

- Pour oil into a skillet and heat until a haze appears. Brown bread in oil on all sides. Remove with a slotted spoon and drain on several thicknesses of paper towels.

The Dressing:
- Combine all ingredients in a blender and whirl until well mixed.

To Assemble and Serve:
- Place blended dressing in the bottom of a wooden salad bowl.

- Add torn greens and toss to coat with dressing. Add Parmesan and toss again. Scatter croutons over salad and serve.

Salad Facile

Sophisticated ingredients and a dressing redolent with herbs

1	teaspoon salt
2	cloves garlic, crushed
1/3	cup olive oil
3	tablespoons red wine vinegar
1	teaspoon dry mustard
1/4	teaspoon freshly ground black pepper
1/2	teaspoon oregano
1/2	teaspoon basil
1/2	cup minced fresh parsley
3	tablespoons minced green onions
4	heads Bibb lettuce, torn into small pieces
1	Belgian endive, sliced
2	tomatoes, sliced
2	tablespoons coarsely chopped walnuts
3	tablespoons capers

Yield: 8 servings

- Sprinkle salt into a large salad bowl. Add garlic, olive oil, vinegar, mustard, pepper, oregano, and basil. Mix with a whisk until smooth.

- Add the parsley, green onions, and lettuce. Toss well.

- Add the endive, tomatoes, walnuts, and capers. Toss lightly.

- Serve immediately.

Five Minute French Dressing

The celery seed makes this an out-of-the ordinary French dressing. It is particularly good on spinach salad.

1	medium onion, cut in eighths
1	cup sugar
1/2	cup vinegar
1	cup vegetable oil
1/3	cup catsup
1	teaspoon salt
1	teaspoon celery seeds

- Combine onion, sugar, and vinegar in a blender. Using several short bursts of power, blend until onion is chopped.

- Add remaining ingredients to blender and whirl until well combined.

- Refrigerate until ready to use.

Yield: 1 quart

Zesty Dressing

Delicious on any combination of mixed greens

1/3	cup sugar
1	teaspoon dry mustard
1	teaspoon salt
1	tablespoon Worcestershire sauce
2	tablespoons catsup
1/2	cup vinegar
3/4	cup vegetable oil
1	tablespoon dehydrated minced onions

- Combine all ingredients in a jar or container with a tight fitting lid.

- Shake well until thoroughly combined. Keep refrigerated.

Yield: 1 1/2 cups

Poppy Seed Dressing

This versatile dressing can be served with vegetable, fruit, or green salads.

1/2   cup sugar
1   teaspoon salt
1   teaspoon dry mustard
1   teaspoon paprika
1   tablespoon grated red onion
1   cup vegetable oil
1/4   cup vinegar
1   tablespoon poppy seeds

Yield: 1 1/2 cups

- Mix sugar, salt, dry mustard, and paprika together. Add onion.
- With a mixer or in a blender, combine mixture with oil and vinegar. When thoroughly combined, add poppy seeds and mix well.
- Refrigerate until ready to serve.

Ginger Dressing For Fruit Salad

Tailor-make your own fresh fruit salad with this versatile dressing.

1   cup plain yogurt or sour cream
1 1/2   tablespoons honey
1 1/2   tablespoons finely minced candied
       ginger

Yield: 1 cup

- Stir all ingredients together and cover. Refrigerate until chilled thoroughly.
- Serve over an arranged fruit salad on individual plates, or for a larger group, serve the dressing beside a large bowl of fresh fruits.

Note: It goes well with a mixture of bananas, oranges, fresh pineapple, papaya and seedless grapes drizzled with lime juice.

VEGETABLES

Vegetables

Steamed Artichokes Verde

An excellent first course for an elegant dinner party.

Artichokes:
8 medium to large artichokes
3 – 4 tablespoons lemon juice
1 small white onion, finely chopped
1 clove garlic, crushed
2 celery stalks
1 bay leaf

Sauce:
1 cup sour cream
1 cup mayonnaise
1 clove garlic
3 sprigs parsley, stem and leaves
juice of 1 lemon
1 (2 ounce) can anchovies
4 whole green onions (tops and all)

Garnish:
thin slices of lemon

Yield: 8 servings

The Artichokes:
- Rinse artichokes. Cut off stems and remove bottom row of tough leaves. With kitchen scissors, trim the tops of remaining leaves. Brush trimmed areas with lemon juice to avoid discoloration.

- Fill a large pot with water to a depth of 2 inches. Add the onion, garlic, celery, bay leaf, and 1½ tablespoons lemon juice. Place artichokes, top side down, in water and steam covered for 40 – 45 minutes. Drain and place individual artichokes on serving plates.

The Sauce:
- Place all ingredients in a blender or food processor and purée. Chill.

- Serve in a small bowl beside each artichoke. Garnish each bowl with a thin slice of lemon.

Jockey Hollow Corn Pudding

Jockey Hollow National Park is the site where George Washington's troops were encamped during the winter of 1777-1778. This encampment is re-enacted in full colonial dress one weekend each year.

12 – 14 ears fresh young corn or 2 cups
      frozen corn
3 tablespoons butter, softened
¼ cup sugar
2 eggs
1 cup milk
½ teaspoon salt

Yield: 6 servings

- Preheat oven to 350°.

- Grate ears of corn to remove kernels.

- Cream butter and sugar with a mixer. Beat in eggs. Add milk and salt until thoroughly combined. Fold in corn.

- Bake in a buttered casserole at 350° for 1 hour, or until pudding is firm.

Herb Garden Green Beans

A wonderful way to prepare beans from your own garden.

1/4   cup olive oil
1/2 – 3/4 cup butter
2   cups chopped onion
3   cloves garlic, minced
1   cup diced celery
2   cups chopped parsley
1   teaspoon dried rosemary
1   teaspoon dried basil
1   teaspoon salt
4   pounds fresh green beans, cut into 2″
       pieces
freshly ground black pepper

Garnish:
chopped parsley
edible flowers such as: pansies,
       nasturtiums, snapdragons, azaleas,
       or freesias

Yield: *12 – 14 servings*

- Melt oil and butter in a sauté pan. Add onion, garlic, and celery. Cook over medium heat for 5 minutes. Add parsley and spices. Cover and simmer for 10 minutes.
- Cook beans in boiling water until tender. Drain well and toss with sauce. Top with freshly ground black pepper. Garnish with chopped parsley and edible flowers.

Broccoli Stir Fry with Sesame

Stir frying preserves the fresh flavor and texture of vegetables being cooked.

1   bunch broccoli
2   tablespoons vegetable oil
1   (8 ounce) can water chestnuts, sliced
1/2   teaspoon salt
1/2   teaspoon sugar
1   tablespoon water
1/2   tablespoon soy sauce
2   tablespoons sesame seeds

Yield: *6 – 8 servings*

- Slice off broccoli flowerets. Reserve. Slice broccoli stems on the diagonal, about 1/4″ thick.
- Heat oil in a wok or large frying pan over high heat until very hot. Add broccoli stems. Stir fry until crisp-tender.
- When stems are almost cooked, add flowerets and continue to stir fry until broccoli is done.
- Add water chestnuts, salt, sugar, water, and soy sauce. Cover. Turn off heat and let vegetables steam for a few minutes.
- When ready to serve, transfer to serving dish, sprinkle with sesame seeds and stir gently.

Carrots à la Champagne

Carrots that are tenderly dressed with champagne and dill.

2	pounds carrots
4	tablespoons butter
1/2	cup beef broth
1	cup very dry champagne
2	tablespoons freshly squeezed lemon juice
1 1/2	teaspoons dried dill weed

Garnish:
thin slices of lemon
sprigs of fresh dill weed

Yield: 6–8 servings

- Clean and scrape carrots. Slice finely, by hand or in a food processor, into rounds.

- Melt butter in a saucepan. Sauté carrots until they just begin to brown. Add beef broth and champagne. Cover and cook over medium heat until just tender, *but still firm.* Remove cover, turn up heat to high and cook until most of the liquid is cooked away. Remove from heat.

- Add lemon juice and dill weed. Toss well and serve.

- Garnish individual servings or vegetable bowl with thin slices of lemon and sprigs of fresh dill weed.

Festive Carrot Ring

This is attractive enough to be a centerpiece for your table.

2	cups mashed cooked carrots (about 2 pounds)
1	cup seasoned bread crumbs
1	cup milk
3/4	cup grated sharp cheddar cheese
1/2	cup butter, softened
1/4	cup grated onion
1	teaspoon salt
1/8	teaspoon cayenne pepper
3	eggs
2	cups cooked peas

Garnish:
parsley sprigs
nasturtiums

Yield: 8 servings

- Preheat oven to 350°. Grease a 1 1/2 quart metal ring mold.

- Combine mashed carrots, bread crumbs, milk, cheese, butter, onion, salt, and pepper.

- Beat eggs with a mixer until light and fluffy. Fold into carrot mixture.

- Pour into prepared mold. Bake at 350° for 40–50 minutes, or until firm but not dried out.

- Unmold onto a serving platter, fill the center with peas.

- Garnish with parsley sprigs and nasturtiums.

Mushrooms Florentine

A sophisticated side dish that looks complicated but is really easy to prepare.

1	pound fresh mushrooms
3	tablespoons butter
2	(10 ounce) packages frozen chopped spinach, defrosted
1	teaspoon salt
1	clove garlic, minced
1/3	cup minced onion
1/4	cup melted butter
1	cup grated cheddar cheese

Garnish:
sliced black olives

Yield: 4–6 servings

- Preheat oven to 350°. Lightly grease a 1 quart casserole dish.

- Wipe mushrooms with a damp paper towel. Separate stems from caps. Slice stems and very large caps. Leave medium and small caps whole.

- Melt butter in a sauté pan, add mushrooms, and sauté until mushrooms are nicely browned, but not limp.

- Drain spinach and squeeze as dry as possible. Mix spinach with salt, garlic, onion, and melted butter. Spread spinach mixture in prepared casserole dish. Sprinkle with 1/2 cup cheese.

- Spoon mushrooms on top. Sprinkle with the rest of the cheese. (Casserole may be refrigerated at this point.)

- Bake at 350° for 20–30 minutes or until cheese is nicely browned and bubbly. Garnish with sliced black olives.

Blue Cheese Onions Gratin

A zesty accompaniment to grilled or broiled steak.

2	large Spanish onions (about 1 pound)
6	ounces blue cheese, broken into pieces
6	tablespoons unsalted butter, at room temperature
2	teaspoons worcestershire sauce
1/2	teaspoon dried dill weed

freshly ground black pepper

Yield: 4 servings

- Preheat oven to 425° and position oven rack to the center of oven. Generously butter a 9″ × 13″ baking dish.

- Slice onions and place evenly in prepared baking dish. Mix remaining ingredients together and spread evenly over onions with a spatula.

- Bake at 425° for 20 minutes, then broil briefly until top is browned and bubbly. (Watch carefully to avoid burning.)

Sherried Mushrooms

A wonderful addition to any harvest or holiday table.

3/4	cup butter
1/2	cup chopped green onion
1 1/2	pounds mushrooms, sliced 1/2″ thick
1/4	cup dry sherry
2	tablespoons flour
1	cup sour cream
1/2	teaspoon salt
1/2	teaspoon pepper
2	tablespoons chopped fresh parsley
1/4	cup bread crumbs

Garnish:
finely chopped parsley

Yield: 6 servings

- Preheat oven to 350°. Generously grease a shallow 2 quart casserole dish with butter.

- Melt 1/2 cup butter in a skillet and sauté onions until limp. Add mushrooms and sauté until tender.

- Add sherry to pan. Sprinkle flour over all and mix well. Continue to cook until mixture is bubbly.

- Turn heat to very low and add sour cream, salt, pepper, and parsley.

- Turn into prepared casserole dish.

- Melt remaining 1/4 cup butter. Pour over bread crumbs and toss until well combined. Sprinkle buttered crumbs over mushroom mixture. Bake uncovered at 350° for 30 minutes.

- Garnish with a sprinkling of finely chopped parsley.

Scalloped Potatoes with Garlic and Cream

A perfect accompaniment to Filet Mignon Superb (page 189).

2	pounds medium size white potatoes
2	cups milk
1 1/2	cups heavy cream
1	large clove garlic, minced
3/4	teaspoon salt
1/2	teaspoon white pepper
1/2	cup grated Swiss cheese

Yield: 8 servings

- Preheat oven to 350°. Grease a shallow baking dish with butter.
- Peel, wash, and dry potatoes. Slice about 1/8″ thick. (A food processor would do this well.)
- Place the potatoes in a large saucepan. Add the milk, cream, garlic, salt, and pepper. Bring to a boil over medium heat, stirring occasionally. Remove from heat after it boils.
- Pour the potato mixture into prepared baking dish. Sprinkle cheese on top and bake at 350° for 1 hour.
- Potatoes are done when they can be pierced with a fork and are golden brown on top.

Potatoes Fromage

The combination of cheese and chives enhances the flavor of the potatoes.

6	medium potatoes
1/4	cup butter
2	cups shredded cheddar cheese
1 1/2	cups sour cream
1/3	cup finely chopped chives
1	teaspoon salt
1/4	teaspoon freshly ground black pepper
2	tablespoons butter
1/2	teaspoon (or more) paprika

Yield: 8 servings

- Preheat oven to 350°. Grease a 2 quart casserole with butter.
- Boil potatoes in their skins. Peel and coarsely shred cooked potatoes.
- In a saucepan, over low heat, combine butter and cheese. Stir occasionally until almost melted. Remove from heat and blend in sour cream, chives, salt, and pepper.
- Fold potatoes into mixture, combining well. Turn into prepared casserole. Dot with butter and sprinkle with paprika. (Can be refrigerated at this point.)
- Bake at 350° for 30 minutes.

Fresh Lemon Rice

A colorful confetti toss of yellow, green, and white

4   tablespoons butter
2½   cups rice
½   cup dry white vermouth
4½   cups chicken broth
1½   teaspoons salt
pinch of white pepper
grated zest of 2 large lemons
¼   cup minced fresh parsley

Yield: 8 servings

- In a heavy pan, melt the butter over low heat. Add rice and stir until all grains are coated with butter (about 2 minutes).

- Add vermouth, broth, salt, and pepper.

- Bring to a boil, cover, and reduce heat. Simmer over low heat for 20 minutes, or until all liquid is absorbed.

- Toss rice with lemon zest and parsley. Serve immediately.

Pilaf Potpourri

An earthy blend of aromas and flavors . . . a nice change of pace from potatoes or plain rice.

1   medium onion, chopped
3   tablespoons butter
1   clove garlic, minced
½   pound mushrooms, sliced
1   cup uncooked rice
2   cups chicken broth
½–1 teaspoon salt
¼   teaspoon freshly ground black pepper

Yield: 4 servings

- Sauté onion in butter until transparent. Add garlic and mushrooms and sauté for 2–3 minutes.

- Add rice and continue to sauté over high heat for 3–5 minutes, until rice is golden brown.

- Bring chicken broth to a boil. Add to rice mixture and keep at a simmer. Add salt (the quantity depends on the saltiness of the chicken broth) and pepper.

- Cover pan tightly and continue to simmer over low heat for 20 minutes, or until liquid is absorbed.

Sweet Potato and Pear Purée

The sweet potato is another of nature's bounty commercially grown in New Jersey.

4   pounds sweet potatoes
4   firm, ripe medium size pears
1/2   lemon
4   medium size tangerines, squeezed for
        juice
1/2   cup unsalted butter
1/2   cup light brown sugar
1   teaspoon ground ginger
salt
freshly ground black pepper

Garnish:
1   teaspoon grated lemon zest

Yield: 8–10 servings

- Peel potatoes and cut into thirds. Boil in a large pot until tender, about 45 minutes. Drain well.

- Pare, core, and halve pears.

- Squeeze juice from lemon into a medium saucepan. Add pears and enough water to fill bottom 2" of pan. Poach pears over medium-high heat until tender, about 15 minutes. Drain well.

- Preheat oven to 350°. Grease a 13" × 9" baking dish with butter.

- Put half of the sweet potatoes, pears, tangerine juice, butter, sugar, and ginger in a food processor or blender. Purée until smooth.

- Transfer purée into prepared baking dish, and repeat with remaining mixture. Stir purée to blend and season with salt and pepper to taste.

- Smooth top of purée with a spatula and bake at 350° until heated through, about 25 minutes.

- Garnish with lemon zest and serve.

Fosterfields Fresh Marinated Vegetables

Fosterfields is a living historic farm located in Morris County. It is farmed as it was circa 1890–1910 using steam engines and antique equipment.

Marinade:
1½ cups red wine vinegar
1 cup virgin olive oil
¼ cup sugar
2 teaspoons salt
2 cloves garlic, finely chopped

Vegetables:
1 large sweet onion
2 large red bell peppers
2 large green bell peppers
1 pound fresh green beans
1 head cauliflower
1 bunch broccoli
1 pound fresh mushrooms, sliced
1 pint cherry tomatoes

Yield: *10–14 servings*

The Marinade:
- Mix all ingredients and boil for 5 minutes. Cool.

The Vegetables:
- Cut onions into rings. Cut red and green peppers into chunks. Slice green beans in half and blanch them in boiling water for one minute. Cut cauliflower and broccoli into bite size flowerets and pieces.

- Combine all vegetables, except for mushrooms and tomatoes, in a glass bowl. Pour marinade over and mix until vegetables are thoroughly coated.

- Marinate for 2 days, stirring 2 or 3 times a day.

- On the last day, add the mushrooms and tomatoes. Stir until combined. Drain before serving.

Pineapple Puff

This is a wonderful side dish with chicken, roast pork, or ham.

5 slices of bread
½ cup butter, softened
¾ cup sugar
4 eggs
1 (20 ounce) can crushed pineapple, drained

Yield: *4 servings*

- Preheat oven to 350°. Grease a 1½ quart casserole.

- Trim crusts from bread and cut into 1″ cubes.

- Cream butter and sugar together. Add eggs, one at a time, and mix until well combined. Stir in pineapple. Fold in bread cubes.

- Bake in prepared casserole at 350° for 1 hour, or until brown on top.

Three Vegetable Pâté

A spectrum of subtle colors and flavors

Base Mixture:
1/2	cup water
5	envelopes unflavored gelatin
3	tablespoons vegetable oil
1/4	cup flour
1	cup milk

Spinach Mixture:
1	pound fresh spinach
1	tablespoon fresh parsley
1	tablespoon vegetable oil
1/2	cup chopped onion
1	clove garlic, minced
4	ounces fresh mushrooms, coarsely chopped
2	teaspoons lemon juice
1/4	teaspoon salt

Cauliflower Mixture:
4	cups cauliflower flowerets
1/2 – 1	teaspoon seasoned salt or herb salt

Carrot Mixture:
4	cups sliced carrots
1	tablespoon vegetable oil
1/2	cup chopped onion
1/4	teaspoon nutmeg
1/4	teaspoon salt
1/4	cup chopped walnuts or pistachios

Garnish:
coarsely chopped aspic, parsley, or
    watercress

Yield: 12 servings

The Base:
- Put 1/2 cup water in a 2 cup Pyrex measuring cup. Sprinkle gelatin over water to soften. Place Pyrex cup in a saucepan with 2" of hot water over low heat. Stir mixture occasionally until gelatin is dissolved.

- Heat 3 tablespoons of oil over medium heat. Whisk flour into oil until well combined. Cook over medium heat for 1 minute. Blend in milk. Cook until bubbly and quite thick.

- Remove from heat and add gelatin mixture. Stir until well combined. Pour mixture back into Pyrex cup and set cup in hot water while you prepare vegetables.

The Spinach Mixture:
- Wash spinach well and trim stems.

- Cook in a large saucepan, using only the water clinging to the leaves, until barely wilted. Drain in colander and press out as much water as possible with the back of a spoon. Then squeeze spinach in a double thickness of paper towels until it is quite dry.

- Purée spinach and parsley in food processor. Add one third of the base mixture (approximately 2/3 cup) to processor and purée.

- Sauté onion and garlic in oil until onion is transparent. Add mushrooms and sauté for 2 more minutes. Add mushroom mixture, lemon juice, and salt to processor. Combine, using a few short spurts.

Continued on next page

The Cauliflower Mixture:
- Steam cauliflower until barely tender. Purée in food processor with one third of base mixture and seasoned salt.

The Carrot Mixture:
- Steam carrots until crisp-tender. Purée in food processor.

- Sauté onion in oil until transparent. Add to processor with one third of the base mixture, nutmeg, and salt. Purée. Add nuts and combine, using a few short spurts.

To Assemble Pâté:
- You may use any of the following items to line a 6 cup, well oiled loaf pan: puff pastry (available frozen), grape vine leaves, lasagna noodles (al denté), or you may leave the loaf pan unlined, but well oiled.

- Preheat oven to 325°.

- Layer each vegetable mixture, carefully smoothing before adding next layer.

- Cover loaf pan with aluminum foil and set in roasting pan. Pour in enough hot water to come halfway up sides of pan. Bake at 325° for 2 hours, or until set.

- Remove pan from oven and cool to room temperature. Keep tightly wrapped. Weight the pâté by placing a heavy object on top of loaf pan and refrigerate for 12 hours.

- When ready to serve, unmold and garnish with coarsely chopped aspic, parsley, or watercress.

Note: Once you learn the technique of making this, you can combine the base mixture with other vegetables, such as broccoli or mushrooms. Remember to make this at least a day before you plan to serve it.

Tomatoes Brookhollow

Fragrant baked tomatoes that compliment grilled or roasted meats.

4	large ripe tomatoes
1	cup Italian salad dressing
1	(6 ounce) jar marinated artichoke hearts
1	tablespoon chopped fresh basil
1/2	cup Italian flavored bread crumbs
1/2	cup Parmesan cheese
4	tablespoons butter

Yield: 8 servings

- Peel and slice tomatoes in half early in the day and place in a glass baking dish. Pour Italian dressing over tomato halves and refrigerate until 1 hour before serving.

- Preheat oven to 350°.

- Drain artichoke hearts and slice. Put on top of tomato halves. Sprinkle each half with basil, bread crumbs, and Parmesan. Top each with a pat of butter.

- Bake at 350° for 20 minutes.

Tomatoes Florentine

Delightful to look at, delicious to eat, and easy to assemble.

2	(10 ounce) packages frozen chopped spinach
2	cups herb seasoned stuffing mix
1	medium onion, finely chopped
2	eggs
3/4	cup butter, melted
1/2	cup Parmesan cheese
1/2	tablespoon garlic salt
1	teaspoon thyme
1/2	tablespoon freshly ground black pepper
4–5	ripe tomatoes, thickly sliced

Yield: 10 servings

- Preheat oven to 350°.

- Cook and drain spinach.

- Mix together all ingredients except tomatoes.

- Arrange tomatoes in a baking dish. Using an ice cream scoop to form mounds, place a mound of dressing on each tomato slice.

- Bake at 350° for 20 minutes.

Zucchini Genovese

This versatile dish may be served as a side dish, a first course, or as a main course.

1/3	loaf Italian bread, broken into small pieces
1	cup cream or milk
9	small to medium zucchini
6	tablespoons olive oil
2	cups ground beef
3	links Italian sausage, casing removed
1	egg yolk
1 1/2	cups grated Parmesan cheese
1	tablespoon chopped fresh parsley
1	pinch dried thyme
1	pinch dried basil
2	leaves dried sage, crumbled
salt	
freshly ground black pepper	
1/2	cup chicken broth
1 1/2	cups tomato sauce

Yield: 8 servings as a side dish
     6 servings as a first course
     4 servings as a main course

- Soak bread in milk or cream for several minutes.

- Cut ends off zucchini and slice in half, lengthwise. Scoop out pulp, leaving a shell, approximately 1/2" thick. Set aside 2 tablespoons of pulp and discard the rest.

- Using 2 1/2 tablespoons olive oil, sauté beef and sausage with reserved pulp, leaving the mixture slightly under-cooked.

- Place mixture in a large bowl and combine with soaked bread, egg yolk, 1 cup of cheese (reserving the remaining 1/2 cup), parsley, herbs, salt, and pepper. Mix with hands, leaving mixture rather coarse.

- Preheat oven to 350°. Coat the bottom of a broiler pan with 3 1/2 tablespoons of olive oil.

- Stuff zucchini shells generously with mixture and place, stuffing side up, in prepared pan. Add chicken broth.

- Bake at 350° for 25–35 minutes, or until shells are tender and stuffing is well browned.

- Drain liquid from pan and pour tomato sauce evenly over zucchini. Sprinkle with remaining Parmesan cheese.

- Broil for 3 minutes, or until cheese is melted and brown.

Zucchini Lasagna

Lasagna without the pasta. A great way to serve vegetables to your family.

4   large zucchini
2   teaspoons extra virgin olive oil
2   cloves garlic, minced
1/2   cup chopped onion
1/4   pound mushrooms, sliced
1/2   pound ground beef
1   (16 ounce) can tomatoes
1   (6 ounce) can tomato paste
3/4   cup dry red wine
1 1/2   teaspoons oregano
1/4   teaspoon thyme
1/4   teaspoon basil
salt
freshly ground black pepper
8   ounces mozzarella cheese, thinly sliced
8   ounces ricotta cheese
1/2   cup freshly grated Parmesan cheese

Yield: 4–6 servings

- Cut zucchini horizontally into 1/4″ thick strips. Place on double thickness of paper towels and sprinkle with salt. Place another double thickness of paper towels over zucchini, weight down with dinner plates, and let sit for half an hour to remove excess moisture.

- Heat oil in a large skillet over medium heat. Add garlic, onion, and mushrooms and cook until onion is tender, but not brown.

- Add meat to skillet and cook, stirring until brown. Drain drippings from skillet. Stir in tomatoes, tomato paste, wine, oregano, thyme, basil, salt, and pepper. Simmer uncovered for 1 1/2 hours.

- Preheat oven to 350°. Generously oil a lasagna pan or shallow casserole dish.

- Place half of the zucchini strips in prepared baking dish. Top with half of the mozzarella and ricotta cheeses. Spread half the meat sauce over the cheese. Repeat layers. Sprinkle with Parmesan cheese.

- Bake at 350° for 30 minutes or until bubbly.

EGGS
and
PASTA

Eggs and Pasta

Emperor's Omelet

An elegant brunch entrée that is a little bit out of the ordinary.

3 tablespoons dried currants
1/4 cup boiling water
3 large eggs, separated, at room
    temperature
2 1/2 tablespoons sugar
1/8 teaspoon salt
1 1/2 cups milk
1/4 teaspoon vanilla extract
3/4 cup flour
4 tablespoons unsalted butter
1 tablespoon confectioners sugar

Yield: 4 omelets

- Plump currants in boiling water for 15 minutes. Drain well and set aside.

- In a blender combine egg yolk, sugar, salt, milk, vanilla, and flour. Whirl at high speed until smooth.

- Beat egg whites until soft peaks hold. Fold the milk mixture into the egg whites.

- Over medium heat, melt a thin slice of butter in an omelet pan, rotating pan to cover evenly with butter. Pour 1 cup of batter into the pan and sprinkle 3/4 tablespoon of currants over the top. Cook 2–3 minutes until the bottom of the omelet is golden brown.

- Slide the omelet, cooked side down, onto a heated plate.

- Add a thin slice of butter to the pan, again rotating pan to cover evenly with butter. Invert omelet into the pan, return to the heat for 45–60 seconds until the bottom is golden brown. Slide onto a serving plate.

- Sift a small amount of confectioners sugar on top and serve immediately. Repeat with remaining batter.

Note: To speed cooking and serving, use 2 omelet pans at once.

Sunday Brunch Special

Assemble this on Saturday night and have an easy brunch dish on Sunday.

3	cups cooked ham, cubed
3	cups trimmed and cubed French bread
1/2	pound cheddar cheese, cubed
3	tablespoons flour
3	teaspoons dry mustard
3	tablespoons butter, melted
4	eggs, beaten
3	cups milk
2	dashes Tabasco

dash garlic salt

Yield: 6 servings

- Toss ham, bread cubes, and cheddar cheese together. Put 1/3 of the mixture in the bottom of a buttered 13" × 9" × 2" casserole.

- Sprinkle with 1 tablespoon flour, 1 teaspoon dry mustard, and 1 tablespoon melted butter.

- Repeat these steps until you have 3 layers.

- In a mixing bowl, combine eggs, milk, Tabasco, and garlic salt. Whisk until thoroughly blended. Pour over casserole. Cover and chill 4 hours or overnight.

- Bake uncovered in a preheated 350° oven for 1 hour or until set and slightly brown on top.

Beverage: Banana Frost (page 32)

Artichokes au Gratin

A wonderful, zesty, and spicy vegetarian entrée for brunch or lunch.

2	(9 ounce) boxes frozen artichoke hearts
1½	cups Italian dressing or 3 (6 ounce) jars marinated artichoke hearts
12	green onions, chopped
2	large cloves garlic, minced
½	pound fresh mushrooms, sliced
15	eggs, beaten
16	soda crackers, crushed
10	dashes Tabasco
4	tablespoons dried parsley
1	pound shredded cheddar cheese.

Yield: 10 servings

- Thaw artichoke hearts and cut in half or quarters. Marinate artichoke hearts in Italian dressing overnight. Or, if using jars of marinated artichoke hearts, simply cut into halves or quarters, reserving the marinade.

- Pour dressing from artichoke hearts into a skillet. Heat on medium setting and add green onions and garlic. Sauté until tender.

- Preheat oven to 325°. Lightly butter a casserole dish or a 10″ × 13″ baking pan.

- Combine artichokes, dressing, onions, garlic, and remaining ingredients, except cheese. Transfer to baking dish and sprinkle top with cheese. (You may assemble casserole completely and refrigerate overnight, or until ready to bake.)

- Bake at 325° for 40 minutes.

Note: For a perfect brunch, serve with stewed fruit, Canadian bacon, and Apricot Delight (page 35).

Fluffy Ham Quiche

A quiche that raises the egg from the ordinary to the extraordinary.

Pastry:

1¹/₂	cups sifted flour
¹/₂	teaspoon salt
¹/₂	cup butter
1	egg yolk
3	tablespoons water

Filling:

¹/₂	pound boiled ham, chopped
³/₄	pound grated Swiss cheese
5	eggs
2	tablespoons flour
1¹/₄	cups milk
²/₃	cup heavy cream
	freshly ground black pepper
3	tablespoons butter, melted

Yield: 6 servings

The Pastry:
- Sift flour and salt into a bowl. Cut in butter with a pastry blender. Stir in egg yolk and water. Form into a ball and chill for 30 minutes.

- With fingers, press pastry into a 10″ pie plate. (You may also use a small glass to roll it in the pie plate.) Crimp edge of pie shell with a fork or fingers.

- Preheat oven to 400°.

The Filling:
- Place ham and cheese in the bottom of pie shell.

- Combine all other ingredients, except melted butter, in a mixing bowl. Beat until large bubbles form on top of mixture. Pour over ham and cheese.

- Drizzle melted butter over the top of quiche and bake at 400° for 30–40 minutes, or until golden brown and a toothpick inserted in pie comes out clean.

Curried Cream Eggs

Next time you entertain, why not consider having a brunch; a time when friends can comfortably gather before the fast pace of the day catches up with them.

1/4	cup butter
1	small apple, peeled, cored, and chopped
1	small onion, chopped
1/4	cup flour
1	cup light cream
1 1/2	cups chicken broth
1/4	teaspoon curry powder
salt	
freshly ground black pepper	
12	hard boiled eggs, sliced
toast points or puff pastry patty shells	

Garnish:
chopped fresh parsley

Yield: *6 servings*

- Melt butter in a skillet and sauté apple and onion over medium heat until tender. Stir in flour, blending until smooth.

- Slowly add cream and chicken broth, stirring until smooth and thickened. Sprinkle in curry powder, salt, and pepper. Stir until blended. Simmer for 8 minutes.

- Gently fold in hard boiled eggs until well combined with sauce.

- Serve over toast points or fill warm baked patty shells with mixture. Garnish with fresh parsley.

Note: Serve this with asparagus for a meatless dinner, or with ham, fresh citrus fruit, and coffee cake for a brunch.

Crêpecakes

A delicate pancake that turns breakfast into bliss.

5   large or 6 medium eggs
¹/₄   cup sugar
pinch of salt
4   cups milk
3   cups sifted flour
¹/₂   cup butter, melted
vegetable oil
seedless raspberry or strawberry preserves

Garnish:
confectioners sugar
fresh berries

Yield: 6 servings

- Beat eggs with sugar and salt. Alternately add milk and flour in small amounts, beating after each addition. Stir in melted butter. Batter may be covered and refrigerated overnight.

- Preheat oven to 200°.

- Heat a 9″, or slightly larger, lightly oiled skillet. Pour in ³/₄ to 1 cup of batter (batter should lightly coat the skillet). Cook over moderate heat until batter firms up, flip to the other side and cook until golden brown. The crêpecake is done when it begins to bubble.

- Remove from pan and keep warm in oven. Repeat process, with the skillet always lightly oiled, until all the batter is used.

- To serve, spread each crêpecake with a thin layer of preserves and roll up. Dust with confectioners sugar, scatter with a few fresh berries (match with preserves), and serve immediately.

Orangery French Toast

If you are going to the trouble of making something this delicious, make it wonderful by using slices of Pinwheel Loaves (page 40) instead of store bought bread.

French Toast:
6   egg yolks
1/2   cup half and half
1/3   cup orange juice
1   tablespoon grated orange peel
1/4   teaspoon salt
12   slices bread
1/4   cup vegetable oil

Orange Syrup:
1   cup brown sugar
1/2   cup orange juice
2   tablespoons grated orange peel

Yield: 6 servings

The Toast:
• Beat together egg yolks, half and half, orange juice, orange peel, and salt. Dip bread slices in batter to coat both sides.

• Heat oil in a skillet and when hot, add coated bread and cook on both sides until golden brown. Transfer to a warm serving platter.

The Syrup:
• In a small saucepan, combine brown sugar, orange juice, and orange peel. Heat and simmer for 5 minutes. Serve over hot toast.

Note: Flavor can be enhanced by using freshly squeezed orange juice.

Linguini Medley

This eye-appealing pasta dish can be served as an elegant first course as well as an entrée.

1	pound fresh asparagus
1	pound chicken breasts, skinned, boned, and cut into cubes
2	tablespoons butter
3	tablespoons finely chopped shallots
1	red pepper, cut into strips
1	cup heavy cream
1/2	teaspoon crushed red pepper
1/4	pound blue cheese, crumbled
1/2	teaspoon crushed dried tarragon

freshly ground black pepper

1/4	pound spinach linguini
1/4	pound tomato linguini
1/4	pound egg linguini
1/2	cup freshly grated Parmesan cheese

Yield: 4 servings

- Clean the asparagus well, break off the tough ends and cut the spears on the diagonal into 1 1/2″ lengths. Drop the asparagus pieces into 1 quart of boiling water. Drain immediately and set aside.

- Melt the butter in a large skillet. Add the chicken and cook quickly, just until the chicken turns white. Add the shallots and red pepper and sauté, stirring for 1 minute.

- Toss in the asparagus and stir until heated through. Stir in the cream and crushed red pepper. Add the blue cheese and tarragon and a generous grinding of fresh black pepper. Cook just until the cheese melts.

- Cook the pasta, according to directions for "al denté." Drain well and toss with the cheese sauce in a large warm bowl.

- Sprinkle with Parmesan or serve Parmesan on the side.

Wine: California Sauvignon Blanc

Fettuccine Toss with Cream Sauce

Rich and flavorful, with a velvet cream sauce.

¹/₂ cup unsalted butter
¹/₄ cup finely chopped shallots
³/₄ pound fresh mushrooms, quartered
1 teaspoon salt
freshly ground black pepper
¹/₄ pound prosciutto, chopped
1 cup heavy cream
¹/₂ cup fresh or frozen peas
³/₄ pound fresh egg fettuccine
¹/₂ pound fresh spinach fettuccine
1 cup freshly grated Parmesan cheese

Garnish:
fresh or roasted red bell peppers

Yield: 6–8 servings

- In a large skillet, melt 4 tablespoons of butter. Sauté the shallots over medium heat until they have turned pale gold. Turn up the heat and add the mushrooms. Cook over medium-high heat until the mushrooms absorb the butter, then lower the heat to medium.

- Sprinkle 1 teaspoon salt, and pepper to taste over the mushrooms. Stir the mushrooms with a wooden spoon until they render their juice. When that happens, turn up the heat and cook mushrooms for 3 minutes, stirring often.

- Reduce the heat, add the prosciutto and cook for 1 minute. Add ¹/₂ cup of the heavy cream and cook until cream thickens slightly. Taste and add more salt and pepper, if necessary. Remove from heat.

- In a very large saucepan, melt the remaining 4 tablespoons of butter. Add the remaining cream. Cook, stirring over low heat until the butter is melted and combined with the cream. Remove from heat.

- Steam fresh or frozen peas until lightly cooked, but still green.

- Cook the two pastas in separate pots. Drain well and transfer both to the pan with the butter and cream. Turn heat to low and toss to coat the fettucine well.

- Add the peas and half of the mushroom cream sauce. Combine gently but thoroughly with the fettucine. Add ¹/₂ cup of Parmesan and quickly mix into the pasta.

- Remove pan from heat, transfer the fettuccine to a warm bowl. Pour the rest of the mushroom cream sauce on top and sprinkle with more Parmesan to taste. Garnish with red peppers.

Wine: Italian Soave

Spaghetti Misto

Pasta has recently been rediscovered all across America and the preparations seem limitless. Here for your enjoyment is a pasta and vegetable combination.

3   tablespoons virgin olive oil
3   large cloves garlic, minced
2   large carrots, cut into 1" pieces
3   green onions, chopped
2   cups fresh broccoli flowerets
3   fresh plum tomatoes, chopped
1   medium yellow bell pepper, julienned
1   medium red bell pepper, julienned
1   small green bell pepper, julienned
1   (16 ounce) can extra large pitted
        black olives, sliced
1   pint light cream
¹/₄ teaspoon freshly ground black pepper
¹/₄ teaspoon grated nutmeg
¹/₄ teaspoon crushed dried basil or 3
        large fresh basil leaves, chopped
³/₄ pound spaghetti
freshly grated Parmesan and Romano
        cheese
salt
freshly ground black pepper

Yield: 6 servings

- In a large skillet, heat olive oil over medium-high heat. When oil is hot, add garlic and stir for 1-2 minutes. Toss in carrots and green onions and sauté until tender. Add all other vegetables, tossing over medium-high heat until well combined.

- Cover pan and lower heat to medium to steam vegetables until tender, about 10-12 minutes.

- Add cream, pepper, nutmeg, and basil, stirring well to coat vegetables. Cook until bubbly and slightly thickened. Keep warm and covered until ready to serve.

- In a large pot of boiling salted water, cook spaghetti until it is "al denté." Drain well, mound on a warm serving platter, and top with vegetable sauce. Serve with Parmesan and Romano cheese and freshly ground pepper.

Wine: Italian Red Dolcetto

Red Pepper Pasta

Macaroni and cheese for grownups!

5	tablespoons butter
2/3	cup vodka
1/4	teaspoon hot red pepper flakes
1 1/2	cups crushed Italian canned tomatoes
3/4	cup heavy cream
1/2	teaspoon salt
1	pound rotelle noodles
3/4	cup freshly grated Parmesan cheese

Yield: 4 servings

- Melt butter in a large skillet over medium heat. Add vodka and red pepper flakes and simmer for 2 minutes. Stir in tomatoes and cream and simmer, covered, for 5 more minutes. Season with salt.

- Cook rotelle according to package directions for "al denté." Drain well and pour into skillet with red pepper sauce. Reduce heat to low, sprinkle in cheese, and mix thoroughly.

Note: For a spicier dish, add additional hot pepper flakes to sauce. Serve with Italian sausage and peppers.

Fettuccine with Garlic

This will warm the hearts of garlic lovers everywhere.

1/2	cup butter
2	tablespoons parsley flakes
1	teaspoon crushed basil
1	(8 ounce) container cottage cheese
1/4	teaspoon salt
1/2	teaspoon freshly ground black pepper
2/3	cup milk, warmed
3	cloves garlic, crushed
1	pound fettuccine
1/2	cup freshly grated Parmesan cheese

Yield: 4 servings

- In a saucepan over low heat, melt 1/4 cup butter. Stir in parsley flakes, basil, cottage cheese, salt, and pepper. Blend in milk. Keep sauce warm.

- Melt remaining butter in a small sauté pan. Add crushed garlic and cook for 1–2 minutes over medium heat.

- Cook fettuccine according to package directions for "al denté." Drain well.

- Pour garlic butter over the cooked pasta. Toss lightly and quickly until well combined. Sprinkle the Parmesan cheese on the pasta, coating thoroughly. Spoon the warm cheese sauce over the top and mix well.

Wine: Italian Soave

Pasta Envelopes

When you taste this, you will know it is well worth the effort.

Filling:
1   (10 ounce) package frozen chopped
      spinach, defrosted
2   eggs, beaten
1   cup minced cooked chicken
1/2   cup bread crumbs
1/4   cup heavy cream
1/3   cup grated Parmesan cheese
2   teaspoons finely chopped parsley
1   clove garlic, minced
1/4   teaspoon nutmeg
salt
freshly ground black pepper

Pasta Envelopes:
3   eggs, beaten
1 1/4   cups milk
3/4   cup flour
1/2   teaspoon salt
1   tablespoon vegetable oil

Béchamel Sauce:
4   tablespoons butter
1/4   cup flour
2   1/2 cups half and half
3/4   teaspoon salt
3/4   teaspoon white pepper
1/8   teaspoon nutmeg

Yield: 6 servings

The Filling:
- Place spinach in a colander and press with the back of a spoon to extract as much moisture as possible. Remove from colander and squeeze between several layers of paper towels until quite dry.

- In a large bowl, mix spinach with remaining ingredients, combining thoroughly.

The Pasta Envelopes:
- Combine all ingredients and beat well until batter is smooth.

- Heat a griddle or crêpe pan until drops of water "dance" when sprinkled on the surface. Lightly oil the cooking surface.

- Pour approximately 2 tablespoons of batter on pan and cook only until set. *It should not brown.* Remove from pan and layer crêpes between sheets of wax paper. Repeat until all batter is used.

- Place 1 tablespoon of spinach mixture in the lower third of each circle. Roll up, encasing filling and set aside.

The Sauce:
- In a saucepan, melt the butter. When it sizzles, whisk in flour until well blended. Cook for 1 minute.

- Add the half and half, whisking constantly. Cook and stir for a few minutes, until sauce is thickened. Add salt, pepper, and nutmeg. Stir until thoroughly combined. Cover and keep warm.

Continued on next page

- Preheat oven to 325°. Butter a lasagna pan or shallow casserole dish.

- Pour ½ cup of sauce on the bottom of the baking pan. Arrange pasta envelopes in a single layer over sauce. Pour another ½ cup of sauce over the envelopes. Repeat with one more layer.

- Bake at 325° for 20 minutes. Serve with additional Béchamel sauce on the side.

Note: The filling can be used for your favorite ravioli recipe as well.

Linguini with Basil and Brie

Translated literally, "al denté" means "to the teeth." This signifies that perfectly cooked pasta should offer some resistance to the bite, rather than being soft and mushy.

4   large ripe tomatoes
1   pound Brie cheese
1   cup chopped fresh basil
3   cloves garlic, minced
1   cup plus 1 tablespoon virgin olive oil
½   teaspoon salt
freshly ground black pepper
1½   pounds linguini
freshly grated Parmesan cheese

Yield: 6–8 servings

- Peel and seed tomatoes and cut into ½″ cubes. Remove the rind from the Brie and discard. Tear or shred the Brie into small pieces.

- In a large bowl, combine tomatoes, Brie, basil, garlic, 1 cup olive oil, salt, and pepper to taste. Cover and set aside for 2–4 hours at room temperature, for flavors to meld.

- Cook linguini until "al denté" in a large pot of boiling salted water, to which you have added 1 tablespoon olive oil.

- Drain linguini and toss immediately with basil and Brie sauce. Serve with Parmesan cheese and freshly ground black pepper.

Wine: Australian Fumé Blanc

Crabmeat Lasagna

A departure from the ordinary, this is lasagna with a gift from the sea.

2   tablespoons butter
1/2   cup chopped onion
1   (4 ounce) can sliced mushrooms,
            drained
1   clove garlic, minced
2   (15 ounce) cans tomato sauce
1   tablespoon chopped fresh parsley
2   tablespoons dried dill weed
1/2   teaspoon dried oregano
1/4   teaspoon crushed basil
1   teaspoon salt
2   (7 1/2 ounce) cans crabmeat, drained
            and flaked
1   pound lasagna noodles
1   cup sour cream
1   cup shredded mozzarella cheese
2   cups shredded sharp cheddar cheese

Yield: 8–10 servings

- Melt butter in a large skillet over medium-high heat. Add onions, mushrooms, and garlic. Cook until onions are tender.

- Stir in tomato sauce, parsley, dill, oregano, basil, and salt. Cover and simmer for 20 minutes. Add crabmeat and blend well with sauce. Remove from heat.

- Cook lasagna noodles according to package directions. Drain and return noodles to pot of cold water to keep them from sticking together.

- Preheat oven to 350°. Butter a 3 quart baking dish.

- Arrange a layer of noodles in the bottom of prepared baking dish. Pour half of the crabmeat sauce over the noodles. Spread half of the sour cream over the sauce. Sprinkle with half of the mozzarella and half of the cheddar. Repeat with another layer of noodles, sauce, sour cream, and cheeses.

- Bake, covered, in a 350° oven for 1 hour, or until lasagna is bubbly. Let stand for 5 minutes after removing from oven before cutting into serving portions.

Wine: French Cru Beaujolais

Cannelloni Florentine

This is a very rich pasta dish that needs only a light salad and a good Italian bread to complete the meal.

Sauce:
1/4   cup butter
1   clove garlic, minced
1/4   cup flour
1 1/2   teaspoons instant chicken bouillon
1/8   teaspoon white pepper
4   cups light cream or half and half
1/2   cup combined freshly grated
       Parmesan and Romano cheese

Cannelloni:
1   (10 ounce) package frozen chopped
       spinach, defrosted
6–8   cannelloni shells, or 20 jumbo pasta
       shells
2   tablespoons butter
3   tablespoons sliced green onion
1   cup finely chopped cooked chicken
1   cup finely chopped cooked ham
1/2   cup combined freshly grated
       Parmesan and Romano cheese
2   eggs, beaten
3/4   teaspoon Italian seasoning
1/4   teaspoon pepper

Yield: *3–4 servings*

The Sauce:
- In a large skillet, melt butter over medium heat. Add garlic and sauté for 3 minutes. Stir in flour, chicken bouillon, and pepper. Whisk until well combined.

- Remove from heat, gradually stir in cream and return to medium heat. Bring to a boil, stirring constantly. Boil and stir for 1 minute until thickened. Reduce heat to low, add cheese and stir until melted.

The Cannelloni:
- Place spinach in a colander and press it with the back of a large spoon to extract as much water as possible.

- Parboil cannelloni shells according to package directions. (Cook extras, in case of tears.) Drain shells and rinse under cold water to prevent sticking.

- Preheat oven to 350°. Butter a 2 quart rectangular baking dish.

- In a large skillet, melt butter over medium heat. Sauté onion until tender, about 3 minutes. Remove pan from heat; stir in spinach and remaining ingredients.

- Fill shells with spinach mixture. Place in baking dish. Spoon sauce over cannelloni. Bake at 350° for 20 minutes, then broil several inches from heat for 5 minutes, or until sauce browns and bubbles.

Wine: Italian Soave

Chicken Pecan Fettuccine

This is a mouth-watering combination of ingredients.

1   pound chicken breasts, skinned and boned
3/4   cup butter
3   cups sliced fresh mushrooms
1   cup sliced green onions
3/4   teaspoon salt
1/2   teaspoon freshly ground black pepper
1/2   teaspoon garlic powder
10   ounces fresh fettuccine
1   egg yolk
2/3   cup half and half
2   tablespoons freshly chopped parsley
1/2   cup freshly grated Parmesan cheese
1   cup chopped pecans, toasted

Yield: *6 servings*

- Cut chicken into 3/4″ pieces. Melt 1/4 cup butter in a large skillet. Sauté chicken until lightly browned. Remove chicken from skillet and set aside.

- To drippings in skillet, add mushrooms, green onions, 1/2 teaspoon salt, 1/4 teaspoon pepper, and 1/4 teaspoon garlic powder. Sauté until mushrooms are tender. Return chicken to skillet and simmer for 20 minutes, or until chicken is done.

- Cook fettuccine in boiling salted water until "al denté." Drain well.

- Melt 1/2 cup butter and combine with egg yolk, half and half, parsley, and remaining salt, pepper, and garlic powder. Stir butter sauce into fettuccine. Sprinkle with cheese, tossing until well mixed. Add chicken and mushroom mixture; toss until combined.

- To serve, arrange fettuccine on a warm platter and sprinkle with toasted pecans.

Wine: California Chardonnay

Pasta and Prawns

Trying to cut down on salt? This recipe accomplishes it without sacrificing flavor.

2   tablespoons low sodium soy sauce
1   cup water
1   pound prawns or medium sized
       shrimp, peeled and deveined
1/4   cup unsalted butter
1/2   cup thinly sliced green onions
3   large cloves garlic, minced
1 1/2 teaspoons cornstarch
4   teaspoons lemon juice
1/4   cup (packed) finely chopped fresh
       basil leaves
1/2   pound capellini
2   tablespoons minced fresh parsley
1/2   teaspoon crushed red pepper

Yield: 4 servings

- Combine soy sauce with water in a small pan. Bring to a boil. Add cleaned shrimp and cook for 2 minutes, or until shrimp just turn pink. Remove shrimp and keep warm, reserving the liquid.

- Melt butter in a large skillet over medium heat. Add green onions and garlic. Sauté for 2 minutes.

- Stir reserved shrimp liquid into skillet. Combine cornstarch and lemon juice. Add to skillet and bring to a boil. Stir in basil and simmer for 1 minute until thickened.

- Cook capellini according to package directions. Drain well and toss with sauce and shrimp. Sprinkle with parsley and red pepper.

Wine: California Chardonnay

King Crab Fettuccine

An impressive dish that is easy to prepare; perfect for a dinner party.

1/2   cup butter
1   clove garlic, minced
6–8 Alaskan King Crab Legs
1/2   cup freshly grated Parmesan cheese
3/4   cup heavy cream
1/2   teaspoon freshly ground black pepper
12   ounces fresh fettuccine
1   tablespoon chopped fresh parsley

Yield: 6 servings

- In a large saucepan, melt butter over medium heat. Sauté garlic for 2 minutes. Add crabmeat, cheese, cream, and pepper. Cook, stirring occasionally, for about 5–7 minutes. Keep warm.

- Cook fettuccine in a large pot of boiling salted water until "al denté." Drain and toss with crab sauce. Garnish with parsley. Serve with additional Parmesan on the side.

Wine: California Chardonnay

Spaghetti Cacciatore

An Italian masterpiece interpreted for today's cook.

1/4   cup extra virgin olive oil
2   whole chicken breasts, skinned,
      boned, and cut into small pieces
1/2   pound mushrooms, sliced
1   small green bell pepper, chopped
1   small onion, chopped
2   cloves garlic, minced
1   (15 ounce) can tomato sauce
1/4   cup white wine, such as Italian Soave
1   bay leaf
2   tablespoons parsley flakes
2   teaspoons oregano
dash Tabasco
1   pound spaghetti
grated Romano cheese

Yield: 4 servings

- Heat oil in a large skillet. Sauté chicken until golden. Remove from skillet.

- Add mushrooms, green pepper, onion, and garlic to skillet and sauté for 2 minutes.

- Reduce heat to low, add tomato sauce, wine, bay leaf, parsley, oregano, and Tabasco. Cover skillet and simmer for 25 minutes. Add chicken and continue simmering for 15 minutes.

- Prepare spaghetti according to package directions, until "al denté." Mound pasta on a warm serving platter.

- Pour cacciatore mixture on top of spaghetti and sprinkle with grated Romano.

Pedigree Pasta

Just a short while ago, it seemed than no one outside of Italy and California had ever heard of sun dried tomatoes. Now they are everywhere!

4   tablespoons unsalted butter
2   tablespoons chopped onions
6   ounces fresh mushrooms, sliced
6   whole sun dried tomatoes
2   cups whipping cream
freshly ground white pepper
1 1/2   pounds fresh fettuccine

Yield: 4 servings

- Melt butter in skillet over medium heat. Add onions and sauté until limp. Add mushrooms and tomatoes, stirring for 3 minutes.

- Pour cream into pan and bring to a boil. Reduce heat and simmer until sauce is thick enough to coat the back of a spoon or is reduced by 1/4.

- Cook fettuccine in a large pot of boiling salted water until "al denté." Drain and transfer to a large warm bowl.

- Add sauce and toss until well combined. Top with freshly ground pepper.

Wine: Italian Barolo

Pesto Presto

When basil is in season, make several batches of this and freeze for future use.

2   cloves garlic
2   cups fresh basil leaves
1/2   cup olive oil
2   tablespoons pine nuts
1   teaspoon salt
1/2   cup freshly grated Parmesan cheese
3   tablespoons butter, softened
1   tablespoon or more hot water

Yield: 1 cup

Food Processor Method:
- Put the garlic cloves in processor and mince at high speed.

- Add basil and process until basil is finely chopped. With processor running, add olive oil through feeder tube in a steady stream. Process until well blended. Add salt and pine nuts and process until combined. Transfer to a bowl.

- Sprinkle Parmesan over pesto, blend well. Add softened butter and stir until combined thoroughly.

Blender Method:
- Crush the garlic cloves and add to blender with the basil. Whirl until chopped.

- With blender running on low speed, add olive oil in a steady stream until well blended. Add salt and pine nuts and whirl at high speed until well combined. Transfer to bowl and add cheese and butter as above.

Note: Cook your favorite pasta as package directs. To the pesto, add a tablespoon or more of hot water in which the pasta has been boiled. Spoon pesto over pasta and toss until well combined.

POULTRY

Poultry

Chicken in Balsamic Vinegar

Balsamic vinegar is very popular right now. Find it in gourmet food shops or gourmet catalogues.

2	chicken breasts, boned and skinned (about 1½ pounds)
2	tablespoons flour
	salt
	freshly ground black pepper
3	tablespoons virgin olive oil
6	cloves garlic, peeled
¾	pound small mushrooms
4	tablespoons balsamic vinegar
¾	cup chicken broth
1	bay leaf
¼	teaspoon dried thyme
1	tablespoon butter

Garnish:
black olives
fresh parsley

Yield: 2–4 servings

- Split each chicken breast in half. Season the flour with the salt and pepper. Dredge chicken in the flour and shake off excess.

- Heat oil over medium heat in a heavy skillet and cook the chicken breasts until browned nicely on one side, about 4 minutes. Add the garlic and cook for 1–2 more minutes.

- Turn chicken over and scatter mushrooms on top. Cook for another few minutes, until the mushrooms have cooked down a bit. Add the balsamic vinegar, chicken broth, bay leaf, and thyme.

- Cover tightly and cook over low heat for 10 minutes, turning pieces occasionally as they cook.

- Remove chicken with a slotted spoon to a warm serving platter.

- Continue cooking the mushrooms and sauce over medium heat for about 7 minutes. Swirl in the butter. Remove the bay leaf and garlic cloves.

- Arrange chicken on platter. Spoon mushrooms and sauce down center of chicken. Garnish with black olives and parsley.

Wine: Italian Vernaccia

Chicken and Corn Pot Pie

The newest of food trends is unpretentious American home cooking. Chicken pot pies are even being served at formal dinners.

Cornmeal-Chive Pastry:
1½ cups unbleached flour
⅔ cup yellow cornmeal
¼ cup cake flour
½ teaspoon salt
3 tablespoons minced chives
½ cup plus 2 tablespoons cold, unsalted
     butter
½ cup cold water

Filling:
1 pound small white onions
2 tablespoons butter
¼ pound country smoked bacon, diced
1 (3 pound) chicken, quartered
¼ cup flour
2 large carrots, diced
1¼ cups condensed chicken broth
3 whole cloves
2 whole cardamom pods
½ teaspoon rosemary
salt
freshly ground black pepper
½ pound fresh or frozen corn kernels

1 egg, beaten

Garnish:
minced chives

Yield: 6–8 servings

The Pastry:
- Combine all dry ingredients. Cut butter into small pieces and mix into dry ingredients with a fork. Add water, tossing with the fork until just moistened and dough can be gathered into a ball. *Do not over mix.*

- Wrap dough in plastic wrap and chill overnight in refrigerator.

The Filling:
- Bring a large pot of water to a boil. Add unpeeled onions and blanch for 2 minutes. Drain and rinse thoroughly with cold water. Trim off tops and bottoms. Slip off skins.

- Melt butter in a large skillet over medium heat. Add bacon and cook until crisp. Remove with slotted spoon and set aside on paper towels.

- Lightly dredge chicken pieces in flour. Increase heat to medium-high and brown chicken on all sides in skillet. Remove chicken and pour off all but 3 tablespoons drippings.

- Add carrots and onions to skillet and cook for about 3 minutes over medium heat. Stir in chicken broth, cloves, cardamom, rosemary, salt, and pepper. Add chicken and bacon and bring to a gentle simmer. Cover and cook for 30 minutes, or until chicken is tender.

Continued on next page

- Remove chicken and set aside to cool. Skim fat and reduce sauce over high heat until flavor is intense. Season to taste with salt and pepper.

- When chicken is cool, remove skin and bone and cut into bite size chunks. Transfer to a bowl and add sauce. Cover and refrigerate overnight. The next day, skim off any fat that rises to the surface.

- Preheat oven to 400°. Generously grease a 6 cup soufflé dish.

- Stir corn into chicken mixture. Turn into prepared dish.

- Roll out pastry to a 14″ square, ⅛″thick. Cut into lattice strips. Lay the strips over the top of the soufflé dish, weaving one over the other to make a dense weave, not an open lattice. (You will have a completely covered pie with a woven crust.) Crimp edges all around to seal in the chicken mixture.

- Brush entire surface with beaten egg. Bake for 1–1¼ hours, or until sauce is bubbly and crust is golden brown and crisp. (Cover with foil if it starts to brown too quickly.)

- Remove from oven, sprinkle with a little bit of minced chives and serve with your best silver serving pieces.

Wine: California Sauvignon Blanc

Chicken Paprika

Paprika can vary in strength from mild to pungent and its flavor intensifies as you cook.

1/3   cup vegetable or peanut oil
2   large chicken breasts, boned, skinned, and halved (about 1 pound each)
4–6   chicken thighs, skinned
2   large onions, diced
2   large green bell peppers, diced
1   teaspoon salt
2   medium tomatoes, peeled, seeded, and diced
2   tablespoons Hungarian paprika
1/2   cup sour cream
1/4   cup milk
2   tablespoons flour

Yield: 6 servings

- In a large skillet, heat oil and brown chicken over medium heat. Add onions to skillet and cook until they are transparent. Toss in green peppers, add salt and stir until well combined. Cover and cook over low heat for a few minutes, until peppers are tender.

- Stir in tomatoes and continue to cook, covered, for 40 minutes. Remove cover and raise temperature to medium and heat until liquid is reduced by half. Blend in paprika.

- Mix sour cream with enough milk to make it pour (up to 1/4 cup). Blend in flour until there are no lumps. (It should be the consistency of honey.) Pour mixture into skillet. Stir until it comes to a boil and thickens.

- Serve with broad egg noodles. Sprinkle extra paprika on top before serving.

Wine: Hungarian Egri Bikaver

Neapolitan Chicken

Looking for the perfect Super Bowl Sunday supper . . . here it is! This can be doubled or tripled, made in advance, and reheated quickly.

1/4	cup chopped onion
1	clove garlic, minced
1	tablespoon virgin olive oil
1/2	pound sweet Italian sausage, cut into 1″ pieces
1	(6 ounce) can tomato paste
1	(28 ounce) can Italian tomatoes
1	tablespoon parsley
1/8	teaspoon rosemary
2	whole chicken breasts, skinned, boned, and cubed
1	red bell pepper, cut into strips
1	green bell pepper, cut into strips
3/4	cup dry white wine, such as Italian Gavi

Yield: 4–6 servings

- In a large skillet, sauté onion and garlic in olive oil over medium heat until tender. Add sausage and lightly brown. Add tomato paste and cook for a few minutes. Add tomatoes, spices, chicken, red and green pepper, and wine.

- Simmer for 1 hour. Transfer to a tureen or a large bowl.

- Serve with garlic bread and Romaine Toss (page 100).

Wine: Italian Gavi

Chicken Scallopine

This can be prepared with very little notice. You probably have all the ingredients on hand.

2	whole chicken breasts, boned, skinned, and halved
3	tablespoons flour
salt	
freshly ground black pepper	
1 1/2	tablespoons virgin olive oil
1	tablespoon butter
1/4	cup dry white wine, such as French Blanc de Blanc
1	lemon, thinly sliced
2	teaspoons capers

Garnish:
lemon peel roses

Yield: 2 servings

- Pound chicken breasts with mallet until very thin.

- Mix flour with salt and pepper to taste. Dredge chicken breasts in flour mixture.

- Combine oil and butter in a large skillet over medium-high heat. Brown chicken pieces quickly, about 3 minutes on each side.

- Pour off pan drippings. Add wine, lemon, and capers. Simmer for 10 minutes over low heat until tender.

- Arrange chicken on a warm platter. Garnish with lemon peel roses.

Wine: Italian Orvieto

Poulet à la Crème Cognac

Just right for your next intimate dinner party

1½ pounds chicken breasts, boned and
    skinned
2   tablespoons butter
1½ tablespoons finely chopped shallots
¼   pound mushrooms, sliced
3   tablespoons cognac
1   avocado
1⅓ cups heavy cream
salt
freshly ground black pepper

Garnish:
carrot curls
lemon peel roses

Yield: 4 servings

- Cut chicken into strips. Sprinkle with salt and pepper.

- Melt butter in a heavy skillet and cook chicken over high heat, shaking and stirring until chicken turns white, about 3–4 minutes. Remove chicken with slotted spoon and set aside.

- Add shallots and mushrooms to skillet. Cook, stirring, until onions are transparent. Sprinkle with cognac.

- Pour cream into skillet and cook over high heat for 5 minutes, until somewhat reduced. Add salt and pepper to taste.

- Peel and seed avocado. Cut into ½″ strips.

- Add avocado and chicken to skillet and cook, very gently, until heated through. Transfer to a warm serving platter.

- Garnish with carrot curls and lemon peel roses. Serve with rice.

Wine: California Chardonnay

Deep Fried Walnut Chicken

The Chinese name for this dish is "He T'ao Chi P'ien."

3   chicken breasts, boned and skinned
       (about 1½ pounds)
2   tablespoons rice wine
3   green onions
3   slices fresh ginger root (size of a
       quarter)
1½ teaspoons salt
1   teaspoon sesame oil
¼   teaspoon pepper
2   cups walnuts
1   egg, slightly beaten
1   cup cornstarch
4–6 cups peanut oil

Yield: 6 servings

- Cut chicken into 1″ chunks.

- Pour rice wine into a large bowl. Flatten green onions and ginger root with the flat side of a cleaver and add to bowl. Add salt, sesame oil, and pepper. Mix well.

- Add chicken to bowl, toss to coat well, and let marinate for at least 30 minutes.

- Blanch the walnuts in a pot of boiling water for 15 seconds. Drain and pat dry with paper towels. Chop fine.

- Remove the green onions and ginger from the marinating chicken. Add the beaten egg and toss to coat the chicken evenly. Remove chicken from marinade, dredge in cornstarch and roll in the walnuts to coat.

- Pour peanut oil into a wok or deep fryer and heat to 350°. Brown the chicken pieces in batches for about 2 minutes, or until light brown on all sides. Remove and drain on paper towels.

- When all the chicken has been browned, heat the oil to 400° and add the chicken all at once. Fry for 1–2 minutes, until deep golden brown and heated through. Drain on paper towels. Arrange chicken pieces on a platter, ring with cooked rice and steamed broccoli. Serve immediately.

Note: As an appetizer, serve on a tray with wooden picks. You may prepare this dish ahead of time up to the second frying. However, chicken must be at room temperature or warmer before second frying.

Wine: California Sauvignon Blanc

Chicken Cachet

When the results of the cooking contest were in, this was the prize winning preparation.

4   tablespoons vegetable oil
1   whole chicken, skinned and cut into
       pieces
2   teaspoons minced onion
1   teaspoon flour
1   teaspoon salt
1/2 teaspoon sugar
1/2 teaspoon paprika
1/4 teaspoon garlic powder
1/4 teaspoon ground thyme
1/4 teaspoon pepper
1/8 teaspoon curry powder

Yield: 4–6 servings

- Preheat oven to 350°. Spread 2 tablespoons of oil in the bottom of a large, shallow baking dish. Place chicken pieces on top in a single layer. Pour remaining 2 tablespoons oil over all pieces.

- Combine remaining ingredients in a small bowl. Sprinkle half of this mixture over chicken.

- Bake, uncovered, at 350° for 30 minutes. Remove from oven.

- Turn chicken over and sprinkle remaining mixture over all pieces. Return to oven and bake for 30 minutes more, or until tender.

Wine: French Loire Sancerre

Chicken Delite

Spa cooking at its best — a low fat, low calorie dish that tastes scrumptious.

Marinade:
1/2 cup low calorie French or Russian
      dressing
1/2 cup plain low fat yogurt
2   tablespoons lemon juice
2   teaspoons (or more) curry powder
1   clove garlic, minced

4   chicken breasts, boned and skinned

Garnish:
raisins

Yield: 4 servings

- Combine all marinade ingredients. Butter a shallow casserole. Cut chicken breasts in half and place in casserole.

- Pour marinade over chicken, turning to coat well. Refrigerate, covered, for at least 2 hours.

- Preheat oven to 300°.

- Bake chicken at 300° for 1 1/2 hours or until tender. Garnish with raisins and serve with couscous.

Curried Stuffed Chicken Breasts

Why save entertaining for the weekends when you can treat yourself and a few friends to a wonderful weeknight dinner.

4 chicken breasts, boned and skinned
3 tablespoons seedless golden raisins
1/4 cup hot water
3 tablespoons butter
1/2 cup finely chopped onion
1/2 cup finely chopped celery
1/4 teaspoon finely minced garlic
1 bay leaf
1 apple, peeled, cored, and cut into 1/4" cubes
3 tablespoons chutney
salt
freshly ground black pepper
1 cup heavy cream
1 1/2 teaspoons curry powder
2 tablespoons dry sherry

Garnish:
golden raisins
sliced almonds, toasted

Yield: 4-6 servings

- Flatten chicken breasts with a mallet.

- Place raisins in a small container. Add hot water and cover for 10-15 minutes while raisins plump.

- Preheat oven to 425°.

- Melt 1 tablespoon butter in a skillet over medium heat. Add onion, celery, and garlic. Cook, stirring often, until onion is transparent. Add bay leaf and apple. Stir and cook for 1 minute.

- Squeeze raisins gently in a paper towel to remove excess liquid. Add to onion mixture. Stir in chutney. Remove from heat and let mixture cool.

- Sprinkle chicken with salt and pepper. Spoon equal amounts of the filling in the center of each chicken breast. Bring up edges and fold chicken over the filling, securing with a toothpick.

- Melt remaining 2 tablespoons butter in a shallow baking dish by placing it in a preheated oven for a few minutes.

- Transfer chicken to baking dish, seam side down. Brush tops with melted butter. Bake at 425° for 10-15 minutes, basting occasionally during cooking. (Dish may be prepared ahead of time up to this point and refrigerated.)

- Blend cream, curry powder, and sherry thoroughly. Pour over chicken. Bake 10-15 minutes more, basting once or twice.

- Remove baking pan from oven. Transfer individual servings to warm plates. Garnish each with golden raisins and toasted sliced almonds.

Wine: French Pouilly Fumé

Poulet Roti et Pommes

Inspired by the roast chicken served at the famous Parisian bistro, Chez Ami Louis.

1   roasting chicken (3–4 pounds)
4   tablespoons butter
2   cloves garlic
2–3 shallots, peeled and quartered
4–6 medium potatoes, peeled and cut
       into 1″ cubes
salt
freshly ground black pepper
1/2 teaspoon fresh or dried tarragon

Yield: 4 servings

- Truss the chicken so that it can be handled easily.

- Melt 1 tablespoon of butter in a large skillet. Brown chicken all over on medium heat. Remove from skillet.

- Preheat oven to 325°.

- Discard drippings from skillet. Add 2 tablespoons butter and return to medium heat. Add 1 clove garlic, shallots, and potatoes and stir briefly until coated with butter. Season to taste with salt and pepper.

- Place 1 tablespoon butter, 1 clove of garlic, and a bit of salt in the cavity of the chicken. Sprinkle outside of chicken with salt, pepper, and tarragon.

- Transfer chicken to a roasting pan and surround with potato mixture. Roast at 325°, uncovered, for 1 hour and 15 minutes, or until juices run clear when thigh is pricked with a fork. Turn chicken 5 times during roasting.

- Remove string trussing and transfer chicken to a warm serving platter. Surround with potatoes and shallots.

Wine: French Macon Blanc Villages

Chicken Grand Marnier

A skillful combination of complimenting flavors

8   whole chicken breasts, boned and
       skinned
¹/₄   cup flour
salt
freshly ground black pepper
¹/₃   cup butter
1¹/₂   teaspoons rosemary, crushed
1   small onion, minced
¹/₂   cup chopped onion
1   cup orange juice
¹/₂   cup Grand Marnier (orange liqueur)
orange slices

Garnish:
orange blossoms

Yield: 6–8 servings

- Preheat oven to 350°. Butter a large, shallow baking dish.

- Cut whole chicken breasts in half. Combine flour, salt, and pepper. Dredge chicken breasts in flour mixture.

- Melt butter in a large skillet over medium heat. Add chicken. Sprinkle with rosemary and add minced onion. Brown chicken on all sides. Place in baking dish.

- Add chopped onion to skillet and sauté until tender. Stir in orange juice and Grand Marnier. Bring to a boil while stirring. Pour sauce over chicken. Top with orange slices. Cover and roast for 1 hour at 350°.

- Remove from oven and arrange on a platter. Garnish with a sprinkling of orange blossoms. Serve Grand Marnier sauce from pan on the side.

Wine: French St. Veran

Walnut Stuffed Chicken Breasts

After the football game, enjoy this tasty Autumn dinner.

6   whole chicken breasts, boned and
        skinned
1   cup grated cheddar cheese
1/2 cup coarsely chopped walnuts
1/2 cup fresh bread crumbs
2   tablespoons minced onion
1/4 teaspoon salt
1/8 teaspoon freshly ground black pepper
5   tablespoons butter
1/2 cup flour
1   cup chicken broth
1/2 cup dry white wine, such as Blanc
        de Blanc
2   tablespoons chopped fresh parsley
4   cups cooked wild rice

Garnish:
chopped walnuts

Yield: 6–8 servings

- Flatten each chicken breast with a mallet until 1/8″ thick. In a small bowl, combine cheese, walnuts, bread crumbs, onion, salt, pepper, and 2 tablespoons melted butter.

- Spoon 1–2 tablespoons of this filling on the center of each chicken breast. Roll up, enclosing filling, and secure with a toothpick.

- Roll chicken breasts in flour. Melt 3 tablespoons butter in a skillet over medium heat. Sauté chicken on all sides until brown. Pour chicken broth and wine into skillet. Cook over low heat for 20 minutes.

- Transfer chicken to a platter. Remove toothpicks and keep warm.

- Increase heat to high and reduce sauce somewhat while stirring. Add chopped parsley to sauce.

- Arrange wild rice on a warm platter. Top with chicken breasts. Pour some of the sauce over the chicken and scatter chopped walnuts over the top. Serve additional sauce on the side.

Wine: California Chardonnay

Chicken Scallopine with Basil Sauce

Candlelight, music, and dinner for just the two of you.

1   whole chicken breast, boned and
        skinned
¼   cup fresh lemon juice
3   tablespoons unsalted butter
salt
freshly ground black pepper
1   tablespoon dry white wine, such as
        Italian Gavi
¼   cup water
¼   cup heavy cream
¼   cup finely chopped fresh basil leaves

Garnish:
basil leaves
lemon slices

Yield: 2 servings

- Cut the chicken breast in half. Flatten with a mallet to ⅛″ thickness.

- Place chicken in a shallow dish and pour lemon juice over it. Turn to coat well and marinate for 15 minutes.

- Melt 1 tablespoon of the butter in a large skillet over medium heat. Drain chicken, reserving lemon juice. Season chicken with salt and pepper and add to skillet. Cook for 3 minutes on each side, or until just firm to the touch.

- Transfer to a serving plate and keep warm.

- Add the reserved lemon juice to the skillet, stir in the wine and the water. Bring the mixture to a boil over moderate heat. Lower heat, stir, and simmer for 1 minute.

- Pour in cream and any juices that have accumulated on chicken plate. Bring to a boil, cook for 2 minutes, until slightly thickened. Remove from heat and whisk in remaining 2 tablespoons of butter. Fold in basil and warm through.

- Arrange chicken on individual plates. Spoon sauce over cutlets. Garnish with small fresh basil leaves and paper thin slices of lemon.

Wine: Italian Gavi

Chicken Marsala

A wonderful, economical substitute for Veal Marsala.

2   *whole chicken breasts, boned,
      skinned, and halved (about 1¹/₂
      pounds)*
salt
freshly ground black pepper
¹/₄   *cup flour*
4   *tablespoons butter*
2   *shallots, chopped*
¹/₄   *cup Marsala wine*
¹/₂   *cup condensed chicken broth*
lemon juice

Garnish:
chopped parsley
lemon slices

Yield: 4 servings

- Pound chicken breasts with a mallet until uniformly ¹/₈″ thick. Salt and pepper chicken, then dredge in flour. Shake to remove excess.

- Melt 2 tablespoons butter in a skillet over medium-high heat. Quickly brown chicken on both sides. (It need not be completely cooked at this time.) Remove from pan and keep warm.

- Discard drippings from skillet and melt remaining butter over medium-high heat. Add shallots and sauté for 1 minute. Pour in wine and chicken broth and bring to a boil. Continue to boil until liquid is reduced by half.

- Add lemon juice, salt and pepper to taste. Return cutlets to pan and heat through.

- Arrange cutlets on a platter and pour sauce over them. Garnish with a sprinkling of parsley and paper thin slices of lemon.

Wine: French White Burgundy

Apple Mustard Chicken

Perfect for a harvest moon supper; serve this with rice and baked acorn squash.

2	whole chicken breasts, boned, skinned, and halved
2	tablespoons butter
1	cup apple juice
1	medium onion, chopped
1	clove garlic, minced
1/2	teaspoon thyme
5	teaspoons Dijon mustard
1	or 2 apples, cored and sliced thin

Garnish:
red and green apple slices

Yield: *4 servings*

- Pound chicken breasts with a mallet to flatten. In a large skillet melt butter over medium heat. Add chicken breasts and brown lightly.

- Add apple juice, onion, garlic, and thyme. Cover and cook until chicken is tender (about 10 minutes). Remove chicken to a platter and keep warm.

- Bring liquid in skillet to a boil. Blend in mustard. Add apple slices and warm through.

- Arrange chicken on platter, pour some sauce over chicken, and garnish with red and green apple slices. Serve remaining sauce on the side.

Wine: California Sauvignon Blanc

Mustard Fried Chicken Breasts

In a hurry? Here's a dish that takes only thirty minutes from start to finish.

4	chicken breasts, boned and skinned
1/2	teaspoon salt
	freshly ground black pepper
1	egg
2	tablespoons Dijon mustard
1/4	cup Parmesan cheese
1/4	cup bread crumbs
2	tablespoons vegetable oil

Garnish:
capers
carrot curls

Yield: *4 servings*

- Sprinkle chicken breasts with salt and pepper. In a small bowl, beat together egg and mustard. In another bowl, combine Parmesan cheese and bread crumbs.

- Dip each chicken breast in egg mixture, then roll it evenly in the cheese mixture. Allow coating to set for about 10 minutes or longer.

- Heat oil in a skillet over medium heat. Sauté chicken on both sides for 15-20 minutes, or until tender.

- Arrange chicken breasts on a platter. Garnish with capers and carrot curls. Serve with sautéed mushrooms and petite vegetables.

Wine: French Sancerre

Chicken Mozzarella

Yearning for an Italian dinner, but tired of pasta? This may be your answer.

1/4 cup flour
salt
freshly ground black pepper
9   chicken breast halves, boned and skinned
4   tablespoons butter
3/4   pound mushrooms, sliced thin
1   (8 ounce) package mozzarella cheese

Garnish:
red and green bell pepper rings

Yield: 6–8 servings

- Preheat oven to 325°.

- Combine flour, salt and pepper. Dredge chicken in flour mixture.

- Melt 2 tablespoons butter in a large skillet over medium heat. Sauté chicken breasts until golden brown. Transfer to a shallow, oven-proof casserole dish.

- Melt remaining butter in the same skillet and sauté mushrooms until tender. Cover each chicken breast with an equal portion of mushrooms.

- Cut mozzarella into 9 slices. Top each chicken breast with cheese. Bake at 325° for 20 minutes, then put under broiler for 1–2 minutes to brown cheese.

- Garnish with red and green pepper rings.

Wine: Italian Vernaccia

Turkey Florentine

An imaginative preparation and presentation

1   cup grated Parmesan cheese
4   tablespoons fine, dry bread crumbs
2   teaspoons Italian seasoning
1   teaspoon salt
1   pound turkey breast, boned and
     skinned
2   eggs, well beaten
2   tablespoons butter
2   tablespoons vegetable oil
1   (10 ounce) package frozen chopped
     spinach, cooked
4   ounces Swiss or Mozzarella cheese,
     shredded

Yield: 4 servings

- Mix together Parmesan cheese, bread crumbs, seasoning, and salt in a large, shallow dish.

- Slice turkey breast, crosswise, into ½" thick slices. Pound with a mallet until thin.

- Dip turkey into egg and coat with crumb mixture, pressing firmly.

- Heat butter and oil over medium heat in a large skillet. Add turkey cutlets and brown on both sides. Transfer to a flameproof casserole or baking dish and keep warm.

- Drain spinach in a colander, pressing with the back of a spoon to remove as much moisture as possible. Mix spinach with cheese. Spoon spinach down center of turkey cutlets. (Dish may be refrigerated at this point. Just remove from refrigerator and bake at 300° for 20 minutes, then continue as follows.)

- Broil in oven for a few minutes, watching carefully, until cheese melts.

Wine: California Zinfandel

Glazed Cornish Hens with Drambuie Stuffing

Careful . . . romantic dinners may be habit forming.

2   cornish game hens

Stuffing:
1/2   navel orange, seeded
1 1/2   cups bread stuffing mix
1   small onion, finely chopped
2   tablespoons butter, melted
2   tablespoons golden raisins
2   tablespoons almond slivers
3   tablespoons Drambuie

Glaze:
1/3   cup orange juice
1/3   cup Drambuie
1/3   cup butter, melted
1   tablespoon honey

1   tablespoon flour
1/2   cup chicken broth

Garnish:
red and green grapes

Yield: 2 servings

The Stuffing:
- Finely chop orange half in a food processor, or by hand, saving juice. Transfer orange and juice to a large bowl and add bread stuffing, onion, and butter. Blend in raisins and almonds. Moisten with Drambuie and combine well.

- Preheat oven to 350°.

- Stuff the hens with the stuffing mix and truss.

The Glaze:
- In a small saucepan, combine orange juice, Drambuie, butter, and honey. Heat on medium for about 5 minutes.

- Brush glaze over hens and place hens in a roasting pan. Bake at 350° for 45 minutes.

- Brush hens with glaze every 10 minutes during roasting, but reserve some of the glaze for later use.

- When hens are done, transfer to a platter and keep warm.

- Pour pan drippings into a small saucepan. Whisk in flour, add chicken broth, and heat over medium heat until sauce thickens. Stir in 2 tablespoons glaze mixture. Serve sauce on the side with the Cornish hens.

- Dip red and green grapes in remaining glaze and roll in granulated sugar. Garnish platter of hens with frosted grapes.

Wine: French White Burgundy

Game Hens à l'Orange

A pair of delicious little birds with an appealing, savory sauce.

2   cornish game hens
1   (6 ounce) can frozen orange juice
        concentrate
4   tablespoons butter
1   tablespoon parsley or chervil
1–2 large cloves garlic, minced

Garnish:
parsley
orange slices
wild rice

Yield: 2 servings

- Preheat oven to 350°.

- Place hens breast side up in a baking pan.

- Combine remaining ingredients in a saucepan. Blend well and simmer over medium heat. Simmer for a few minutes to release garlic and herb flavors.

- Pour sauce over hens. Bake at 350° for 30–45 minutes, or until tender, basting frequently to keep moist.

- Place cooked hens on a bed of wild rice and garnish with parsley and thin slices of orange. Serve with sauce on the side.

Honey Glazed Duckling

The invitation reads, dinner at eight, dressed to the nines.

2   ducklings (about 4¹/₂ pounds each)
2   medium onions, chopped
2   cloves garlic
¹/₄ cup soy sauce
¹/₂ cup dry sherry
¹/₂ cup honey
¹/₂ teaspoon ground ginger
¹/₄ teaspoon freshly ground black pepper
dash Tabasco

Garnish:
orange slices
grapes
parsley

Yield: 4–6 servings

- Preheat oven to 350°.

- Snip off wing tips and wipe inside and outside of ducklings with paper towels.

- Combine remaining ingredients in a blender and whirl on high until thoroughly liquified.

- Place ducklings, breast side up, on a rack in a roasting pan. Brush ducks generoulsy with honey glaze.

- Roast ducks at 350° for 20 minutes per pound. Brush with glaze every 15–20 minutes during roasting.

- When done, remove ducks to a platter and garnish with orange slices, grapes, and parsley.

Wine: California Chardonnay

Spiced Cranberry Citrus Conserve

Don't wait until Thanksgiving to try this as it is good with any poultry recipe.

1	pound cranberries
²/₃	cup cold water
5	whole cloves
1	(3 inch) stick cinnamon

pinch salt

¹/₄	teaspoon allspice
¹/₄	teaspoon ground ginger
¹/₂	teaspoon mace
¹/₂	teaspoon nutmeg
1	large orange
1	lemon
²/₃	cup raisins
²/₃	cup boiling water
2¹/₂	cups sugar
²/₃	cup chopped nuts

Yield: 6 cups

- Combine cranberries, cold water, and spices in a saucepan. Bring to a boil over medium heat and continue to boil until cranberry skins burst.

- Quarter orange and lemon. Remove seeds and pithy centers. Cut into thin slices, rind and all. Chop raisins into small pieces.

- Add lemon, orange, raisins, boiling water, and sugar to cranberry pulp. Stir over low heat until sugar is dissolved.

- Increase heat and boil rapidly for 10–15 minutes, stirring constantly. Syrup should thicken only slightly. Do not overcook. Remove from heat and stir in chopped nuts.

- Pour into jelly jars and refrigerate, or follow approved method for canning.

Pilgrim Berry Sauce

New Jersey is the third largest producer of cranberries in the world. The Pilgrim Cranberry is one variety grown in this state.

1¹/₂	cups pure maple syrup
¹/₂	cup water
1	teaspoon ground ginger
4	cups fresh cranberries

Yield: 4 cups

- Bring maple syrup, water, and ginger to a boil in a large heavy saucepan over medium heat. Stir in cranberries.

- Simmer until berries burst, about 5 minutes, stirring occasionally.

- Transfer to a serving bowl, cover the surface of the mixture with plastic wrap (so a skin won't form), and let cool.

- Refrigerate until serving time.

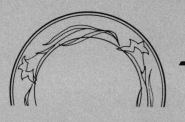

FISH
and
SEAFOOD

Fish and Seafood

Turbot with Fresh Salsa

For those aficionados of spicy, zippy, and zesty foods

Salsa:
2	large ripe tomatoes, peeled, seeded, and chopped
3	tablespoons finely chopped onion
3	tablespoons finely chopped green bell pepper
3	tablespoons or more finely chopped jalapeño pepper
1	tablespoon red wine vinegar
1	tablespoon fresh coriander, or 1 teaspoon dried
$1/4$	teaspoon salt
2	cloves garlic, minced
2 – 3	dashes Tabasco

Fish:
1	large onion, cut into $1/4''$ rings
2	tablespoons olive or vegetable oil
1	green bell pepper, cut into $1/4''$ rings
$1/2$	pound mushrooms, sliced $1/4''$ thick
	salt
	white pepper
$1^1/2$	pounds turbot fillets
4	cloves garlic, minced
$1/4$	cup olive oil
	paprika

Yield: *4 servings*

The Salsa:
- Combine all salsa ingredients in a large bowl. Cover and chill for several hours or overnight, stirring occasionally.

The Fish:
- In a medium skillet, sauté onion in oil until transparent. Add green pepper and mushrooms and sauté until tender. Season with salt and pepper to taste. Add half of the salsa mixture and heat through.

- Rub fish with salt and pepper. Mix garlic and olive oil. Spread over fish. Sprinkle with paprika.

- Broil fish 6″ from flame for 6 minutes.

- Place fish on warmed serving platter and top with remaining salsa mixture.

- Serve with steamed summer and zucchini squash.

Beverage: Molson Brador Malt Liquor

Flounder Almondine

A delicious classic reintroduced by popular demand.

1	pound fresh flounder fillets
1/2	cup flour
1	tablespoon butter
1	tablespoon vegetable oil
1/2	teaspoon minced garlic
1/4	cup sliced almonds
2	tablespoon dry white wine, such as French Muscadet
1	tablespoon lemon juice
1	tablespoon minced fresh parsley

Yield: 2 servings

- Lightly dust the flounder with flour.

- Heat 1/2 tablespoon of butter and 1/2 tablespoon oil in a 10″ or 12″ non-stick skillet. Sauté flounder for 2–3 minutes on each side. Remove to a warm platter.

- Add remaining butter and oil to skillet. Sauté garlic and almonds for 1 minute. Add wine and lemon juice. Stir until combined.

- Pour sauce over fillets and sprinkle with parsley.

- Serve with wild rice and Carrots à la Champagne (page 111).

Wine: Italian Vernaccia

Broiled Flounder Fromage

A New Jersey fisherman's "catch-of-the-day" could be: tile fish, sea bass, whiting, or flounder.

1 1/2	pounds flounder fillets
	salt
	freshly ground black pepper
1/2	cup mayonnaise
1/2	cup shredded Swiss cheese
	dash cayenne pepper
1	egg white
	fresh parsley

Yield: 4 servings

- Sprinkle fish with salt and pepper. Place fillets on broiler pan and broil 4″ from flame for about 10 minutes.

- Mix mayonnaise, cheese, and cayenne together.

- Beat egg white until stiff and fold into cheese mixture.

- Spread cheese mixture on fish and return to the broiler until puffed and lightly browned. Sprinkle with fresh parsley.

Wine: California Fumé Blanc

Sole Piccata

Fabulous!

1	large egg
3/4	cup flour
1	teaspoon salt
1/4	teaspoon pepper
1/4	teaspoon paprika
1 1/2	pounds grey sole fillets
1/2	cup butter
3	tablespoons olive oil
1/3	cup Madeira wine
1/4	cup fresh lemon juice
1/4	cup small capers, drained

Yield: 4 servings

- In a bowl, beat the egg lightly. On a large plate, combine the flour, salt, pepper, and paprika. Dip the fillets in the egg, then in the flour mixture.

- Heat the butter and oil in a large skillet over medium high heat until hot but not smoking.

- Cook the fillets for 3 minutes on each side, or until they are lightly browned. Transfer the fillets to a warm platter and cover.

- Discard all but 3 tablespoons of the fat in the skillet. Add the Madeira and bring to a boil. Keep at a boil for one minute over high heat. Add lemon juice and bring to a boil.

- Pour the sauce over the fillets and sprinkle with capers.

- Serve with Fresh Lemon Rice (page 115).

Wine: French White Graves

Grilled Tuna Teriyaki

The longer the tuna marinates, the richer the flavor becomes.

Marinade:
1/4	cup soy sauce
1/4	cup dry sherry
2	tablespoons sugar
2	tablespoons vegetable oil
3/4	teaspoon ground ginger
1	clove garlic, minced

Fish:
4	medium tuna steaks, about 1″ thick

Yield: 4 servings

The Marinade:
- Combine marinade ingredients in a blender and whirl until thoroughly mixed. Pour over the tuna and marinate for at least 1 hour, preferably longer.

The Fish:
- Put tuna steaks in a well oiled, hinged fish grill or brush a barbecue grill with oil after the coals are hot. Grill tuna for 6–8 minutes per side, basting several times with the marinade.

- Tuna may also be prepared in the broiler. Broil for 6–8 minutes per side, basting frequently.

Wine: California Chardonnay or Kirin Beer

Trout Elsinore

New Jersey is a fisherman's paradise where both fresh water and salt water fishing abound.

4	small fresh trout (1/2 – 3/4 pound each)
	fresh lemon juice
2	teaspoons salt
1/2	teaspoon thyme
1 1/2	teaspoons powdered caraway
1	teaspoon celery seed
1	teaspoon fennel
1/4	teaspoon cayenne pepper
1/2	teaspoon garlic powder
1/8	teaspoon fine herbs
4	bacon strips

Yield: 4 servings

- Place trout on a lightly oiled broiler pan. Sprinkle generously, inside and out, with fresh lemon juice.

- Combine salt and all other spices in a bowl. Sprinkle trout liberally with mixture.

- Broil fish for 10 minutes about 1″ from flame.

- Turn trout, lower rack to 3″ from flame. Lay one strip of bacon on each trout. Broil until bacon is crisp.

- Serve immediately with pan juices.

Wine: Long Island Chardonnay

Crab Stuffed Sole

A medley of ingredients producing perfect harmony

¹/₄ cup butter
¹/₄ cup chopped onions
³/₄ cup chopped mushrooms
13 ounces crabmeat, canned or frozen
¹/₂ cup crushed saltine crackers
2 tablespoons chopped fresh parsley
8 fillets of sole (about 2 pounds)
3 tablespoons butter
2 tablespoons flour
¹/₄ teaspoon salt
1¹/₂ cups milk
¹/₃ cup dry sherry
4 ounces Swiss cheese, grated
¹/₂ teaspoon paprika

Yield: 8 servings

- Preheat oven to 350°. Lightly grease a 9″ × 13″ casserole.

- Melt butter in skillet and sauté onions until translucent. Add mushrooms and sauté until tender.

- Remove from heat and add crabmeat, crushed saltines, and parsley.

- Spread mixture on each fillet. Roll up and place, seam side down, in prepared casserole. (You may use toothpicks to secure fillet rolls.)

- Melt butter in a small saucepan. Whisk in flour and salt. Add milk and stir until smooth. Add sherry and stir for 3–5 minutes until sauce thickens.

- Pour sauce over fillets and bake, uncovered at 350° for 20 minutes or until sauce bubbles.

- Sprinkle with grated cheese and paprika and bake 5 minutes more, or until cheese melts.

Wine: California Johannisberg Riesling

Blackened Grilled Swordfish

For a sizzling summer night, serve Cajun style with black beans and rice.

1/2	teaspoon onion powder
1/2	teaspoon garlic salt
1/2	teaspoon cayenne pepper
1/2	teaspoon crushed dried basil
1/4	teaspoon white pepper
1/4	teaspoon crushed dried thyme
1/4	teaspoon black pepper
1/8	teaspoon ground sage
1/4	cup butter
2	pounds swordfish steaks

lemon juice

Yield: 4 servings

- Mix together all spices. Sprinkle evenly over a large flat platter.

- Melt butter and brush over swordfish steaks. Dip fish in seasonings and coat well on both sides.

- *To cook on a grill:* make sure grill is very hot and rack is close to coals. Barbecue for 5 minutes per side.

- *To cook indoors:* place a cast iron skillet over a high flame and heat for 10 minutes until searing hot. Place fish in skillet and cook for 5 minutes on each side.

- When done, sprinkle with lemon juice.

Wine: Australian Chardonnay

Swordfish with Julienne Vegetables

A fresh tasting healthy entrée, just add a rice pilaf.

1 1/2	cups julienned carrots
1 1/2	cups julienned green onions or leeks
1/2	pound fresh mushrooms, sliced
2	tablespoons finely chopped fresh parsley
1	teaspoon crushed thyme

salt
freshly ground black pepper

2	pounds thick swordfish steaks
1	large lemon
3	tablespoons butter
3/4	cup dry white wine, such as French Blanc de Blanc

Yield: 4 servings

- Preheat oven to 375° and butter a shallow casserole.

- Spread carrots evenly over casserole bottom. Distribute the green onions or leeks over carrots. Scatter mushrooms on top of vegetables. Sprinkle with parsley, thyme, salt, and pepper.

- Place swordfish steaks on top of casserole. Slice lemon wafer-thin and spread on top of fish. Dot with butter. Pour wine over fish.

- Bake at 375° for 25 – 30 minutes. Baste the fish with pan juices 2 – 3 times during cooking to keep moist.

Wine: California Fumé Blanc

Elegant Barbecued Salmon

Who says a barbecue can't be elegant?

Marinade:
1/4	cup fresh apple cider
6	tablespoons soy sauce
2	tablespoons unsalted butter
1	large clove garlic, finely minced

Fish:
2   salmon fillets (2 1/2 – 3 pounds each)
or
5 – 6 pounds salmon steaks, 1″ thick

Yield: 8 – 10 servings

The Marinade:
- Combine apple cider and soy sauce in a saucepan. Bring to a boil and simmer for 3 – 5 minutes. Add butter and garlic and simmer, stirring occasionally for about 20 minutes or until mixture is thick enough to coat the back of the spoon (almost as thick as molasses). Remove from heat. Cool to room temperature.

The Fish:
- Pat salmon fillets or steaks with a paper towel. Place them in a shallow pan and brush generously on both sides with marinade. Refrigerate for at least 1 hour.

- When ready to cook, let stand at room temperature for 30 minutes.

To Barbecue:
- Use mesquite flavored chips if possible. When coals are hot, brush grill with oil.

- Place salmon fillets on grill, skin side down. Tent with aluminum foil and grill for about 15 – 20 minutes, or until fish is still slightly translucent in the thickest part.

- If using salmon steaks, grill for 7 – 8 minutes on each side, turning once very carefully with a large spatula.

Wine: Beaujolais Grand Cru

Sauce Grenoble

A chef's secret recipe that is now yours to enjoy.

8	tablespoons butter
1/4	pound shrimp, shelled, deveined, and chopped
2	tablespoons capers
2	tablespoons shallots
1	cup white wine, such as French Blanc de Blanc
1	pint heavy cream

salt
freshly ground black pepper

Yield: 3 cups

- Melt 1 tablespoon butter in a sauté pan. Add shrimp, capers, and shallots and sauté until shrimp is pink and shallots are translucent.

- Add white wine and cook over medium heat until wine has almost completely evaporated.

- Stir heavy cream into pan and continue to cook until cream is reduced and slightly thickened. Whisk remaining butter into cream mixture, a little at a time, until thoroughly combined.

- Add salt and pepper to taste.

Note: Serve this over broiled fish, sautéed scallops or on a warm salmon mousse.

Lemon Dill Sauce

This adds zest to any plain broiled, baked, or poached fish.

3	tablespoons butter
3	tablespoons flour
1/2	cup milk or light cream
1	cup fish poaching liquid or water
1/2	teaspoon salt
3	teaspoons fresh dill weed or 1 teaspoon dried
1	tablespoon lemon juice

Yield: 1 1/2 cups

- Melt butter in a heavy saucepan. Whisk in flour until smooth.

- Add milk or cream and poaching liquid or water. Blend well and cook over medium high heat for about 1 minute.

- Add salt, dill, and lemon juice. Cook and stir constantly for another minute or so.

- Remove from heat and pour over the cooked fish of your choice.

Delmarva Crab Cakes

If you take the Cape May ferry from New Jersey across the Delaware Bay, you will land on the "Delmarva Peninsula," a strip of land shared by Delaware, Maryland, and Virginia.

$^1/_2$ cup chopped celery
$^1/_2$ cup chopped onion
1   tablespoon vegetable oil
1   pound fresh crabmeat
2   tablespoons fresh chopped parsley
$^1/_3$ cup mayonnaise
$^1/_2$ teaspoon Old Bay Seasoning
$^1/_2$ teaspoon worcestershire sauce
$^1/_8$ teaspoon Tabasco
3   tablespoons butter, melted
salt
freshly ground black pepper
2 – 3 slices white bread, toasted
1   tablespoon vegetable oil

Garnish:
parsley sprigs
lemon wedges

Yield: 6 – 8 servings

- Sauté celery and onion briefly in vegetable oil. Celery should remain quite crisp.

- Combine crabmeat with remaining ingredients except toast and oil.

- Crumble toast finely and add to crab mixture until there are enough crumbs to hold mixture together.

- Form crabmeat mixture into patties. Heat oil over medium heat in a non-stick pan and fry patties until browned.

- Garnish with parsley and lemon wedges and serve immediately.

Wine: Italian Gavi

Crab Coquille

Native to New Jersey waters, the blue crab is a favorite of seafood fanciers.

1   (14 ounce) can artichoke hearts,
       quartered
1   pound fresh lump crabmeat
5   tablespoons butter
1/2 pound fresh mushrooms, sliced
herbs de Provence
2 1/2 tablespoons flour
1   cup light cream
1/2 teaspoon salt
1   teaspoon worcestershire sauce
1/4 cup dry sherry
pinch cayenne
freshly ground black pepper
1/4 cup grated Parmesan cheese
paprika

Garnish:
parsley sprigs

Yield: 6 servings

- Preheat oven to 375°. Butter 6 large scallop shells or individual gratiné dishes.

- Arrange artichoke hearts in shells. Spread crabmeat on top.

- Melt 1 tablespoon butter in a sauté pan. Add sliced mushrooms and sauté until tender. Layer mushrooms over crab. Sprinkle with herbs de Provence.

- Melt 4 tablespoons butter in saucepan. Add flour and whisk until well combined. Stir in cream, salt, worcestershire, sherry, cayenne, and pepper, whisking well to form a smooth sauce.

- Pour sauce over crab mixture. Sprinkle with Parmesan and top with paprika.

- Arrange shells on a broiling pan and bake at 375° for 15–20 minutes. Garnish with parsley sprigs and serve immediately.

Note: "Sea Legs" can be substituted for crab.

Wine: California Chardonnay

Scallops and Shrimp au Vin

The shellfish harvested off New Jersey's 100 mile coastline include clams, lobsters, oysters, and scallops.

Sauce:

1/4	cup butter
4	ounces mushrooms, sliced
1	small red bell pepper, chopped
2	tablespoons flour
1/2	teaspoon salt
1	cup half and half

Seafood:

1/2	cup dry white wine, such as French Muscadet
1	(14 ounce) can artichoke hearts, drained and quartered
1	pound bay scallops
1	pound shrimp, shelled and deveined
1/4	cup grated Parmesan cheese
2	tablespoons chopped fresh parsley

Yield: 6 servings

The Sauce:

• Melt butter in a sauté pan. Add mushrooms and red pepper and cook, stirring until tender. Remove vegetables with a slotted spoon.

• Whisk flour and salt into butter. Cook, stirring constantly, until smooth and bubbling. Remove from heat. Whisk in half and half. Return to heat and bring sauce to a boil, stirring constantly. Continue to boil and stir for 1 minute.

• Add mushrooms and red pepper. (Sauce may be covered and refrigerated at this point.)

The Seafood:

• Heat sauce until just bubbling. Stir in wine, artichokes, scallops, and shrimp. Heat until shrimp are pink and scallops are cooked.

• Transfer to a serving dish. Sprinkle with Parmesan and parsley.

• Serve with "angel hair" pasta which has been lightly tossed with herbs.

Wine: French Meursault

Tipsy Marinated Shrimp

Large, succulent shrimp, perfect for a seaside barbecue

Marinade:
1/2	cup bourbon
1/2	cup soy sauce
1/2	cup Dijon mustard
1/2	cup light brown sugar
1	teaspoon salt
2	tablespoons worcestershire sauce
1/2	cup finely chopped onion
2	pounds large shrimp, shelled and deveined

Yield: 4 servings

The Marinade:
- Combine all ingredients in a shallow bowl. Whisk until well blended.

The Shrimp:
- Marinate shrimp in bowl for half an hour (no longer).

- Place shrimp on skewers and grill over hot coals until lightly browned. Baste with marinade several times while broiling.

Wine: French Sancerre

Surfside Shrimp

Luscious shrimp in a zesty tomato sauce redolent with basil.

4	tablespoons butter
3	medium onions, chopped
2	green bell peppers, chopped
1	clove garlic, minced
1/8	teaspoon paprika
1/2	teaspoon cayenne pepper
1/2	teaspoon fresh basil
salt	
2	cups stewed tomatoes
1 1/2	pounds medium shrimp, shelled and deveined

Yield: 6 servings

- Melt butter in a large sauté pan. Add the onions, peppers, garlic, paprika, cayenne, and basil. Add salt to taste. Cover and cook on low heat for 10 minutes.

- Add stewed tomatoes to pan and simmer uncovered for 5 minutes.

- Mix in shrimp and simmer for 10 more minutes.

- Serve over a bed of rice with Herb Garden Green Beans (page 110).

Wine: Alsatian Sylvaner

Shrimp with Feta

A one dish meal with a Mediterranean flair

Sauce:

1/4	cup olive oil
1/4	cup chopped green onion
4	large tomatoes, peeled, seeded, and diced
1/3	cup dry white wine, such as French Muscadet
1	clove garlic, minced
1/8	teaspoon oregano
1/2	cup chopped fresh parsley
salt	
freshly ground black pepper	

Shrimp:

1/4	cup olive oil
2 1/2	pounds fresh shrimp, shelled and deveined
2	tablespoons lemon juice
salt	
freshly ground black pepper	
4	tomatoes, peeled and sliced
1/4	pound feta cheese, crumbled

Garnish:
chopped fresh parsley
chopped pitted black olives

Yield: *4 servings*

The Sauce:

- In a heavy skillet, heat oil and sauté the onion over medium heat until soft.

- Add remaining sauce ingredients and simmer uncovered until the sauce thickens, about 20 minutes. Stir occasionally and make sure the sauce does not boil.

The Shrimp:

- Preheat oven to 425°.

- In a large heavy skillet, heat the oil and sauté the shrimp until they are just pink, about 1 minute or less. Toss the shrimp with lemon juice.

- Spread sauce evenly on the bottom of a shallow casserole dish. Layer shrimp on top of sauce. Season with salt and pepper.

- Place sliced tomatoes on top of shrimp. Sprinkle feta cheese on top of tomatoes.

- Bake at 425° for 15 minutes or until cheese is somewhat melted.

- Serve on a bed of "angel hair" pasta and garnish with a sprinkling of chopped parsley and olives.

Wine: *French Muscadet*

Seaside Ceviche

This colorful concoction is wonderful on a hot summer afternoon at the Jersey Shore.

1½   pounds fresh scallops
fresh lime juice to cover scallops
     (about 6–8 limes)
⅓   cup thinly sliced green onions
1   (4 ounce) can chopped green chili
     peppers
¼   cup minced fresh cilantro
¼   cup chopped stuffed green olives
½   cup chopped green bell pepper
2   medium tomatoes, seeded and
     chopped
1   tablespoon virgin olive oil
dash cayenne pepper
¼   teaspoon garlic powder
salt
freshly ground black pepper
2   heaping tablespoons taco sauce
     (optional)
lettuce
lemon wedges

Yield: 8 servings

- Cut scallops into bite size pieces and place in a flat, shallow, glass baking dish. Cover scallops with freshly squeezed lime juice. Marinate in the refrigerator for at least 4 hours (preferably overnight). Drain and discard lime juice.

- In a large bowl, toss scallops with onions, chili peppers, cilantro, olives, green pepper, tomatoes, and olive oil. Season with cayenne and garlic powder. Add salt and pepper to taste and taco sauce, if desired.

- Transfer to a glass serving bowl lined with lettuce and serve with lemon wedges.

Beverage: Dos Equus Beer or Tequilla Snow-cones (page 32).

Hot and Spicy Shrimp

A gorgeous shrimp dish with a Szechaun tang

1½ cups orange juice
1 cup chicken broth
6 tablespoons soy sauce
4 tablespoons grated orange peel
1 tablespoon sugar
3 tablespoons peanut oil
2 medium carrots, julienned
4 jalapeño peppers, seeded and slivered
2 large red bell peppers, julienned
3 large stalks of broccoli
1 (2 inch) piece fresh ginger, peeled and
   minced
8 cloves garlic, minced
4 green onions, chopped diagonally
2½ pounds large shrimp, shelled and
   deveined
1 (8 ounce) package dried Chinese
   noodles
1–2 teaspoons oriental sesame oil
¼ teaspoon cayenne pepper
2 tablespoons cornstarch
¼ cup chicken broth

Yield: *6 servings*

- In a small bowl, combine orange juice, broth, soy sauce, orange peel, and sugar.

- Heat 1 tablespoon peanut oil in a wok and stir fry the carrots, jalapeño peppers, and red peppers until slightly soft, about 4 minutes. Transfer to a bowl.

- Cut the heads off the broccoli and separate into flowerets. Slice the stalks diagonally into 2″ pieces. Steam the broccoli until bright green and still crunchy. Keep warm.

- Heat remaining peanut oil in wok over high heat. Add the ginger, garlic, green onion, and shrimp. Stir fry until the shrimp begin to turn pink, about 1 minute.

- Add the orange juice mixture and cook, stirring occasionally, for about 3 minutes.

- Meanwhile, cook the noodles in a large pot of boiling salted water until just tender, about 3 minutes. Drain, return to pot and toss with sesame oil.

- Return all vegetables, except broccoli, to wok. Cook and stir for 1 minute.

- Dissolve cornstarch in ¼ cup chicken broth. Add to wok. Add cayenne (amount depends on spiciness desired). Stir until the sauce boils, thickens, and coats the vegetables.

- Mound the hot Chinese noodles in the center of a warm platter. Using a slotted spoon, top the noodles with shrimp and vegetable mixture. Ring the platter with the steamed broccoli.

Beverage: Kirin or Asahi Beer.

Scallops with Fresh Ginger

It is hard to imagine that those funny little knobs of ginger can produce such a heavenly flavor and aroma.

1	large carrot
1	small zucchini
1	small leek
2	tablespoons butter
2	tablespoons finely chopped shallots
2	tablespoons finely chopped fresh ginger
1/2	cup dry white wine, such as French Blanc de Blanc
1	cup light cream
salt	
freshly ground black pepper	
1	pound bay scallops

Yield: *4 servings as an entrée*
   6 servings as a first course

- Cut the carrot, zucchini, and leek into julienne strips, about 1/4″ wide and 1–2″ long. You should have about 3/4 cup of carrots, 1 cup of zucchini, and 3/4 cup of leeks.

- Melt butter in a skillet over medium high heat. Add the shallots and cook for 2 minutes, stirring frequently.

- Add the carrots and sauté for about 1 minute more, then add the fresh ginger, cook and stir for another minute.

- Pour the wine into the skillet, bring to a boil and let it cook down almost completely. Stir in the cream, then salt and pepper to taste.

- Add the leeks, cook and stir for 5 minutes, then add the zucchini and scallops and continue to stir until scallops are done, about 5 minutes.

- Serve with rice and Broccoli Stir Fry with Sesame (page 110).

Note: *This can be served in large scallop shells as a fish course in a multi-course dinner.*

Wine: *Alsatian White Gewurztraminer*

Crêpes Coquilles

An impressive luncheon or light supper entrée

Seafood:
2   *tablespoons butter*
3   *tablespoons minced green onions*
1   *pound sea scallops, cut in half*
$^1/_2$ *teaspoon salt*
$^1/_4$ *cup dry white wine, such as French*
      Blanc de Blanc
$^1/_4$ *cup dry vermouth*
2   *tablespoons cornstarch*
2   *tablespoons milk*
$1^1/_2$ *cups heavy cream*
$^3/_4$ *cup grated Swiss cheese*

8   *crêpes*

Garnish:
lavender chive blossoms
chopped chives

Yield: 4 servings

- Melt butter in a large skillet. When it bubbles, add green onions and scallops. Stir for approximately 1 minute.

- Add $^1/_4$ teaspoon salt and white wine. Bring to a boil. Continue to boil until most of liquid is evaporated. Remove from pan.

- Pour vermouth into pan and boil until reduced to 1 tablespoon.

- Combine cornstarch and milk. Reduce heat under skillet and add to vermouth. Stir in cream and remaining salt. Simmer for 2 minutes, stirring constantly. Add $^1/_2$ cup grated Swiss cheese. Stir until melted, then mix in scallops.

- Preheat oven to 425° and butter a large baking pan.

- Spoon some of the scallop filling on a crêpe. Roll up and place, seam side down, in baking dish. Spoon remaining sauce over crêpes. Sprinkle with remaining $^1/_4$ cup of Swiss cheese.

- Bake at 425° for 20 minutes.

- Garnish with blossoms and chopped chives scattered on top and serve with Pilaf Potpourri (page 115).

Wine: California Sauvignon Blanc

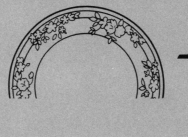

MEATS
and
MAIN DISHES

Meats and Main Dishes

Filet Mignon Superb

A black tie dinner entrée you can enjoy in bluejeans.

3   *cloves garlic, minced*
1   *teaspoon lemon pepper seasoning*
1   *large filet mignon (or 8 filet slices,*
       1½″ thick each)
3   *tablespoons butter*
3   *tablespoons cognac*
¾   *pound mushrooms, sliced*
½   *cup butter*
2   *tablespoons flour*
1   *cup beef bouillon*
1   *tablespoon steak sauce*
1   *tablespoon seasoning and browning*
       sauce
dash Tabasco
¼   *cup dry sherry*
salt
freshly ground black pepper

Yield: 8 servings

- Make a paste of garlic and lemon pepper seasoning. Rub over filet. In skillet, heat 3 tablespoons butter over medium high heat until sizzling. Sear filet quickly all over, until outside is crusty.

- Warm cognac in a small pan. Keeping meat in skillet with heat on, pour cognac over meat and set aflame. When flames die out, remove filet to a large, shallow dish. Arrange mushrooms over meat.

- In the same skillet, melt ½ cup butter. Stir in flour. Slowly add beef bouillon, stirring constantly until thickened. Add steak sauce, seasoning and browning sauce, Tabasco, and sherry. Blend well and simmer for 1 minute. Add salt and pepper to taste. Cool.

- Preheat oven to 375°.

- Pour cooled sauce over filet. Bake at 375° for 30–40 minutes for a large filet or 15 minutes for individual slices.

- Pour reserved sauce into serving bowl to accompany the meat.

Wine: St. Emilion Bordeaux

Filets au Poivre

This is one of our favorite recipes and is sure to be one of yours.

1	red bell pepper
1	yellow bell pepper
1	green bell pepper
4	tablespoons butter
4	slices filet mignon, (1½″ thick each)
salt	
1½	tablespoons black peppercorns, cracked
1	tablespoon olive oil
2	tablespoons brandy
½	cup heavy cream

Yield: 4 servings

- Slice bell peppers into thin strips. Melt 2 tablespoons butter in a skillet over medium heat and sauté peppers until tender, but not soft.

- Sprinkle filets with salt and press cracked peppercorns into both sides of meat. Heat 1 tablespoon of butter and olive oil in another skillet over medium-high heat. Sauté filets for 5 minutes on each side. Remove steaks and keep warm.

- Add brandy to skillet to deglaze, scraping any browned bits from pan and stirring to incorporate liquid.

- Stir in heavy cream. Bring to a boil to reduce slightly. Add remaining tablespoon of butter a little at a time, whisking well to blend. Taste and season with salt and pepper, if necessary.

- Place pepper strips on a serving platter. Arrange filets over them. Pour sauce over steaks and arrange a few pepper strips on top.

Note: Serve with parsley buttered new potatoes and Almost Caesar Salad (page 102).

Wine: Châteauneuf-du-Pape

Chateaubriand with Cognac–Mustard Sauce

Treat yourself to a restaurant meal at home. It is every bit as delicious and much more comfortable.

Meat:
2   beef tenderloins, trimmed (2 to 2½ pounds each)
salt
freshly ground black pepper

Sauce:
1   tablespoon unsalted butter
4   medium shallots, minced
2   cups beef broth
2   tablespoons cognac
2   tablespoons Dijon mustard
3   tablespoons minced fresh parsley
½   cup unsalted butter
salt
freshly ground black pepper

Garnish:
parsley sprigs

Yield: *8 servings*

The Meat:
- Preheat oven to 450°.

- Place tenderloins in a roasting pan and roast at 450° for 15 minutes. Reduce oven temperature to 350° and continue to cook beef for 25 minutes, or until a meat thermometer reaches 130°

The Sauce:
- Melt 1 tablespoon butter in a skillet over medium heat. Add shallots and cook until softened, about 5 minutes. Stir in beef broth. Boil until reduced by half.

- Stir cognac into pan and boil for 1 minute. Reduce heat to low and whisk in mustard. Stir in parsley.

- Divide butter into 8 pieces and whisk in 1 piece at a time. Season with salt and pepper to taste.

- Cut meat into ½″ slices. Arrange slices on individual plates. Spoon sauce over meat and garnish with parsley sprigs.

Wine: French Red Bordeaux (Margaux or Pauillac)

Filets Boursin

A whole filet of beef in puff pastry is usually an involved and extravagant preparation. Our version is easy and every bit as elegant.

2 tablespoons soy sauce
6 (1 to 1¼″ thick) slices beef tenderloin
2 tablespoons extra virgin olive oil
1 (17¼ ounce) package frozen puff pastry, defrosted
¼ cup plus 2 tablespoons fine, dry bread crumbs
4 ounces Boursin cheese (see recipe on following page)

Yield: 6 servings

- Preheat oven to 400°.

- Rub soy sauce on both sides of each filet. Heat oil over medium heat in a heavy skillet. Add filets and sauté in batches for 2 minutes on each side. Remove from skillet and cool to room temperature.

- Cut each of the two pastry sheets into four even squares. Roll out six of the squares to about 10″ each. From the two remaining squares, cut leaf, ribbon, or other decorative shapes for garnish.

- Sprinkle bread crumbs in the center of each pastry square, covering an area the size of a filet. Place filets on top of bread crumbs.

- Place dots of cheese evenly over beef. Gather pastry around filets in folds, moistening pastry on top with water and pinching just below the top edge to form a topknot. Moisten decorative cut pastry shapes and press on to sides of pastry package.

- Place, topknot side up, on a rack in a shallow baking pan. Bake at 400° for 20–25 minutes or until puffed and golden brown.

Wine: California Cabernet Sauvignon

Boursin Cheese

1   large clove garlic or 2 small cloves
      garlic
8   ounces unsalted whipped butter,
      softened
2   (8 ounce) packages cream cheese,
      softened
1/2 teaspoon salt
1/2 teaspoon chopped fresh basil
1/2 teaspoon marjoram
1/2 teaspoon chopped fresh chives
1/4 teaspoon powdered thyme
1/4 teaspoon freshly ground black pepper
1   teaspoon dill weed

Yield: 2 cups

- Add all ingredients to a blender or food
  processor and process until smooth and
  well combined.

- Spoon mixture into a small serving bowl
  and chill overnight.

- Serve at room temperature.

Surf and Turf Kebabs

Whether it's Spring, Summer, or Fall, this is perfect for an epicurean barbecue.

Marinade:
1   (8 ounce) can pineapple chunks
1   (1 1/4 ounce) package dry onion soup
      mix
1/4 cup soy sauce
1/4 cup lemon juice
1/4 cup vegetable oil

1/2 pound shrimp, cleaned and deveined
1/2 pound sirloin, cut into 1" chunks
16 cherry tomatoes
8   mushrooms
2   green bell peppers, cut into chunks

Yield: 4 servings

The Marinade:
- Drain pineapple and reserve 1/4 cup
  syrup. Set chunks aside.

- Combine onion soup, soy sauce, lemon
  juice, oil, and pineapple syrup in a large
  bowl. Add shrimp and meat to bowl.
  Cover and marinate in refrigerator for 2
  hours, preferably longer.

- Alternate meat, shrimp, pineapple
  chunks, and vegetables on kebab
  skewers. Grill over hot coals, basting
  with marinade, until meat reaches
  desired doneness.

Beverage: Samuel Adams Lager Beer.

Barbecued Beef Roast

A moist and savory roast; the cooking aroma is mouth-watering!

3	cloves garlic, pressed
1	teaspoon salt
1/2	teaspoon pepper
1	teaspoon chili powder
1	teaspoon powdered thyme
1/4	teaspoon cayenne pepper
1	cup vegetable oil
1/2	cup red wine vinegar
4	pounds beef rump roast

Yield: 10 servings

- In a bowl slightly larger than the roast, mash garlic with salt, pepper, chili powder, thyme, and cayenne. Gradually beat in oil. Whisk in vinegar.

- Pierce meat all over with a roasting fork and add to marinade. Cover with plastic wrap and let stand in refrigerator for several hours or up to 2 days. Turn periodically.

- Heat barbecue grill. Remove meat from marinade and let excess drip off for 1–2 minutes. Reserve marinade.

- Place meat on a hot grill, 5″–6″ from coals. Brown roast on all sides. Insert a meat thermometer in roast, cover grill with lid and cook until meat thermometer reads 140° for rare.

- While meat is grilling, boil marinade in a small saucepan until reduced to a thick paste. Pour off most of excess oil.

- Brush meat on all sides with the paste and cook for 5 minutes more. Remove from grill and cut across the grain into thin slices.

Beverage: Samuel Adams Lager Beer.

Lobster Stuffed Tenderloin

Surf and Turf for the true gourmet

3–4 pounds whole beef tenderloin
2   (4 ounce) frozen lobster tails
1   tablespoon butter, melted
1½ teaspoons lemon juice
6   slices bacon, partially cooked
½   cup sliced green onion
½   cup butter
½   cup dry white wine, such as
      Sauvignon Blanc
⅛   teaspoon garlic salt
fresh parsley

Yield: 8 servings

- Cut tenderloin horizontally, forming a pocket, but do not slice all the way through. Bottom portion should be about ½″ thick.

- Place frozen lobster tails in boiling salted water to cover. Simmer for 5 minutes. Remove lobster tails from shells. Allow lobster to cool for a few minutes, then cut in half, lengthwise.

- Preheat oven to 425°.

- Mix melted butter and lemon juice. Place lobster pieces, end to end inside beef. Brush with butter mixture. Close meat around lobster and tie roast together with kitchen string.

- Place meat on a rack in a roasting pan. Roast at 425° for 30 minutes. Place bacon on top and roast for 5 minutes longer.

- Melt ½ cup butter in a skillet over medium heat. Sauté onion until tender. Add wine and garlic salt and heat through.

- Remove string from meat, slice roast, and pour wine sauce over it. Garnish with parsley.

Wine: French White Burgundy

Veal and Lobster with Tarragon Cream Sauce

The rich distinctive flavors of this dish are enticing.

2   (1¼ pound) lobsters, cooked
½   cup light cream
1   tablespoon minced fresh tarragon, or
         1 teaspoon dried tarragon
6   tablespoons clarified butter
1¼   pounds veal scallops, pounded thin
½   cup flour
1   cup sliced mushrooms
4   green onions, sliced
¼   cup dry vermouth
salt

Yield: 6 servings

- Remove meat from lobster shells and cut into ¾" pieces. Set aside.

- Simmer cream and tarragon in a small saucepan until reduced to ¼ cup. Set aside.

- Heat clarified butter in a large, heavy skillet over medium-high heat. Dredge veal in flour and add to skillet. Brown lightly on both sides. (Do not crowd, brown in batches, if necessary.) Transfer to heated platter and keep warm.

- Add mushrooms and green onions to skillet. Sauté for 2 minutes. Stir in lobster meat, cream mixture, and vermouth. Reduce heat and simmer for 2 minutes. Season to taste with salt.

- Pour lobster sauce over veal scallops and garnish with tarragon.

Note: Serve with Fresh Lemon Rice (page 115), and Herb Garden Green Beans (page 110).

Wine: California Fumé Blanc

Veal Chops with Pesto

More than barbecued meat, this is an elegant grilled dinner.

Pesto:
⅓	cup extra virgin olive oil
2	cups fresh basil leaves, lightly packed
2	tablespoons pine nuts
2	medium cloves garlic, crushed
½	teaspoon salt
2½	tablespoons butter, softened
2	tablespoons freshly grated Romano cheese
½	cup freshly grated Parmesan cheese

Meat:
4   veal chops, about 2″ thick
salt
freshly ground black pepper

Yield: 4 servings

The Pesto:
- Place the olive oil, basil, pine nuts, garlic, and salt in a food processor or blender and mix into an even paste. Transfer to a bowl and blend in butter and cheeses by hand. Add 2–3 tablespoons warm water to thin, if necessary.

The Meat:
- Season veal chops with salt and pepper. Slice through center of chop on one side and fill with pesto. Close the opening by securing with a toothpick.

- Grill chops over a hot fire for 15 minutes or so, until thoroughly cooked.

Note: Serve with Linguini Medley (page 132) and Tomatoes Brookhollow (page 120).

Wine: California Cabernet Sauvignon

Veal Marengo

A far cry from ordinary beef stew, but every bit as easy to prepare.

3   pounds veal shoulder
2   tablespoons vegetable oil
2   tablespoons virgin olive oil
2   tablespoons flour
salt
freshly ground black pepper
2   tablespoons tomato paste
1   clove garlic, minced
1   cup dry white wine, such as
      Chardonnay
1   (10¹/₂ ounce) can condensed chicken
      broth
1   bouquet garni (2 sprigs parsley, 1 bay
      leaf, 1 celery top, tied together with
      string)
1   teaspoon thyme
2   tablespoons butter
20   small white onions (fresh or frozen)
³/₄   pound mushrooms, quartered
2   tomatoes, peeled and seeded

Garnish:
1   tablespoon fresh chopped parsley
¹/₄   cup thinly sliced pitted black olives

Yield: 10 servings

- Carefully trim fat and sinew from veal. Cut meat into bite size pieces.

- In a large skillet, heat the oils on medium-high heat and brown the veal in several batches. When all is browned, return all the pieces to the pan and sprinkle with flour, salt, and pepper.

- Stir and sauté for a few minutes, then add tomato paste, garlic, wine, chicken broth, bouquet garni, and thyme. Bring to a boil and simmer for 1 hour.

- Melt butter in a skillet on medium heat, add the onions and sauté until they are nicely browned. Add the mushrooms and sauté until tender.

- Add onions and mushrooms to the veal and simmer for another 10 minutes. Cut tomatoes into eighths. Mix into veal and simmer for 20 minutes more. Remove Bouquet Garni.

- Transfer to a serving tureen and garnish with parsley and black olives.

Wine: French Red Burgundy

Veal Chops with Sorrel Sauce

Sorrel is not as readily available here as it is in Europe. Its unique lemon-vinegar taste makes the quest for it well worth your while.

6   tablespoons unsalted butter
2   tablespoons flour
4   veal loin chops
salt
freshly ground black pepper
1   small carrot, chopped
1   large shallot, chopped
1   cup dry white wine, such as Italian
       Gavi
2   tablespoons beef broth
1   cup heavy cream
1   cup finely shredded sorrel leaves

Garnish:
1   slice prosciutto, cut into narrow strips

Yield: 4 servings

- Make beurre manié as follows: knead 2 tablespoons butter with 2 tablespoons flour. Divide into small balls and chill.

- Season veal chops on both sides with salt and pepper. In a heavy skillet, melt 4 tablespoons of butter over medium heat. Sauté veal chops until nicely browned on both sides.

- Reduce heat to low, cover and simmer for 15 minutes or until tender. Remove from pan and keep warm on a large platter.

- Add carrots, shallots, wine, and beef broth to pan, and cook, stirring, until pan drippings are reduced by half. Stir in cream and continue cooking and stirring until liquid is again reduced by half.

- Add sorrel and any juices that may have accumulated on platter of cooked veal chops. Whisk in half of beurre manié and blend until thickened. If sauce is still thin, add more beurre manié and cook, stirring until sauce is thickened.

- Pour sauce over chops and garnish with prosciutto.

Note: When sorrel is unavailable, spinach leaves can be substituted.

Wine: Italian Gavi

Veal Scallops in Mustard Cream

From preparation to presentation in 15 minutes

4   *tablespoons unsalted butter*
2   *tablespoons vegetable oil*
3   *green onions, chopped*
1¹/₂ *pounds veal scallops, pounded thin*
salt
freshly ground black pepper
¹/₃   *cup dry white wine, such as*
      Sauvignon Blanc
¹/₃   *cup Dijon mustard*
¹/₂   *cup heavy cream*

Garnish:
1   *large ripe tomato, peeled, seeded, and*
      chopped

Yield: 4–6 servings

- Preheat oven to 200°.

- Heat butter and oil together in a large skillet. Add onions and sauté over low heat for 5 minutes. Do not brown.

- Raise the heat, add the veal, and season with salt and pepper. Cook veal scallops for 1 minute on each side. (Don't worry if they do not brown.) Remove veal from skillet and keep warm in oven.

- Add wine to skillet and bring to a boil. Cook until mixture is reduced and thickened. Whisk in mustard and heavy cream and boil for 2 minutes.

- Arrange veal on a warm serving platter, spoon on sauce, and garnish with the chopped tomato.

Wine: French White Bordeaux

Veal and Artichoke Casserole

A good main dish for a buffet dinner. It can be assembled in advance and requires only a few minutes of final heating.

6	tablespoons butter
2	(10 ounce) packages frozen artichoke hearts, defrosted
2½	teaspoons salt
½	cup flour
½	teaspoon freshly ground black pepper
18	veal scallops
2	eggs, beaten
6	tablespoons virgin olive oil
½	cup beef broth
½	cup grated Parmesan cheese

Yield: 10 servings

- In a large skillet, melt the butter and sauté the artichokes over medium heat for 5 minutes. Season with 1 teaspoon salt.

- Combine flour, pepper, and remaining salt. Dip the veal scallops in the egg, then in seasoned flour.

- Preheat oven to 375°. Butter a shallow casserole dish.

- Heat the oil in a large skillet. Brown the veal scallops, a few at a time, on both sides.

- Arrange veal in casserole dish, add the beef broth, cover with the artichoke hearts and sprinkle with the Parmesan.

- Bake at 375° for 10 minutes or until lightly browned.

Wine: Italian Dolcetto

Agneau à la Moutarde

For those who like the taste of fresh pepper.

1   *leg of lamb, (4–5 pounds), butterflied*

Marinade:
1   *(8 ounce) jar Dijon mustard*
1/2   *cup olive oil*
1   *clove garlic, minced*
2   *teaspoons dried rosemary*
1   *teaspoon bay leaves, crushed*
1/2   *cup honey*
1/4   *cup ground black pepper*
1   *small onion minced*

Garnish:
fresh rosemary
herb blossoms

Yield: 8 servings

- Carefully trim all fat and sinew from lamb. Open meat and cut small slits in top.

- Mix together all marinade ingredients. Spread generously on all surfaces of lamb. Cover tightly and marinate for at least 24 hours, preferably 2 days.

- Preheat oven to 350° and prepare barbecue grill for cooking.

- Drain lamb, reserving marinade.

- Bake lamb in 350° oven for 20–30 minutes. Remove from oven and finish cooking on grill. (Grilling time will vary according to thickness of the lamb. It should be charred on the outside, but still slightly pink on the inside.)

- Transfer lamb to a platter and cut into thin slices. Warm up marinade and pour some down the center of the slices. Garnish with fresh rosemary and herb blossoms. Serve with additional marinade.

Wine: French Red Bordeaux

Barbecued Butterflied Leg of Lamb

Lamb is available all year long. But, somehow Spring lamb is better, and a Springtime barbecue featuring lamb is best.

Marinade:

1	large onion, quartered
4	cloves garlic
1/2	cup fresh lemon juice
3	bay leaves
2	tablespoons fresh parsley
1	teaspoon dried oregano
1	teaspoon salt
1/2	teaspoon freshly ground black pepper
1/2	cup olive oil
1/2	cup vegetable oil
1	leg of lamb (6–7 pounds), butterflied

Garnish:
edible flowers

Yield: 10 servings

The Marinade:

- Drop onion into food processor and pulse once or twice. With processor running, add garlic cloves and process for 5–10 seconds, until garlic is minced. Add remaining ingredients and process until marinade is thick.

The Meat:

- Trim lamb carefully of all fat and sinew and spread out flat on a broiler pan.

- Brush all surfaces of lamb generously with marinade. Cover tightly with two layers of plastic wrap and one layer of aluminum foil and refrigerate. (Covering securely ensures that the aroma of the marinade will not permeate your refrigerator.) Keep refrigerated for at least 24 hours.

- Two hours before serving, remove lamb from refrigerator. Grill over hot coals until lamb is charred on the outside, but still rosy pink on the inside. (Grilling time will vary according to the thickness of the lamb and heat of the grill, from 10–20 minutes per side.)

- You may also broil the lamb for 10–15 minutes per side in your broiler.

- Remove lamb to a platter, slice thinly against the grain. Garnish with pansies or other edible flowers. Serve with New Potato Salad (page 92).

Beverage: Whatney's English Ale

Vintage Ham with Grapes

Make sure you use a good drinking wine, rather than a cooking wine for this and all other recipes requiring wine. You only get out what you put in.

1	tablespoon butter
2	tablespoons sugar

dash ground ginger

2¼	pound ham slice, cut 1½" thick
¾	cup dry red wine, such as Beaujolais
1	tablespoon cornstarch
¼	cup cold water
1	cup seedless grapes

Yield: *4 servings*

- Melt butter in a large skillet over medium heat. Sprinkle in sugar and ginger. Brown ham quickly on both sides, then remove from skillet.

- Blend wine into butter mixture, cook and stir until boiling.

- Combine cornstarch and water. Add to wine mixture and stir until boiling and thick.

- Return ham to skillet. Cover and cook over low heat for 15 minutes. Add grapes and cook for 1–2 minutes longer.

- Transfer ham to warm serving platter. Spoon wine sauce and grapes on top.

Wine: *French Brouilly*

Pineapple Chutney

Something out of the ordinary to serve with pork or lamb.

1	(20 ounce) can crushed pineapple
1½	cups sugar
3	tablespoons lemon juice
1	tablespoon salt
2	teaspoons fennel
1	teaspoon crushed red pepper
1½	teaspoons ground cumin
¾	teaspoon freshly ground black pepper

Yield: *2 cups*

- Drain half of the liquid from the pineapple. Combine the pineapple and remaining liquid with sugar, lemon juice, and salt in a non-aluminum saucepan. Cook over medium-high heat until it has a jam-like consistency, stirring occasionally. (Mixture will require more frequent stirring toward the end of cooking time.) Remove from heat.

- Crush fennel and red pepper in a mortar or a spice grinder. Mix these and other seasonings with the pineapple mixture.

- Transfer to a serving dish. Store, covered in the refrigerator.

Baked Ham with Port

Say goodbye to the Old Year and ring in the New with a celebration banquet featuring this ham.

1   whole precooked smoked ham with
    bone (15 – 16 pounds)
20 – 30 whole cloves
¹/₃   cup Dijon mustard
1   cup dark brown sugar, packed
2   cups apple juice
2   cups port, such as Sandeman Ruby
    Port
2   cups pitted dates
2   cups pitted dried prunes
2   cups dried figs

Yield: 20 – 25 servings

- Preheat oven to 350°. Trim fat well from ham.

- With a sharp knife, score the ham in a diamond pattern and place in a large, shallow roasting pan. Insert a whole clove at each intersection of the scoring pattern. Pat the mustard evenly over the top and sides of the ham and sprinkle the brown sugar over the top.

- Pour the apple juice into the bottom of the roasting pan and bake at 350° for 1½ hours, basting frequently with apple juice.

- Combine port and fruit in a bowl and let sit to marinate. After the ham has baked for 1½ hours, add port and fruit to pan. Bake for 30 more minutes, basting frequently.

- Remove ham to a warm platter. Stir pan juices. Arrange fruit from the pan on top of the ham. Pour some of the pan juices over the top. Serve the remainder on the side.

Wine: *Grand Cru Beaujolais Moulin à Vent*

Saucy Spareribs

Make sure you serve a good crusty bread with these ribs, the sauce is so delicious you will want to sop it all up!

Sauce:
1   teaspoon salt
1   teaspoon chili powder
1   teaspoon celery seed
¼   cup brown sugar
¼   cup white wine vinegar
¼   cup worcestershire sauce
1   cup catsup
2   cups water
dash Tabasco

Pork:
18   to 20 country style pork spareribs
1   large onion, chopped
salt
freshly ground black pepper
2   lemons, sliced

Yield: 4 servings

- Preheat oven to 500°.

- Combine all sauce ingredients and bring to a boil.

- Separate ribs. Place ribs, meaty side up in a shallow baking pan. Scatter onions, salt, and pepper on top. Brown for 20 minutes in 500° oven.

- Reduce oven temperature to 350° and lay lemon slices on top. Pour sauce over all and cook for 1 - 1½ hours, basting from time to time with the sauce.

- Remove ribs from oven, cool and place in a casserole. Cover and refrigerate for several hours or overnight. Before serving, remove all fat which has risen to the surface. Reheat ribs, covered, in a low oven until hot.

Wine: French Cahors

Black Currant Pork Chops

A low fat, low salt recipe, with a sensational flavor.

1/3 cup water
1/4 cup dried currants
1/4 cup black currant preserves
1 1/2 tablespoons Dijon mustard
1 teaspoon vegetable oil
6 center cut pork chops (1" – 1 1/2" thick)
freshly ground black pepper
1/3 cup apple cider vinegar

Garnish:
parsley sprigs
edible flowers

Yield: 4–6 servings

- In a small saucepan, bring water to a boil. Add currants, cover, and remove from heat. Let sit to plump currants.

- Mix the preserves and mustard together. Set aside.

- Brush a non-stick skillet with vegetable oil. Wipe with a paper towel so that only a thin film remains. Over medium-high heat, brown pork chops lightly on both sides. Season chops with pepper and spoon the mustard mixture over them.

- Cover, reduce heat and cook for 20 minutes or until done. Transfer to a platter and keep warm.

- Remove excess fat from skillet. Deglaze pan with vinegar, scraping the browned bits from the pan and incorporating them into the liquid. Stir over medium heat until the sauce is reduced by one third.

- Pour sauce over the chops. Drain plumped currants and scatter over the top of sauce. Garnish with parsley and edible flowers.

Wine: French Red Burgundy

Pork Tenderloin with Mustard Sauce

The mustard sauce is magnificent and truly enhances the taste of the pork.

Mustard Sauce:
2/3 cup sour cream
2/3 cup mayonnaise
2 tablespoons dry mustard
2 tablespoons chopped green onions
2 teaspoons vinegar

Marinade:
1/2 cup soy sauce
1/2 cup bourbon
4 tablespoons brown sugar

3 pounds pork tenderloin

Yield: *6 servings*

The Mustard Sauce:
• Mix all ingredients together. Refrigerate for several hours or overnight to develop flavors.

The Marinade:
• Combine all ingredients in a bowl large enough to accommodate meat. Pierce tenderloin all over with a large fork and place in marinade for several hours or overnight. Turn occasionally.

• Preheat oven to 375°. Flour a see-through roasting bag.

• Place meat in roasting bag, seal and pierce several times with a fork so that steam can escape. Bake at 375° for one hour.

• Carve meat into thin slices. Serve with mustard sauce, which may be cold or at room temperature.

Wine: *Australian Sheraz*

Bourbon Mustard Marinade

An excellent marinade for beef, pork, lamb, or poultry

1 cup water
1 cup soy sauce
1 tablespoon dry mustard
3 cloves garlic, minced
1/4 cup bourbon whiskey
6 tablespoons brown sugar

Yield: *2 1/2 cups*

• Combine all ingredients and blend well.

• Pour over meat in a shallow dish and marinate for several hours or up to 2 days.

Note: *You can add uncooked meat to marinade and freeze for later use. The meat marinates while it defrosts.*

Cumberland Sauce

This rich, fruity sauce is traditionally served with pork or game.

1	6-ounce can orange juice concentrate
1/4	teaspoon ground ginger
1/8	teaspoon ground cloves
2	teaspoons dry mustard
pinch cayenne pepper	
1/2	cup seedless golden raisins
1/2	cup currant jelly
2	teaspoons cornstarch
2	tablespoons water
1/4	cup Ruby port wine

Yield: 2 cups

- Combine orange juice concentrate with ginger, cloves, mustard, and cayenne in a saucepan. Heat on low until warmed.

- Add raisins and simmer for 5 or more minutes, until raisins are plump and soft.

- Stir in jelly and heat through until it is melted. Dissolve the cornstarch in the water and stir into the sauce. Simmer until it begins to thicken.

- Keep sauce warm until ready to serve. Just before serving, stir in the port. Serve warm with your choice of meats.

Mustard–Caper Sauce

This sauce takes on different characteristics, depending upon the meat with which it is made and served.

pan drippings from cooked meat	
3	tablespoons butter
3	tablespoons dry vermouth or 3 tablespoons dry white wine, such as Sauvignon Blanc
1	tablespoon Dijon mustard
1/4	teaspoon worcestershire sauce
1 1/2	tablespoons capers, drained

Yield: 1 cup

- Remove meat from pan and keep warm. Transfer pan drippings to a saucepan. Add butter and melt over low heat.

- Mix in remaining ingredients, stirring briskly to blend.

- Serve sauce poured over the meat or on the side.

DESSERTS

Desserts

White Chocolate Mousse with Raspberry Sauce

The texture of velvet, the sheen of satin, the taste of heaven

White Chocolate Mousse:
9   ounces imported white chocolate, chopped
3   large egg yolks
1/3   cup confectioners sugar
1 1/4 cups chilled heavy cream

Raspberry Sauce:
1   (10 ounce) package frozen raspberries, defrosted and drained
1/4   cup superfine sugar
2   teaspoons Grand Marnier (orange liqueur)

Garnish:
violet blossoms

Yield: 6 servings

The Mousse:
- Melt white chocolate in the top of a double boiler over barely simmering water. Stir occasionally with a wooden spoon. Remove from heat.

- In a bowl set over a saucepan of simmering water, whisk together the egg yolks and sugar until well combined. Remove bowl from saucepan and beat in 1/4 cup of the cream. Slowly stir in the melted chocolate until well combined.

- Whip the remaining 1 cup of cream until stiff peaks form. Gently fold together whipped cream and white chocolate mixture.

- Spoon into wine goblets and refrigerate until ready to serve.

The Sauce:
- Put the raspberries, sugar, and Grand Marnier in a blender or food processor and purée. Do not strain as the seeds enhance the texture. Chill.

- To serve, top each goblet of white chocolate mousse with raspberry sauce and garnish with a violet blossom.

The Ultimate Chocolate Mousse

The grand finale to satiate the most discerning chocolate lover

Mousse:
8	ounces sweet chocolate
6	large eggs, separated
3	tablespoons water
1/4	cup Bauchant Liqueur (orange liqueur)
2	cups heavy cream
6	tablespoons sugar

Garnish:
whipped cream
semi-sweet chocolate shavings

Yield: 10–12 servings

- Break chocolate into pieces and melt in the top of a double boiler over hot, not boiling water. Pour chocolate into a small container and set aside. Rinse out top of double boiler.

- Put yolks and water in the top of the double boiler over simmering water. Beat constantly with a wire whisk until yolks begin to thicken. Add Bauchant Liqueur and continue to beat until mixture is smooth, thick, and creamy. Remove from heat. *Have a large bowl of ice water nearby in which to set the top of the double boiler if the mixture begins to curdle.*

- Fold melted chocolate into mixture.

- Whip cream until soft peaks form. Add 2 tablespoons sugar and continue whipping until very stiff. Fold chocolate mixture into whipped cream.

- Beat egg whites until stiff peaks form. Add 4 tablespoons sugar and continue beating until very stiff. Fold together chocolate cream and whipped egg whites.

- Spoon into a crystal bowl or balloon wine goblets and chill.

- Serve garnished with additional whipped cream and semi-sweet chocolate shavings.

Charlotte Russe Suprème

An impressive looking ethereal confection

Charlotte Russe:

9	egg yolks
1/2	cup superfine sugar
4	teaspoons unflavored gelatin
1 1/2	cups milk
3	cups heavy cream
1/2	vanilla bean
1/4	cup confectioners sugar
2	packages ladyfingers (about 24)

Raspberry Sauce:

2	(10 ounce) packages frozen raspberries, defrosted
2	tablespoons superfine sugar
1	tablespoon Chambord Liqueur (raspberry liqueur)

Garnish:
fresh raspberries

Yield: 10 servings

The Charlotte:

- With an electric mixer, beat the egg yolks with the superfine sugar until the mixture falls in a ribbon from the beaters.

- Sprinkle the gelatin over 1/2 cup milk. Set aside to soften.

- Combine remaining 1 cup milk with 1 cup of heavy cream in a small saucepan. Add the 1/2 vanilla bean and bring to a boil. Remove from heat. Remove the vanilla bean.

- Thoroughly combine the cream mixture and the yolk mixture. Pour this mixture back into the saucepan and cook over *low heat, stirring constantly* (do not rush or the mixture will curdle), until slightly thickened. *Do not allow to boil.*

- Remove from heat and stir in softened gelatin. Strain into a medium size bowl that is set in a large bowl of ice water. Stir until mixture is almost cold. (Mixture will thicken considerably as it cools.)

- Whip remaining 2 cups heavy cream. When not quite stiff, add confectioners sugar. Continue whipping until very stiff. Fold the whipped cream into the cooled custard.

- Line the sides and bottom of an 8" spring form pan with ladyfingers. Pour the filling into lined pan. Chill overnight, *Do not freeze.*

The Sauce:

- Put raspberries, superfine sugar, and Chambord Liqueur in a blender or food processor and purée. Sieve and strain the sauce to remove seeds. Chill.

- To serve, unmold Charlotte onto a serving plate, garnish with fresh raspberries. Pour sauce on individual slices.

Lime 'n Gin Fizz

Food for leprechauns, fairies, elves, and all the wee people.

4   eggs, separated
$^1/_2$ cup confectioners sugar
1   teaspoon finely grated lime peel
2   teaspoons unflavored gelatin
$^1/_3$ cup freshly squeezed lime juice
2   tablespoons gin
$^2/_3$ cup whipping cream
2   teaspoons confectioners sugar
green food coloring

Garnish:
lime twists

Yield: 6 servings

• Use an electric mixer to beat together egg yolks, confectioners sugar, and lime peel until thick and lemon colored.

• In the top of double boiler, over hot, not boiling water, completely dissolve gelatin in lime juice and gin. Remove from heat and cool to room temperature.

• Beat gelatin mixture into egg mixture.

• Whip cream with 3 drops of green food coloring until soft peaks form. Fold into mixture.

• Beat egg whites until soft peaks form. Beat in 2 teaspoons confectioners sugar until dissolved. Fold into whipped cream mixture. Combine well.

• Spoon into parfait or dessert champagne glasses. Chill for 6 hours or overnight. (If kept any longer, it will begin to toughen and lose its delicate texture.)

• Garnish with a lime twist.

Woodland Maple Mousse

New Jersey maple trees are tapped each year in early Spring. The sap that is harvested will be boiled down to maple syrup, nature's own liquid gold.

4   eggs, separated
1   cup real maple syrup (no substitutes)
1   tablespoon unflavored gelatin
2   tablespoons water
2   drops maple extract or ¼ teaspoon
        maple syrup
2   cups heavy cream
¼   cup finely chopped walnuts

Yield: 8–10 servings

- With an electric mixer, beat egg yolks until thick and light in color.

- Heat ¾ cup of the maple syrup in the top of a double boiler over simmering water.

- Add a fine stream of syrup to yolks while constantly beating. *Be careful not to cook yolks.* Pour mixture back into the top of the double boiler and stir until mixture thickens. Set aside to cool.

- Dissolve gelatin in water and ¼ cup maple syrup. Add gelatin mixture to cooling maple mixture.

- Whip egg whites with 1 drop of maple extract or syrup until quite stiff. Fold in cooled maple mixture.

- Whip cream and 1 drop of maple extract or syrup until stiff peaks form. Fold in maple fluff mixture.

- Spoon into a crystal bowl. Sprinkle with nuts. Chill until set. *Do not freeze.*

- Serve with Victorian Lace Cookies (page 261).

Crème Quadroon

A totally original cream confection

1/2 cup dark brown sugar
1/2 cup heavy cream
1 1/2 teaspoons unflavored gelatin
3 tablespoons water
1 1/2 cups sour cream
2 tablespoons Kirsch (wild cherry
   liqueur)
2 cups sliced strawberries
brown sugar

Garnish:
nasturtium leaves and flowers

Yield: 6 – 8 servings

- Oil a 2 cup ring mold.

- Combine brown sugar and heavy cream in a small saucepan. Heat and stir until sugar dissolves.

- Soften gelatin in water. Add to sugar and cream mixture. Heat and stir until gelatin completely dissolves.

- Remove saucepan from heat and beat in sour cream. Stir in Kirsch. Beat mixture thoroughly until it is well blended and smooth.

- Pour into prepare mold and chill 3 – 4 hours.

- To serve, unmold, fill center cavity with strawberries, and sprinkle with brown sugar. Garnish with nasturtium leaves and flowers.

Brown Sugar Flan

A custard that is soothing to the palate after a hot spicy meal.

3 tablespoons brown sugar
4 eggs
1 (8 ounce) package cream cheese, softened
1 (12 ounce) can evaporated milk
1 (14 ounce) can sweetened condensed milk
1 cup milk
1 teaspoon vanilla extract
2 tablespoons honey

Garnish:
1 (6 ounce) can mandarin oranges

Yield: 6–8 servings

- Preheat oven to 350°. Sprinkle brown sugar evenly over the bottom of a 9″ × 5″ × 3″ loaf pan.

- With an electric mixer, beat together the remaining ingredients until they are well blended and the consistency is smooth. Pour into the loaf pan. Cover and seal the top with heavy aluminum foil.

- On the lowest shelf in the oven, place the loaf pan in a 13″ × 9″ × 2″ pan filled with water. Bake at 350° for 1½ hours. Test to see if the flan is cooked through by inserting a knife half way into the flan. If the knife comes out clean, the flan is cooked.

- Cool well, invert onto a serving dish, cover and refrigerate overnight. Serve at room temperature garnished with mandarin orange slices.

Lemon Tease

Tantalize, tease, and please your taste buds with this scrumptious offering.

1 (3 ounce) package lemon Jello
1 cup boiling water
3 tablespoons fresh lemon juice
1 (8 ounce) package cream cheese, at room temperature
1 cup sugar
½ teaspoon vanilla extract
16 ounces heavy cream
2 packages Ladyfingers (about 24)

Garnish:
lemon peel curls
lemon blossoms

Yield: 10–12 servings

- Dissolve gelatin in boiling water. Stir in lemon juice. Cool to room temperature.

- Cream together cream cheese, sugar, and vanilla. Beat in gelatin mixture.

- Whip cream until stiff peaks form. Fold into cream cheese and gelatin mixture.

- Line the sides and bottom of an 8″ spring form pan with ladyfingers. Pour filling into lined pan. Chill overnight. *Do not freeze.*

- To serve, place on a serving dish and unmold. Garnish with lemon peel curls and lemon blossoms.

Citrus Soufflé with Grand Marnier Sauce

A subtle blend of citrus flavors that is utterly intoxicating.

Citrus Soufflé:
1/4	cup Grand Marnier (orange liqueur)
1	tablespoon fresh lemon juice
3	teaspoons unflavored gelatin
5	eggs, separated
1	cup sugar
3/4	cup fresh orange juice
1/3	cup tart orange marmalade
1/4	teaspoon salt
1/2	teaspoon finely grated lemon peel
1	cup whipping cream

Garnish:
candied violets
lemon peel curls

Grand Marnier Sauce:
3	egg yolks
2/3	cup sugar
2	tablespoons cornstarch
2	cups milk
1/4	cup butter
1	teaspoon vanilla extract
1/3	cup Grand Marnier (orange liqueur)
1/3	cup whipping cream

Yield: 8 servings

The Soufflé:
- Prepare a 1 quart soufflé dish with a lightly oiled 1 1/2" wax paper collar.

- Combine Grand Marnier and lemon juice; sprinkle with gelatin. Let stand until softened.

- In the top of a double boiler, combine egg yolks, 3/4 cup sugar, orange juice, marmalade, and salt. Cook, stirring constantly, over simmering water, until mixture is thickened. Remove from heat and stir in softened gelatin mixture and lemon peel. Let cool to room temperature.

- With an electric mixer, beat egg whites until foamy. Gradually beat in remaining 1/4 cup sugar. Beat until stiff peaks form. Stir some of the egg whites into the cooled custard mixture to lighten texture. Fold in remaining egg whites.

- Beat cream until stiff peaks form. Fold whipped cream into custard mixture. Turn into prepared dish. Refrigerate until firm and spongy.

- Serve chilled, garnished with candied violets and lemon peel curls.

The Sauce:
- With an electric mixer, beat egg yolks with 1/3 cup sugar until thickened. Add cornstarch and beat until lemon colored.

- In a small saucepan heat milk, butter, and remaining 1/3 cup sugar. Stir occasionally until mixture boils. Remove from heat.

Continued on next page

- Stir some hot milk mixture into egg yolk mixture to warm it slightly. Strain all of egg yolk mixture into remaining hot milk mixture. Blend well. Return to heat and bring to a boil. Remove from heat and stir in vanilla.

- Refrigerate until ready to serve.

- Just before serving, add Grand Marnier and cream. Blend well. Heat through, but *do not boil*.

- Turn into a small serving bowl or sauce boat. Spoon over soufflé as it is served.

Glazed Oranges

The most civilized way to eat oranges. Serve in a cut glass bowl or crystal compote.

6   large navel oranges
$1/3$ cup sugar
$1/3$ cup water
2   tablespoons Grand Marnier (orange
      liqueur)

Garnish:
mint leaves
fresh raspberries

Yield: 6 servings

- Peel oranges with a sharp knife, being sure to cut through both the skin and the membrane. Slice into $1/4''$ rounds.

- Place orange slices, sugar, and water in a medium size saucepan and cover. Bring to a boil and simmer for 4 minutes. Remove orange slices and place them in a glass or crystal serving bowl.

- Return liquid to heat and reduce to $1/3$ cup. Pour over oranges. Cool.

- Just before serving, sprinkle with Grand Marnier.

- Garnish with mint leaves and fresh whole raspberries scattered on top. Serve alone or with a slice of Butter Cream Pound Cake (page 245).

Eden Apple Crisp

The rich sour cream topping makes this sinfully delicious.

Crisp:
8	cooking apples
³/₄	cup flour
1	cup brown sugar
1	teaspoon cinnamon
1	teaspoon nutmeg
¹/₂	cup oatmeal
¹/₂	cup margarine

Cream Topping:
¹/₂	cup sour cream
¹/₄	cup heavy cream
¹/₂	teaspoon vanilla extract
1	teaspoon sugar

Yield: 8 servings

The Crisp:
- Preheat oven to 350°. Grease a 10″ diameter quiche dish.
- Peel, core, and slice apples. Turn apples into prepared dish.
- Mix together dry ingredients. With a pastry blender or 2 knives, used scissor fashion, cut in margarine. Sprinkle over apples.
- Bake at 350° for 45 minutes or until golden brown. Serve warm.

The Topping:
- Mix together sour cream, heavy cream, vanilla, and sugar. Spoon over Apple Crisp.

Peach Kuchen

A peach season specialty, fresh from the farm country

¹/₂	cup butter, softened
2	cups flour, sifted
¹/₄	teaspoon baking powder
¹/₂	teaspoon salt
2	tablespoons sugar
6	large fresh peaches, peeled and halved
³/₄	cup brown sugar
1	teaspoon cinnamon
2	egg yolks
1	cup sour cream

Yield: 6–8 servings

- Preheat oven to 400°.
- Mix together butter, flour, baking powder, salt, and sugar in a food processor until mixture resembles coarse corn meal crumbs. Press crumbs into the bottom and on the side of an ungreased 8″ × 8″ baking dish. Place peach halves in the baking dish.
- Combine the brown sugar with the cinnamon. Sprinkle over the peaches. Bake at 400° for 15 minutes. Remove from oven.
- Mix together egg yolks and sour cream. Pour over partially baked peaches. Return to oven and bake 30 minutes longer. Serve warm.

Apple Dumplings with Ginger Crust

Winesap apples originated in New Jersey in 1817. These dumplings highlight their unique flavor.

Ginger Crust:

3	cups flour
1/4	cup non-fat dry milk
1/2	teaspoon salt
1	teaspoon ground ginger
1	teaspoon cinnamon
1/4	teaspoon nutmeg
1	teaspoon ground cloves
1	cup solid all-vegetable shortening, at room temperature
10	tablespoons ice water

Apples:

4	large winesap apples
1	teaspoon cinnamon
1/4	cup brown sugar
2	tablespoons butter
1	cup sugar
2	cups water
3	tablespoons butter

Yield: 4 servings

The Crust:

- Preheat oven to 425°.

- Sift together dry ingredients. With a pastry blender or 2 knives, used scissor fashion, cut in the shortening. Work in the ice water with a fork, 1 tablespoon at at time.

- Shape dough into a ball. Divide dough into 4 equal pieces. On a floured surface, roll each piece into a 9″ square.

The Apples:

- Peel and core apples. Place an apple on each pastry square.

- Mix together cinnamon and sugar. Fill apple core cavity with cinnamon sugar mixture. Dot with butter.

- Moisten pastry edges with water. Bring opposite points of pastry together over apple. Overlap and seal. Place pastry covered apples in a shallow baking dish.

- In a small saucepan combine sugar, water, and butter. Heat to boiling.

- Pour boiling syrup in the bottom of the baking dish. Bake at 425° for 45 minutes or until crust is crisp and brown.

- Serve warm with Cold Sabayon Sauce (page 228).

Watermelon Sparkle

A touch of sparkle on a sizzling summer night

1/2   cup sugar
1/3   cup white rum
3   tablespoons fresh lime juice
6   cups watermelon balls

Garnish:
mint sprigs
pansy blossoms

Yield: 6 servings

- Stir together sugar, rum, and lime juice. Pour over watermelon balls and chill for 2 – 3 hours. Stir occasionally while chilling.

- Serve in balloon wine goblets garnished with a mint sprig and pansy blossom.

Note: *Try using the new seedless variety of watermelon.*

Chocolate Cinnamon Ice Cream

Who ever said ice cream was just for children?

2   (1 ounce) squares unsweetened chocolate
2   (14 ounce) cans Eagle Brand sweetened condensed milk
1   quart light cream
2   tablespoons vanilla extract
2   teaspoons cinnamon
1/8   teaspoon salt
2   cups water

Garnish:
shaved chocolate

Yield: 1 gallon

- Melt chocolate in the top of a double boiler over hot, not boiling, water. Add sweetened condensed milk. Increase heat until water is boiling. Stir melted chocolate and sweetened condensed milk with a wooden spoon until well combined and smooth. Remove from heat and cool.

- Stir in cream. Add vanilla, cinnamon, and salt. Mix well. Stir in water and mix well.

- Pour mixture into electric ice cream maker and follow manufacturer's operating directions.

- Garnish individual portions with shaved chocolate.

Chocolate Gold Brick

If you don't want this to disappear before company arrives, better padlock your freezer and hire an armored guard.

1   box Famous Chocolate Wafers,
      crushed into crumbs
6   tablespoons butter or margarine,
      melted
8   (1 ounce) squares semi-sweet
      chocolate
1/4   cup margarine
3   eggs
1/4   cup sugar
1 1/2 teaspoons almond extract
1   (12 ounce) container Cool Whip
1   cup whipping cream
1   tablespoon sugar
1   tablespoon ground almonds
1   tablespoon shaved chocolate

Yield: 12 servings

- Grease a 9″ × 5″ loaf pan and line with wax paper.

- Mix together cookie crumbs and melted margarine. Set aside.

- Melt chocolate with 1/4 cup margarine in the top of a double boiler over hot, not boiling, water. Stir with a wooden spoon until smooth. Remove from heat and cool slightly.

- In the large bowl of an electric mixer, beat eggs for 10 minutes or until thick. Beat in 1/4 cup sugar.

- Fold the melted chocolate into the egg mixture. Stir in almond extract. Fold in Cool Whip.

- Spoon about 1 cup of the mixture into prepared loaf pan. Add a layer of cookie crumbs. Repeat layers ending with cookie crumbs. Cover with aluminum foil and freeze for at least 6 hours.

- Remove from freezer, peel away foil covering and invert on an oval platter. Peel off wax paper.

- Whip cream with 1 tablespoon of sugar until stiff peaks form. Frost loaf with whipped cream, or using a pastry bag and a star tip, decorate with whipped cream. Sprinkle top with ground almonds and shaved chocolate. Return to freezer until ready to serve.

Very Vanilla Ice Cream

So delicious, it should be called "ice dream."

2	cups milk
4	cups sugar
4	eggs, slightly beaten
1/2	teaspoon salt
1	(14 ounce) can Eagle Brand sweetened condensed milk
2 1/2	quarts half and half
1	tablespoon vanilla extract
1/2	tablespoon lemon extract
1/2	tablespoon white rum

Yield: 1 gallon

- In the top of a double boiler over hot, not boiling water, warm milk. With a wooden spoon stir in sugar until dissolved. With a wire whisk beat in eggs. Cook and stir until slightly thickened.

- Stir in salt, sweetened condensed milk, half and half, vanilla, lemon extract, and rum until well combined and smooth. Remove from heat.

- Pour mixture into an electric ice cream maker and follow manufacturer's operating directions.

Blueberry Sorbet

This can be served as a dessert or as a palate refresher between courses.

1	cup water
1/2	cup sugar
1/4	cup fresh lemon juice
1/4	cup Kirsch (wild cherry liqueur)
1	pint blueberries

Garnish:
candied violets

Yield: 1 quart

- Combine water and sugar in a small saucepan. Bring to a boil and boil for 2 minutes to make a sugar syrup.

- Remove from heat and stir in lemon juice and Kirsch. Cool.

- Purée blueberries in food processor or blender. Add purée to sugar syrup.

- Refrigerate until well chilled.

- Spoon into an electric ice cream maker and follow manufacturer's operating instructions.

- Garnish individual portions with candied violets.

Frozen Amaretto Cream

A simple and elegant cousin to ice cream. Serve in a champagne coupe.

4   egg whites
dash salt
3/4   cup sugar
2   cups whipping cream
1/2   cup Amaretto Liquore (almond
        liqueur)
1/4   cup sliced almonds, toasted

Yield: 1 quart

- With an electric mixer, beat egg whites and salt until foamy. Beat in 1/2 cup sugar, 1 tablespoon at a time, until stiff peaks have formed. Set aside.

- Whip cream until foamy. Beat in the remaining 1/4 cup sugar, 1 tablespoon at a time, until soft peaks form. Gently fold in Amaretto Liquore.

- Gently fold together the egg white and whipped cream mixtures. Fold in almonds. Blend well.

- Spoon into a plastic container large enough to allow for expansion and cover. Freeze at least 4 hours.

Frozen Orange Blossom

A lovely, light, and luscious confection

6   egg yolks
3/4   cup sugar
2 3/4   cups heavy cream
1/3   cup Grand Marnier (orange liqueur)

Garnish:
shaved bitter chocolate
mint leaves
orange blossoms

Yield: 8 servings

- With an electric mixer, beat together egg yolks and sugar until stiff.

- Whip heavy cream until soft peaks form. Fold whipped cream into yolk mixture. Fold in Grand Marnier.

- Spoon into a plastic container large enough to allow for expansion and cover. Freeze for at least 2 hours. Fifteen minutes before serving remove from freezer.

- Whip remaining 3/4 cup heavy cream until soft peaks form.

- To serve, spoon frozen mixture into balloon goblets. Top with a dollop of whipped cream. Sprinkle with chocolate shavings. Garnish with a mint leaf and an orange blossom.

Cold Sabayon Sauce

Drizzle this over a slice of Angel Food Cake and some fresh New Jersey blueberries.

2	cups dry white wine, such as French Blanc de Blanc
1/3	cup water
4	eggs
1/2	cup sugar

Yield: 2½ cups

- Combine wine and water in the top of a double boiler over simmering water. Using a wire whisk, beat in eggs and sugar. Beat constantly until very thick and smooth.
- Remove from heat and cool thoroughly. Just before serving, beat with a wire whisk to recombine until smooth.

Note: *This can also be served hot.*

Hot Fudge Sauce

Serve this sauce with reverence . . . it's divine.

1/2	cup heavy cream
3	tablespoons butter, cut into small pieces
1/3	cup sugar
1/3	cup firmly packed dark brown sugar

dash salt

1/2	cup unsweetened cocoa

Yield: 1 cup

- Combine cream and butter in a 1 quart saucepan. Stir over moderate heat until butter melts. Stir in sugars until completely dissolved.
- Reduce heat. Stir in salt and cocoa until completely dissolved. Serve immediately.

Note: *Can be stored in the refrigerator and reheated over low heat.*

Praline Parfait Sauce

A nostalgic favorite from ice cream parlor days

1	cup firmly packed brown sugar
1/2	cup coarsely chopped pecans
3	tablespoons boiling water
2	teaspoons butter
1	teaspoon vanilla extract

Yield: 1¼ cups

- Combine all ingredients in a small saucepan and bring to a rolling boil.
- Remove from heat. Cool slightly, pour into a glass jar, and seal. Store in refrigerator.
- When ready to serve, remove lid and warm jar in microwave or in a pan of hot water. Serve warm over ice cream.

Jamocha Rum Sauce

Make ice cream sensational with this Carribean inspired sauce.

1/2	cup butter (no substitutes)
1	cup sugar
1/8	teaspoon salt
1	teaspoon instant coffee granules
2 1/2	tablespoons dark rum
1/3	cup cocoa
1	cup heavy cream
1 1/4	teaspoons vanilla extract

Yield: 2 cups

- Melt butter over low heat in a medium size saucepan. Add sugar, salt, coffee granules, rum, and cocoa. Using a wire whisk, blend thoroughly while cooking over low heat. Blend in cream.

- Turn up heat and bring mixture to a slow boil. Simmer for 5 minutes, stirring occasionally. Remove from heat and stir in vanilla.

- Serve warm or at room temperature.

Note: Store in a tightly sealed container in the refrigerator. This sauce thickens as it cools and must be reheated before serving.

Raspberry Fudge Sauce

Treat yourself to chocolate satin with a shimmer of berries.

1/2	cup fresh raspberries
3	(4 ounce) bars semi-sweet chocolate
1/2	cup unsalted butter, cut into small pieces
2	egg yolks, at room temperature
1	cup heavy cream
2	tablespoons Chambord Liqueur (raspberry liqueur)

Yield: 3 cups

- Crush raspberries in a fine sieve. Reserve the pulp and juice that pass through the sieve. Discard seeds.

- Melt chocolate and butter in the top of a double boiler over hot, not boiling water. Stir with a wooden spoon until smooth. Using a wire whisk, blend in the egg yolks.

- Using a wooden spoon, stir in the raspberry pulp, juice, and heavy cream. Sauce should be glossy and thick.

- Remove from heat and stir in Chambord Liqueur.

- Serve hot over ice cream or crêpes.

CAKES
and
PIES

Cakes and Pies

Cakes

Almond Cheesecake, 240

Autumn Pumpkin Roll, 233

Bailey's Irish Cream
Cheesecake, 238

Black and White German Chocolate
Cake, 246

Butter Cream Pound Cake, 245

Carrot Cake Classic, 235

Chocoholics Dream, 243

Chocolate Fleck Cream Cake, 241

Fudge Cake with Chocolate
Silk Frosting, 244

Gingerbread with Hot Lemon
Sauce, 237

Hazelnut Cheesecake, 239

Healthy Apple Cake, 234

Macadamia Fudge Cake, 242

Pecan Dream Cake, 236

Pies

Apricot Amaretto Pie, 251

Buckeye Pie, 254

Chocolate Angel Pie, 257

Chocolate Decadence, 258

Fall Fruit Pie, 249

Fresh Blueberry Pie, 250

Mini Pecan Tarts, 256

Naked Apple Pie, 248

Peaches and Cream Pie, 250

Perfect Pie Crust, 248

Pumpkin Farm Pie, 255

Raspberry Perfection, 252

Strawberry Delight, 253

Autumn Pumpkin Roll

A grand climax to an Autumn harvest celebration

Cake:

3	eggs
1	cup sugar
3/4	cup canned pumpkin
1	teaspoon lemon juice
1/2	teaspoon finely grated lemon peel
3/4	cup flour
1	teaspoon baking powder
2	teaspoons cinnamon
1	teaspoon ground ginger
1/2	teaspoon nutmeg
1/8	teaspoon allspice
1/8	teaspoon ground cloves
1/2	teaspoon salt
1	cup finely chopped walnuts

granulated sugar

Filling:

1	cup confectioners sugar
2	(3 ounce) packages cream cheese, at room temperature
4	tablespoons butter, at room temperature
1	teaspoon vanilla extract
1/4	teaspoon cinnamon
1/2	cup ground walnuts

Garnish:
granulated sugar
brightly colored autumn leaves

Yield: 10–12 servings

The Cake:

- Preheat oven to 350°. Grease and line with wax paper a 15″ × 10″ × 1″ jelly roll pan.

- Beat eggs with an electric mixer set at high speed for 5 minutes. Gradually beat in sugar.

- Stir in pumpkin, lemon juice, and peel.

- Sift together flour, baking powder, spices, and salt. Stir into pumpkin mixture until well combined.

- Spread batter evenly on prepared pan. Sprinkle with walnuts and bake at 350° for 15–20 minutes.

- Dust a clean dish towel with granulated sugar and invert freshly baked cake onto it. Peel off wax paper and gently roll the towel and cake lengthwise. Let cool. *Do not chill.*

The Filling:

- Cream together sugar, cream cheese, and butter. Add vanilla and cinnamon. Beat until spreadable.

- Unroll cooled cake and spread with filling. Sprinkle walnuts over filling.

- Roll up cake and place seam down on a serving platter. Cover with plastic wrap and chill thoroughly.

- To serve, trim ends, dust with confectioners sugar, and place on a platter decorated with autumn leaves.

Healthy Apple Cake

Dense with apples and a hint of caramel, this cake is as nutritious as it is delicious.

2	cups whole wheat flour
1/4	cup wheat germ
2	teaspoons baking soda
1	teaspoon cinnamon
1	teaspoon salt
1/2	teaspoon nutmeg
4–5	cooking apples, peeled, cored, and diced
1	cup sugar
1	cup firmly packed brown sugar
1/2	cup vegetable oil
1	cup chopped walnuts
2	eggs, beaten
1	teaspoon vanilla extract

confectioners sugar

Yield: *12 servings*

- Preheat oven to 350°. Grease a tube pan or a 13″ × 9″ × 2″ baking pan.

- Stir together flour, wheat germ, baking soda, cinnamon, salt, and nutmeg.

- In a large bowl, combine apples, sugar, brown sugar, oil, walnuts, eggs, and vanilla.

- With a wooden spoon, gently blend in flour mixture. Turn into prepared pan.

- Bake at 350° for 50 minutes or until cake pulls away from the sides of the pan. Cool cake completely.

- If a tube pan is used, remove from pan and dust with confectioners sugar. If a rectangular baking pan is used, dust with confectioners sugar, cut into squares and serve.

Carrot Cake Classic

A traditional favorite that can be enjoyed year-round.

Cake:

1¹/₂	cups vegetable oil
2	cups sugar
4	eggs
2	cups flour
2	teaspoons baking soda
2	teaspoons baking powder
1	tablespoon cinnamon
1	teaspoon salt
³/₄	cup finely chopped walnuts
3	cups grated carrots

Frosting:

¹/₂	cup butter (no substitutes), at room temperature
1	(8 ounce) package cream cheese, at room temperature
1	(1 pound) box confectioners sugar
2	teaspoons vanilla extract
¹/₂	cup finely chopped walnuts
¹/₄	cup flaked coconut
³/₄	cup raisins

Yield: 12 servings

The Cake:

- Preheat oven to 350°. Grease and flour a tube pan.

- Stir together oil and sugar until smooth. Beat in eggs, one at a time.

- Sift together flour, baking soda, baking powder, cinnamon, and salt. Add dry ingredients to egg mixture and combine well. Stir in walnuts and carrots.

- Pour batter into prepared pan and bake at 350° for 1 hour. Remove cake from pan and cool completely.

The Frosting:

- Cream together butter and cream cheese. Add sugar and vanilla and beat until smooth. Stir in walnuts, coconut, and raisins.

- Spread thickly over top and down sides of cooled cake.

- Cover and refrigerate for at least 2 hours before serving.

Pecan Dream Cake

A rich confection that sweet dreams are made of . . .

Cake:
¹/₂	cup butter, at room temperature
¹/₂	cup solid all-vegetable shortening, at room temperature
2	cups sugar
5	eggs, separated
2	cups flour
1	teaspoon baking soda
1	cup buttermilk
1	teaspoon vanilla extract
1¹/₄	cups coconut flakes
1	cup chopped pecans

Frosting:
11	ounces cream cheese, softened
6	tablespoons butter, at room temperature
5¹/₂	cups confectioners sugar (1¹/₂ pounds)
2	teaspoons vanilla extract
¹/₃	cup chopped pecans

Yield: 12 servings

The Cake:

- Preheat oven to 350°. Grease and flour three 8″ round cake pans.

- Use an electric mixer to cream together butter and shortening. Add sugar and beat until mixture is smooth. Beat in egg yolks.

- Combine flour and baking soda. Add to cream mixture alternately with buttermilk. Stir in vanilla, coconut, and pecans.

- Beat egg whites until stiff. Fold into batter.

- Pour into prepared pans and bake at 350° for 20–25 minutes. Remove from pans and cool completely before frosting.

The Frosting:

- Cream together cream cheese and butter. Gradually add sugar and beat until smooth. Beat in vanilla.

- Spread frosting on top of each layer. Stack layers and spread frosting on sides. Put a little extra frosting on the top of the cake and sprinkle with pecans.

Gingerbread with Hot Lemon Sauce

"Over the river and through the woods to Grandmother's house we go . . ."

Gingerbread:
1 1/2 cups sifted flour
1/2 cup sugar
1/2 teaspoon baking soda
1/2 teaspoon baking powder
1/2 teaspoon salt
1 teaspoon ground ginger
1 teaspoon cinnamon
1/4 teaspoon allspice
1/4 teaspoon nutmeg
1 tablespoon lemon juice
1/2 cup milk
1/4 cup solid all-vegetable shortening, melted
1/4 cup maple syrup
1 egg, well beaten

Sauce:
3/4 cup sugar
1 tablespoon plus 2 teaspoons cornstarch
pinch salt
1 1/2 cups water
1 teaspoon grated lemon peel
3 tablespoons lemon juice
3 tablespoons butter

Yield: 9 servings

The Gingerbread:
• Preheat oven to 350°. Grease and flour an 8″ square cake pan.

• In a large mixing bowl, sift together the dry ingredients.

• Pour 1 tablespoon lemon juice in a measuring cup and then fill to the 1/2 cup measure with milk. Stir together and let stand for 10 minutes.

• In a small bowl stir together milk mixture with melted shortening, maple syrup, and egg.

• Pour into the dry ingredients and beat until batter is smooth and creamy, approximately 2 minutes. Pour batter into prepared pan.

• Bake at 350° for 30–35 minutes or until cake springs back when lightly touched. Cool slightly and cut into squares.

The Sauce:
• In a small saucepan, stir together sugar, cornstarch, and salt. Turn on heat. Gradually stir in the water. Bring to a boil and cook for 10 minutes, stirring often.

• Add lemon peel, lemon juice, and butter. Cook for another 1–2 minutes or until butter is melted. Serve hot over warm gingerbread.

Bailey's Irish Cream Cheesecake

A little bit of Irish with your cream and "Top of the evening to you!"

Crust:
1   (8½ ounce) package chocolate wafers
1   tablespoon sugar
⅓   cup margarine, melted

Cake:
2   (8 ounce) packages "light" cream
      cheese, at room temperature
1   cup sugar
1⅓ cups "light" sour cream
3   eggs
1   teaspoon vanilla extract
1½ teaspoons unsweetened cocoa powder
pinch salt
¾   cup Bailey's Original Irish Cream
      Liqueur

Yield: 8–10 servings

The Crust:
- Crush wafers in a food processor.

- Combine cookie crumbs, sugar, and margarine. Stir well with a fork.

- Set aside 2 tablespoons of the mixture.

- Press the rest of the mixture evenly over the bottom and a little up the sides of an 8″ spring form pan.

The Cake:
- Preheat oven to 375°.

- Using a food processor, cream together the cream cheese and sugar. Continue processing while you gradually add the sour cream and each egg.

- When well combined and smooth add the vanilla, cocoa powder, and salt. Pour in the liqueur and blend well.

- Turn into prepared pan and bake at 375° for 35 minutes. Turn oven off and let cheesecake stay in the oven for 1 more hour.

- Remove from oven and sprinkle with reserved crumb mixture. Cool on a cake rack. Cover and chill thoroughly. Just before serving, remove spring sides of pan.

Hazelnut Cheesecake

For the cheesecake connoisseur, a cut above classic

¹/2   pound hazelnuts or filberts
softened butter
graham cracker crumbs
4   (8 ounce) packages cream cheese, at
*   room temperature*
1¹/3 cups sugar
4   eggs
1   cup heavy cream
1   teaspoon vanilla extract

Garnish:
small bunches of green and red sugar
*   glazed grapes*

Yield: 8–10 servings

- Blanch hazelnuts by alternately pouring boiling water then cold water over them and pinching or rubbing off the skins. Toast hazelnuts in a 300° oven until just golden. Shake pan or stir nuts frequently to avoid burning. Finely grind toasted hazelnuts.

- Preheat oven to 300°. Spread butter generously over the bottom and sides of an 8″ diameter × 3″ high cake pan.

- Coat bottom and sides of cake pan with graham cracker crumbs.

- Use an electric mixer to cream together 2 packages of cream cheese and sugar. Blend in eggs, heavy cream, and vanilla.

- Add 2 remaining packages of cream cheese and gradually increase speed.

- When mixture is smooth, turn down mixer and add ground nuts. Continue to beat at a low speed while scraping down sides.

- Pour into prepared pan. Set into a larger pan and place on the center rack of the oven.

- Pour boiling water to 1″ level in the larger pan. Bake at 300° for 2 hours. Turn off oven and let cheesecake stay in the oven for 1 more hour.

- Remove from oven and cool completely. Chill.

- To serve, invert on a cake plate, remove pan and garnish with bunches of sugar glazed grapes.

Almond Cheesecake

A melange of chocolate, cream, and almonds . . . simply superb.

Crust:

1	(8½ ounce) package chocolate wafers
1	cup finely chopped blanched almonds
⅓	cup sugar
2	tablespoons butter, softened

Cake:

3	(8 ounce) packages cream cheese
1	cup sugar
4	eggs
⅓	cup heavy cream
¼	cup Amaretto Liquore (almond liqueur)
1	teaspoon vanilla extract
¼	cup flour

Topping:

2	cups sour cream
1	teaspoon vanilla extract
1	tablespoon sugar

blanched slivered almonds

Yield: 12–14 servings

The Crust:
- Grease a 9″ springform pan.

- Crush wafers in a food processor.

- Combine crumbs, almonds, sugar, and butter. Stir well with a fork. Press evenly over the bottom and up the sides of prepared pan.

The Cake:
- Preheat oven to 375°.

- Use an electric mixer to cream together cream cheese and sugar. Add eggs, one at a time, beating well after each addition.

- Add cream, Amaretto, vanilla, and flour. Beat until light in consistency.

- Pour into crust and bake at 375° for 35 minutes. Remove from oven and let stand on a cake rack for 5 minutes. (Cake will not be set at this point.)

The Topping:
- Combine sour cream, vanilla, and sugar.

- Gently spread over cake and return to oven for 5 minutes.

- Remove from oven and cool completely on a cake rack. Cover and chill overnight.

- Just before serving, remove spring sides of pan. Mound almonds on the top of the cake.

Chocolate Fleck Cream Cake

Chocolate and cream transformed to heaven on earth.

Crust:
22   "Oreo" type cookies
1/3   cup melted butter

Cake:
1   cup whipping cream, chilled
2   (8 ounce) packages cream cheese, at
         room temperature
2/3   cup sugar
1   tablespoon vanilla extract
2   ounces semi-sweet chocolate, grated

Garnish:
semi-sweet chocolate cut-outs*
dark and milk chocolate curls**

Yield: 16 servings

The Crust:
- Crush cookies in a food processor.

- Combine cookie crumbs and butter. Stir well with a fork.

- Press evenly over bottom and a little up the sides of a 9″ springform pan.

The Cake:
- Whip cream until soft peaks form.

- Beat the cream cheese until light and fluffy. Gradually add the sugar. Blend in the vanilla.

- Gently, but thoroughly, fold in the whipped cream. Fold in the grated chocolate.

- *Do not over mix* or the mixture will be all chocolate instead of white with chocolate flecks scattered throughout.

- Spoon into crust. Level the surface. Cover and chill at least 2 hours. Remove spring sides of pan.

- Decorate and garnish with chocolate cut-outs or curls.

Note: *To make chocolate cut-outs, melt 3–4 ounces chocolate in the top of a double boiler over hot, not boiling water. Pour melted chocolate onto a wax paper lined cookie sheet. Refrigerate for 10 minutes. Remove from refrigerator and return to room temperature. Using small cookie cutters, cut out desired shapes. Lift carefully from the cookie sheet with a spatula and place on cake.*

Note: **To make chocolate curls, wrap a square of chocolate in wax paper and hold it in your hands to warm it slightly. Unwrap and shave with long thin strokes using a vegetable peeler. Lift curls with a toothpick and place on cake.*

Macadamia Fudge Cake

There are nut cakes and there are fudge cakes . . . this superb combination is one in a million.

Cake:
1   cup flour
3/4 cup sugar
3/4 cup sour cream
1/2 cup butter, softened
1/4 cup unsweetened cocoa powder
1 1/2 teaspoons freeze dried coffee granules
1/2 teaspoon baking soda
1/2 teaspoon baking powder
1/2 teaspoon vanilla extract
1/4 teaspoon salt
1   egg

Frosting:
1   cup heavy cream
1/2 cup sugar
2   tablespoons butter
1   tablespoon corn syrup
4   (1 ounce) squares semi-sweet
       chocolate
1   teaspoon vanilla extract
1   (7 ounce) jar macadamia nuts

Yield: 12 servings

The Cake:
- Preheat oven to 350°. Grease a 9″ diameter cake pan. Line the bottom with wax paper and grease the wax paper.

- Combine all ingredients in a large bowl and beat with an electric mixer at low speed.

- Pour into prepared cake pan and bake at 350° for 30–35 minutes or until a toothpick inserted in the center comes out clean. Cool on a cake rack for 10 minutes.

- Remove cake from pan, peel off wax paper and place on a large serving plate to cool completely (approximately 3 hours).

The Frosting:
- In a 2 quart saucepan over medium high heat, combine cream, sugar, butter, corn syrup, and chocolate, stirring constantly.

- When mixture boils, reduce heat to medium and cook, stirring, 5 minutes longer. Remove from heat and stir in vanilla. Cool for 10 minutes.

- Stir in macadamia nuts.

- Pour frosting quickly over the top of the completely cooled cake, allowing frosting to run down sides. Refrigerate for 1 hour or until frosting is firm.

Chocoholics Dream

True chocoholics will experience Nirvana when tasting this fabulous cake.

Cake:
1/2	cup strong brewed coffee
8	ounces semi-sweet chocolate, cut into pieces
1	cup granulated sugar
1	cup unsalted butter
4	eggs

Topping:
1	cup whipping cream
1/4	cup confectioners sugar
1/4	teaspoon vanilla extract
2	tablespoons shaved semi-sweet chocolate

Garnish:
fresh raspberries
fresh strawberries
candied violets

Yield: 8-10 servings

The Cake:
- Preheat oven to 350°. Grease a 9″ × 5″ × 3″ loaf pan. Line with parchment and grease parchment well.

- In a small saucepan, combine coffee, chocolate, sugar, and butter. Cook over medium heat until butter and chocolate are melted. Stir occasionally.

- Remove from heat and stir in eggs. Blend well and pour into prepared pan.

- Bake at 350° for 55-65 minutes or until cake cracks around sides and is crisp on top. Remove from oven and cool in pan.

- Cover with foil and refrigerate overnight or for up to one week.

- At serving time, invert chilled cake on an oval serving platter, remove pan and carefully peel off the parchment.

The Topping:
- Whip cream with sugar and vanilla until soft peaks hold their form.

- Frost the top of the cake with whipped cream. Dust with grated chocolate.

- Mound berries at either end of the cake on the plate. Place a few berries on top of the cake. Stud berry mounds with candied violets and place a few on the top of the cake.

Fudge Cake with Chocolate Silk Frosting

A rich brownie-like cake with a silky smooth frosting.

Cake:
1   (12 ounce) package semi-sweet
        chocolate chips
1   tablespoon freeze dried coffee granules
5   tablespoons water
1½ cups butter, softened
2   cups sugar
6   eggs, separated
1   cup flour
8   pecan halves

Frosting:
2   (1 ounce) squares semi-sweet
        chocolate
1   teaspoon freeze dried coffee granules
¼   cup water
1   egg yolk
1   cup margarine, at room temperature
4   tablespoons unsalted butter, at room
        temperature
1   (3 ounce) package cream cheese, at
        room temperature
3   cups confectioners sugar
2   tablespoons plus 2 teaspoons
        unsweetened cocoa powder

Yield: 10 servings

The Cake:
- Preheat oven to 350°. Butter a 10″ springform pan. Dust with flour.

- Melt chocolate chips with coffee granules and water in the top of a double boiler over hot, not boiling water. Stir with a wooden spoon until smooth.

- Remove from heat and pour chocolate mixture into a medium size bowl to cool.

- Use an electric mixer to cream together butter and sugar in a large bowl. Add egg yolks, one at a time, mixing well after each addition. Gradually beat in flour.

- In a small bowl, beat egg whites until soft peaks hold their form. Fold into cooled chocolate mixture. Carefully fold into batter.

- Spoon into prepared pan. Arrange pecans in 3 rings on the top and bake at 350° for 50–55 minutes.

- Remove from oven and cool in the pan. When completely cool remove spring sides of pan.

- Carefully split cake into two layers.

The Frosting:
- Melt chocolate with coffee granules and water in the top of a double boiler over hot, not boiling water. Stir with a wooden spoon until smooth. Pour and scrape into a cup and set in the freezer to cool for 2–3 minutes.

- Remove from freezer and cool completely at room temperature.

Continued on next page

- Use an electric mixer to beat egg yolk until thick.

- Add margarine, butter, and cream cheese. Cream until light and fluffy.

- Add cooled chocolate to mixture and beat until thoroughly blended. Beat in confectioners sugar and cocoa powder.

- Spread frosting on bottom layer of cake. Cover with top layer. Frost sides. *Do not frost top.* (If frosting is left over, it can be kept for a few days in the refrigerator.) Chill for at least 2 hours.

Butter Cream Pound Cake

Richer than regular pound cakes, this one melts in your mouth.

Cake:
1   (8 ounce) package cream cheese
1   cup butter
2   cups sugar
2   tablespoons vanilla extract
6   eggs
2   cups Presto cake flour
confectioners sugar
cocoa powder

Yield: 8–10 servings

- Have all ingredients at room temperature.

- Preheat oven to 350°.

- Use an electric mixer to cream together cream cheese and butter. Beat in sugar and vanilla. Add eggs, one at a time, beating after each addition. Continue beating until mixture is almost doubled in volume.

- Using lowest speed, fold in flour. *Do not over beat.*

- Pour batter into an ungreased tube pan and bake at 350° for 45 minutes or until a toothpick inserted comes out clean. Remove from oven and immediately invert and cool. Cooled cake can be wrapped and frozen.

- Serve at room temperature, sprinkled with confectioners sugar or cocoa powder.

Note: Serve with fresh berries or Glazed Oranges (page 221).

Black and White German Chocolate Cake

An "Old World" recipe for you and your family to enjoy and cherish.

Cake:
1	cup margarine, at room temperature
2	cups sugar
4	eggs, separated
1	teaspoon vanilla
1	(4 ounce) package German chocolate
1/2	cup boiling water
2 1/2	cups cake flour
1/2	teaspoon salt
1	cup buttermilk
1	teaspoon baking soda

Frosting:
3	cups sugar
1 1/2	tablespoons flour
1 1/2	cups evaporated milk
1 1/2	tablespoons butter
1 1/2	cups chopped pecans
1 1/2	cups flaked coconut
3/4	teaspoon salt
1 1/2	teaspoons vanilla extract

Garnish:
dark chocolate curls

Yield: 12 servings

The Cake:

- Preheat oven to 350°. Butter three 8″ diameter cake pans. Line the bottoms with wax paper and butter the wax paper. Dust pans with flour.

- Cream together margarine and sugar. Beat in egg yolks, one at a time. Stir in vanilla.

- Melt chocolate in boiling water and set aside to cool completely.

- Stir together flour and salt. Alternately add flour and 1/2 cup buttermilk to cream mixture in small amounts, beating after each addition.

- Stir baking soda in remaining 1/2 cup buttermilk and set aside for 3–5 minutes. (A chemical reaction produces almost a full cup of buttermilk again.)

- Continue alternating flour and buttermilk until all is combined.

- Beat in the melted chocolate mixture.

- Beat egg whites until stiff peaks hold. Fold into batter.

- Spoon equal portions of batter into the three prepared pans and bake at 350° for 35–40 minutes. Cool layers completely, then remove from pans.

Continued on next page

The Frosting:

- In a medium size saucepan, mix together sugar, flour, evaporated milk, and butter. Bring mixture to a boil over medium heat while stirring constantly with a whisk.

- Boil, stirring constantly for 8–9 minutes. (If frosting turns quite thick and reduces in volume, remove from heat immediately and proceed with rest of the recipe.)

- Remove from heat, stir in pecans, coconut, salt, and vanilla. Cool completely.

- Spread evenly on the top of each layer. Stack layers and spread on sides of cake. Refrigerate to set.

- To garnish, arrange chocolate curls on top of cake and serve.

Note: Pay particular attention while boiling frosting as it will become very hard if overcooked.

Perfect Pie Crust

The basis for a perfect pie: a light, delectable flaky crust

1/2 cup water
1 tablespoon distilled vinegar
1 egg
4 cups flour
1 tablespoon granulated sugar
2 teaspoons salt
1 3/4 cups solid all-vegetable shortening

Yield: 5 single crusts

- In a small bowl, combine the water, vinegar, and egg. Beat well and set aside.
- Use a food processor to combine flour, sugar, and salt. Process for 30 seconds.
- Add the shortening and process until a crumbly consistency is reached. Pour in the liquid mixture and process until a dough ball is formed.
- Wrap in plastic wrap and chill for 30 minutes before using.

Note: This dough can be kept in an airtight refrigerated container for 1 week.

Naked Apple Pie

X-rated. Extra good, extra fine, and extra compliments for the chef!

1/2 cup flour
1 1/2 teaspoons baking powder
1 egg
1/2 cup brown sugar
1/2 cup sugar
1 teaspoon vanilla extract
pinch salt
2 large tart apples
1/2 cup chopped walnuts or pecans

Yield: 1 pie

- Preheat oven to 350°. Grease a 9″ pie pan.
- Sift together flour and baking powder.
- Use an electric mixer to beat the egg. Add brown sugar, sugar, vanilla, and salt. Beat at medium speed for 1 minute. With the beater running, add flour mixture.
- Peel, core, and thinly slice apples. Fold apples and nuts into batter. Spoon into prepared pie pan.
- Bake at 350° for 30 minutes.
- Cool completely and serve with whipped cream or ice cream.

Note: Do not cover pie or it will become soggy. Serve it the same day it is baked.

Fall Fruit Pie

An intriguing flavor finale replete with Autumn's bounty.

Pastry lined 9″ pie pan
1/4   cup flour
1/3   cup sugar
1   tablespoon butter, at room
         temperature
2   tart apples
1   (28 ounce) jar mincemeat fruit
         conserve
1 1/4 cups fresh or frozen cranberries
2   tablespoons sugar

Yield: 1 pie

- Preheat oven to 425°. Sprinkle 2 table-spoons flour over the pastry lined pie pan.

- Combine remaining flour with sugar and butter in a small bowl, mashing with a fork until crumbly in consistency. Set aside.

- Peel, core, and slice apples into 1/2″ wedges.

- In a large saucepan, combine mincemeat, cranberries, and sugar. Stir together and bring to a boil. Boil for one minute and remove from heat. Spoon into prepared pie pastry.

- Lay apple wedges on top in concentric circles. Sprinkle with crumb mixture. Cover rim of pastry with aluminum foil to prevent burning.

- Bake at 425° for 30 minutes. Remove foil and bake an additional 5 – 10 minutes or until pie crust rim is golden. Cool before serving.

Fresh Blueberry Pie

Blueberry pie is one of the simple pleasures.

2 tablespoons cornstarch
1/8 teaspoon salt
3/4 cup sugar
1/4 cup water
4 1/2 cups (1 quart) blueberries, rinsed and
    picked over
1 tablespoon butter
1 tablespoon lemon juice
9" prebaked pie shell, cooled

Garnish:
freshly whipped cream
1 teaspoon finely grated lemon peel
fresh blueberries

Yield: 1 pie

- In a medium size saucepan, mix together cornstarch, salt, and sugar. Stir in water. Add 2 1/4 cups blueberries and cook over medium heat, stirring constantly, until mixture becomes thick. Stir in butter and lemon juice. Remove from heat and cool.

- Put the remaining blueberries in the bottom of the prebaked pie shell. Over these, spoon thickened blueberry mixture. Chill.

- Just before serving, garnish with dollops of whipped cream dusted with lemon peel and studded with blueberries.

Peaches and Cream Pie

Luscious Jersey peaches make this a delectable late summer dessert.

pastry lined 9" pie pan
5 or 6 ripe peaches
1 cup light cream or half and half
1 teaspoon almond extract
1/2 cup sugar
2 eggs
2 tablespoons butter

Yield: 1 pie

- Preheat oven to 350°.

- Arrange peeled, halved, and pitted peaches, cut side up, in a pastry lined pie shell.

- Blend together cream, almond extract, 1/4 cup sugar, and eggs. Pour over and around peaches. Dot peaches with small pieces of butter.

- Sprinkle with remaining 1/4 cup sugar.

- Bake at 350° for 1 hour or until crust is golden and filling is set.

- Serve warm or at room temperature with ice cream or whipped cream.

Apricot Amaretto Pie

As special and sweet as the first flowers of Spring.

Pie Filling:

2	(17 ounce) cans apricot halves
1	tablespoon unflavored gelatin
6	egg yolks
1	cup sugar
3	tablespoons Amaretto Liquore (almond liqueur)
2	cups heavy cream, chilled
1	teaspoon almond extract

graham cracker crust

Glaze:

1/3	cup apricot preserves
1/2	teaspoon lemon juice

Yield: 1 pie

The Pie Filling:

- Drain apricots, reserving only 1/4 cup of liquid. Sprinkle gelatin over liquid in a small heat-proof bowl. Set aside to soften.

- Cut up one half the quantity of apricots and reserve the rest.

- Use an electric mixer to beat egg yolks at high speed until light and lemon colored. Continue to beat and gradually add the sugar. Beat 3–5 minutes longer, until it ribbons.

- Place the dish of gelatin mixture in a few inches of simmering water to dissolve completely.

- Pour a thin stream of the dissolved gelatin into the yolk mixture, beating constantly. Stir in Amaretto.

- Whip the cream until soft peaks form. Add almond extract and fold into mixture.

- Fold in the cut apricots.

- Spoon into pie shell and chill for 1 hour or until set.

The Glaze:

- In a small saucepan, slowly bring apricot preserves to a boil. Remove from heat and stir in lemon juice.

- Place reserved apricot halves in concentric circles over filling.

- Brush glaze over the top of the pie and chill.

Raspberry Perfection

Remember picking raspberries and eating one for every one you collected to bring home? After a taste of this you will.

4   cups fresh raspberries
*Pastry for a double crust
5   tablespoons flour
1   cup sugar
1   tablespoon lemon juice

Yield: 1 pie

- Slightly crush raspberries and let them sit for several hours at room temperature.

- Preheat oven to 400°. Line a 9″ pie pan with one round of dough, reserving the second round.

- Gently combine flour, sugar, and lemon juice with the crushed berries and resulting juice. Spoon into pastry lined pan.

- Cover berries with the remaining pastry round. Trim edges evenly and flute decoratively. Cut four steam vents in the pastry. Cover rim of pastry with aluminum foil to prevent burning.

- Bake at 400° for 10 minutes, reduce heat to 350° and bake an additional 30 – 40 minutes or until the top is golden brown.

- Serve lukewarm with Very Vanilla Ice Cream (page 226).

- *Use our Perfect Pie Crust recipe (page 248).

Note: Place a cookie sheet on a rack under pie pan during baking to catch any berry juice that might spill over.

Strawberry Delight

Luscious ripe strawberries atop a creamy lemon filling . . . what a perfect combination!

Crust:
1/2	cup butter, at room temperature
1	cup flour
2	tablespoons confectioners sugar

Filling:
1	(8 ounce) package cream cheese, at room temperature
2	tablespoons lemon yogurt
1	quart strawberries
1	cup sugar
3	tablespoons cornstarch

Yield: 1 pie

The Crust:

- In a food processor, combine crust ingredients and process until crumbly. Form into a ball, wrap in plastic wrap, and refrigerate until firm.

- Unwrap dough and place in a 9″ pie pan. Press and mold to form a shell.

- Bake at 375° for 10 minutes or until light golden brown. (Check often as crust burns easily.) Cool completely.

The Filling:

- Mix together cream cheese and yogurt until smooth and spreadable. Spoon into pie crust and spread evenly over the bottom.

- Wash, hull, and drain berries. Place half of the berries upright in the cream cheese. Purée the remaining strawberries in a food processor. Strain purée to remove pulp and seeds from juice.

- In a small saucepan, bring strawberry juice to the boiling point.

- Stir together sugar and cornstarch.

- Using a whisk, gradually stir sugar mixture into the juice. Cook over low heat for 10 minutes, stirring occasionally.

- Cool and pour over upright berries. Chill until set.

Buckeye Pie

A scrumptious combination to bring out the kid in you.

6	ounces semi-sweet chocolate
4	eggs
1	cup butter, softened
2	cups confectioners sugar
3/4	cup smooth peanut butter
1	cup heavy cream, chilled
10"	prebaked pie shell

Garnish:
1	tablespoon grated semi-sweet chocolate
1	teaspoon finely chopped dry roasted unsalted peanuts

Yield: 1 pie

- Melt chocolate in the top of a double boiler over hot, not boiling water. Remove from heat and cool.

- With an electric mixer, beat eggs with 3/4 cup butter, melted chocolate, and sugar for 5 minutes until thick and creamy.

- In a separate bowl, beat peanut butter with remaining 1/4 cup butter and up to 1/3 cup cream until peanut butter is spreadable and thin enough to swirl with chocolate mixture.

- Spoon chocolate mixture into pie shell. Swirl peanut butter into chocolate mixture. Refrigerate until set.

- Whip remaining chilled cream until soft peaks form. Spread over filling.

- Garnish with a sprinkling of grated chocolate and chopped peanuts.

Pumpkin Farm Pie

The farms of New Jersey are particularly colorful in the Fall. Brightly colored trees outline the fields, and mountains of pumpkins are ready for market.

Crust:
1/2	cup finely ground walnuts
3	tablespoons sugar
2	tablespoons butter

Filling:
1 1/2	cups fresh puréed pumpkin
3/4	cup firmly packed brown sugar
1/2	cup milk
2	eggs, separated
1	(1/4 ounce) package unflavored gelatin
1 1/2	teaspoons cinnamon
1/2	teaspoon ground ginger
1/4	teaspoon ground cloves
1/3	cup sugar
3/4	cup sour cream
1 1/4	teaspoons grated orange peel

Garnish:
orange flavored whipped cream
grated orange peel
nutmeg

Yield: 1 pie

The Crust:
- Preheat oven to 400°. Lightly butter a 9″ pie pan.

- Combine nuts, sugar, and butter. Press firmly into bottom and sides of prepared pie pan.

- Bake at 400° for 6–8 minutes. Cool completely before filling.

The Filling:
- Combine pumpkin, sugar, milk, egg yolks, gelatin, cinnamon, ginger, and cloves in a medium saucepan. Cook over medium heat, stirring constantly, until just about to boil. *Do not boil.* Remove from heat.

- Let cool to room temperature and then chill.

- Using an electric mixer, beat egg whites until soft peaks form. Gradually add sugar and continue beating until stiff and glossy.

- Fold into pumpkin mixture, then fold in sour cream and orange peel. Spoon into crust, forming a mound. Chill several hours or overnight.

- Garnish with whipped cream sprinkled with orange peel and nutmeg.

Mini Pecan Tarts

Dainty delicacies that are rich, attractive, and flavorful.

Crust:
1   (3 ounce) package cream cheese, at
       room temperature
¹/₂ cup butter, at room temperature
1   cup flour

Filling:
³/₄ cup brown sugar
1   egg
1   tablespoon butter
1   cup chopped pecans
confectioners sugar

Yield: 2 dozen

The Crust:
- Combine cream cheese, butter, and flour in a food processor. Process until a dough ball forms. Wrap dough in plastic wrap and chill thoroughly.

- Preheat oven to 375°. Divide dough ball into 24 equal pieces. Roll each piece into a ball. Press balls into miniature cupcake pans to form tart shells.

The Filling:
- Using a food processor, combine brown sugar, egg, and butter. Add the chopped nuts and process until just combined.

- Place 1 teaspoon of nut mixture in each tart shell.

- Bake at 375° for 30 – 35 minutes. Remove from oven and cool completely.

- Just before serving, dust with confectioners sugar.

Chocolate Angel Pie

As light as a cloud and just as heavenly

Meringue Shell:
3   egg whites, at room temperature
1/8   teaspoon cream of tartar
pinch salt
3/4   cup sugar
1   cup chopped pecans
1   teaspoon vanilla extract

Filling:
1   (4 ounce) bar German chocolate
1   teaspoon vanilla extract
2   tablespoons Crème de Cacao Liqueur
    (chocolate liqueur)
3   cups heavy cream, chilled
sugar

Garnish:
chocolate shavings or curls

Yield: 1 pie

The Shell:
- Preheat oven to 300°. Butter a 9″ pie pan.

- Use an electric mixer to beat egg whites until foamy. Add cream of tartar and salt and beat until soft peaks form. Gradually beat in sugar and continue beating until stiff peaks form. Fold in pecans and vanilla.

- Turn into prepared pie pan and build up sides 1/2″ higher than the rim of the pan. Bake at 300° for 50–55 minutes. Cool completely.

The Filling:
- Melt chocolate in the top of a double boiler over hot, not boiling water. Cool slightly and stir in vanilla and Crème de Cacao. Cool completely.

- Whip cream until soft peaks form. Sweeten with a bit of sugar. Reserve 1/2 cup whipped cream.

- Fold together chocolate mixture and cream. Spoon into meringue shell.

- Decorate with dollops of reserved whipped cream and garnish with chocolate shavings or curls. Refrigerate.

Note: Do not make on a rainy or humid day.

Chocolate Decadence

A decadently delicious chocolate mousse torte.

1   tablespoon butter
fine dry bread crumbs (unseasoned)
1   tablespoon instant coffee
¹/₄   cup boiling water
8   ounces semi-sweet chocolate
8   eggs, separated, at room temperature
²/₃   cup superfine sugar
1   teaspoon vanilla extract
¹/₈   teaspoon salt

Garnish:
whipped cream
chocolate shavings

Yield: 1 pie

- Preheat oven to 350°. Grease a 9″ glass pie dish with 1 tablespoon butter. Dust with bread crumbs.

- In the top of a double boiler over hot, not boiling water, combine coffee, water, and chocolate. Stir with a wooden spoon until chocolate is melted and mixture is smooth. Remove from heat and cool mixture completely.

- Use an electric mixer to beat egg yolks at high speed for 5 minutes, until pale and thickened. Gradually add sugar while beating on low speed. Increase speed to high and beat for 5 more minutes, until very thick. Add vanilla and chocolate, beating on low until smooth.

- In a separate bowl with clean beaters, beat egg whites and salt until soft peaks hold. Fold a generous amount of the egg whites into chocolate, then quickly fold chocolate mixture into remaining egg whites until no white streaks remain.

- Remove 4 cups of the chocolate mixture and refrigerate.

- Pour the remaining mixture into prepared pie dish. Smooth and level top.

- Bake at 350° for 25 minutes. Turn off oven, but leave torte in oven for 5 additional minutes. Remove from oven and cool completely. (The center of the torte will settle.)

- Pour the reserved chocolate mixture over torte. Refrigerate for 2–3 hours.

- Garnish with whipped cream and chocolate shavings.

COOKIES
and
CANDY

Cookies and Candy

Victorian Lace Cookies

Anyone can successfully make this cookie, just follow the directions carefully.

2¼ cups old fashioned oats (not quick or
     instant)
2¼ cups firmly packed light brown sugar
3   level tablespoons flour
½   teaspoon salt
1   cup butter (no substitutes)
1   egg, slightly beaten
1   teaspoon vanilla extract

Yield: 6 dozen

- Preheat oven to 350°. Heavily grease 2 cookie sheets.

- Stir together oats, sugar, flour, and salt.

- Melt butter and then add to the oat mixture. Mix thoroughly. Add egg and vanilla. Mix thoroughly.

- Drop dough by ½ teaspoonsful onto prepared cookie sheets. (These cookies really spread in the baking, so space at least 2″ apart on the cookie sheets.)

- Bake at 350° for 6–7 minutes. Remove cookie sheets from oven and set aside for 1 or 2 minutes. Remove cookies from cookie sheets with thin spatula and cool on wax paper or roll into a cylindrical shape and then cool on wax paper. Work quickly. If cookies begin to harden before they are removed from the cookie sheet, return to oven for one half minute.

- Heavily regrease cookie sheets before beginning second batch.

- Store cookies in air tight container in a cool dry place.

Meringue Kisses

A delicate confection that melts in your mouth . . .

2 egg whites, at room temperature
1 pinch salt
1 teaspoon vanilla extract
²/₃ cup sugar
1 cup finely chopped pecans
1 cup semi-sweet chocolate chips

Yield: 2 dozen

- Preheat oven to 350°. Line 2 cookie sheets with aluminum foil.

- With an electric mixer, beat egg whites until foamy. Continue beating and add salt and vanilla. When soft peaks form, add sugar one tablespoon at a time. Beat until stiff peaks form.

- With a wooden spoon, gently fold in the pecans and chocolate chips.

- Place heaping teaspoonsful of the batter on prepared cookie sheets.

- Put in preheated oven, close door and turn oven off. Do not open for at least 6 hours. May be left in oven over night. Store in an air tight container in a cool dry place.

Note: Cannot be made on a humid or rainy day.

Country Shortbread

These are more delicate than traditional shortbread.

1 cup butter (no substitutes)
²/₃ cup sugar
2 cups flour
¹/₂ cup whole wheat flour

Yield: 1 dozen

- Preheat oven to 300°.
- Cream together butter and sugar in food processor.
- Add both flours and mix thoroughly.
- Press dough into an 8″ × 8″ ungreased pan. Bake at 300° for 50–60 minutes or until shortbread is pale beige in color.
- Remove from oven, cool 5 minutes on a wire rack. Cut into squares while still warm.

Mini-Chip Cookies

More chips to the cookie . . . an idea whose time has come.

2	cups flour
1	teaspoon baking soda
1	teaspoon salt
1	cup butter, softened
1	cup brown sugar
1/2	cup sugar
1	egg
1	teaspoon vanilla extract
1	(12 ounce) package semi-sweet mini chocolate chips

Yield: 5 dozen

- Preheat oven to 350°.

- Mix together flour, baking soda, and salt. Set aside.

- Cream together butter and sugars. Add egg and vanilla and mix well. Add flour mixture and mix well. Stir in mini chocolate chips.

- Roll dough into small (3/4″ diameter) balls. Place balls 2″ apart on ungreased cookie sheets.

- Bake at 350° for 9–10 minutes. Watch cookies carefully. Remove them from the oven just as the edges begin to brown. The centers of the cookies will look almost uncooked.

Ginger Snaps

The kind your grandmother made. Enjoy them with a glass of milk and a few apple slices dusted with cinnamon sugar.

3/4	cup margarine
1	cup sugar
1	egg, beaten
4	tablespoons molasses
2	teaspoons baking soda
2	cups flour
1	teaspoon salt
1	teaspoon ground ginger
1	teaspoon ground cloves
1	teaspoon cinnamon
sugar	

Yield: 6 dozen

- In a food processor, cream together margarine and 1 cup sugar. Add egg and molasses. Process until well combined.

- Sift dry ingredients together. Add to creamed mixture and process until well combined.

- Chill dough for 2 hours.

- Preheat oven to 325°.

- Roll dough into small (3/4″ diameter) balls. Then roll in sugar, being sure to coat evenly.

- Place 2″ apart on ungreased cookie sheets and bake at 325° for 15 minutes.

Holly Cookies

You may vary the artwork on this cookie with the season or holiday . . . hearts for Valentines Day, daisies for Spring . . .

Cookies:

2	cups flour
1	cup sugar
1	teaspoon cinnamon
3/4	teaspoon baking powder
1/4	teaspoon salt
1/2	cup butter
1	egg, slightly beaten
1/4	cup milk
2/3	cup seedless raspberry jam

Icing:

2   cups confectioners sugar, sifted
1/2   teaspoon vanilla extract
2 – 3 tablespoons milk
red cinnamon candies
green food coloring

Yield: 4 1/2 dozen

The Cookies:

- Combine flour, sugar, cinnamon, baking powder, and salt. With a pastry blender or 2 knives used scissor fashion, cut in butter until small particles form. Make a well in the center of the mixture.

- Mix together the egg and milk. Pour into the well. Mix until dough is formed.

- Divide dough into 2 parts. Cover each part with plastic wrap and chill 3 – 5 hours.

- Preheat oven to 375°. Spray cookie sheets with non-stick spray.

- On a lightly floured surface, using a floured rolling pin, roll the dough to 1/8″ thickness. Using a 2″ diameter cookie cutter, cut into rounds.

- Place on prepared cookie sheet and bake at 375° for 8 – 10 minutes or until light brown around the edges.

- Remove cookies immediately from cookie sheet and cool on wax paper.

- Repeat rolling, cutting, and baking procedures until all the dough has been used.

- Spread 1/2 teaspoon of jam on one cookie and top with another. Repeat with all cookies.

Continued on next page

The Icing:

- In a small bowl, stir together confectioners sugar, vanilla, and enough milk to make a spreadable icing.

- Spread top of each cookie with icing. While icing is still wet place 3 cinnamon candies on top of each cookie. Allow icing to dry.

- Using a fine paint brush and the green food coloring, paint holly leaves and a stem on each cookie.

Snowballs

A holiday season tradition from generation to generation

1   cup unsalted butter, at room
       temperature
1/2   cup confectioners sugar
2   teaspoons almond extract
2   cups flour, sifted
1/4   teaspoon salt
1/2   cup chopped pecans
1/2   cup chopped almonds
confectioner's sugar

Yield: 6 dozen

- Preheat oven to 325°.

- In a food processor, cream together butter and 1/2 cup sugar. Add almond extract, flour, and salt. Process until well combined.

- Add nuts and process only until combined.

- Remove dough from processor. Roll dough into small (3/4″ diameter) balls.

- Place balls on an ungreased cookie sheet and bake at 325° for 20 minutes.

- Cool cookies on wax paper. When completely cool, roll in confectioners sugar. Store in an airtight cookie tin with wax paper between the layers of cookies.

Sugar Crisps

The measuring and the instructions are so easy that children love to make and eat these.

$^1/_2$ cup white sugar
$^1/_2$ cup brown sugar
$^1/_2$ cup margarine, softened
$^1/_2$ cup corn oil
1   egg
$^1/_2$ cup Rice Krispies cereal
$^1/_2$ cup oatmeal
$^1/_2$ cup coconut
$^1/_2$ cup chopped walnuts
1   teaspoon vanilla extract
$^1/_2$ teaspoon salt
$^1/_2$ teaspoon baking soda
$^1/_2$ teaspoon cream of tartar
$1^3/_4$ cups flour
sugar

Yield: 5 dozen

- Preheat oven to 350°.

- Combine all ingredients except extra sugar. Mix well.

- Roll into large ($1^1/_4$″ diameter) balls. Dip in extra sugar.

- Place balls, sugar side up, 2″ apart on ungreased cookie sheets. Bake at 350° for 10–15 minutes or until golden brown.

Sugar Cakes

A perfectly lovely, light, afternoon tea cookie

$^3/_8$ cup solid all-vegetable shortening
1   cup sugar
2   eggs
$^1/_2$ cup sour cream
1   teaspoon baking soda
$^1/_2$ teaspoon cream of tartar
$^1/_2$ teaspoon vanilla extract
$1^3/_4$ cups flour

Yield: 5 dozen

- Preheat oven to 375°.

- In a food processor, cream together shortening and sugar. Add eggs and sour cream. Process. Add baking soda, cream of tartar, vanilla, and flour. Process until well combined.

- Drop by teaspoonsful on ungreased cookie sheets.

- Bake at 375° for 8–10 minutes or until golden brown.

Oatmeal Apricot Bars

A good mid-morning snack with a cup of freshly brewed coffee

1½ cups unbleached flour
1½ cups old fashioned rolled oats,
    (not instant)
1   cup firmly packed brown sugar
½   teaspoon baking soda
¾   cup butter, at room temperature
1   cup apricot preserves

Yield: 1 dozen

- Preheat oven to 375°.
- Stir together flour, oats, sugar, and soda. With a pastry blender or 2 knives used scissor fashion, cut in butter until mixture resembles course crumbs.
- Press two-thirds of mixture into a 9″ × 9″ ungreased pan. Spread preserves over mixture. Sprinkle remaining third of mixture on top of preserves.
- Bake at 375° for 20 minutes. Remove from oven, cool and cut into bars. (Take extra care when cutting and removing bars from baking pan as the bars are easily broken.)

Back-to-Basic Brownies

Before store bought, packaged or instant brownies, there were brownies like these made at home.

2   (1 ounce) squares unsweetened
    chocolate
7   tablespoons butter
2   eggs
1   cup sugar
½   cup flour
½   cup chopped walnuts
1   teaspoon vanilla extract

Yield: 1 dozen

- Preheat oven to 350°. Grease and flour an 8″ × 8″ pan.
- Melt chocolate and butter in the top of a double boiler over hot, but not boiling water. Stir with a wooden spoon until smooth and well combined. Remove from heat and let cool.
- Beat the eggs well. Add the chocolate mixture and beat again. Blend in sugar, flour, nuts, and vanilla.
- Pour into prepared pan and bake at 350° for 25–30 minutes. Remove from oven, cool and cut into squares.

Crème de Menthe Brownies

An elegant dessert cookie that would compliment a parfait or accent a cookie assortment on a Viennese table.

Cake Layer:

1/2   cup butter, softened

1   cup sugar

4   eggs

1   cup flour

1/2   teaspoon salt

1   (16 ounce) can chocolate syrup

1   teaspoon vanilla extract

Mint Layer:

1/2   cup butter, softened

2   cups confectioners sugar

4   tablespoons green crème de menthe
      liqueur

Frosting:

1   (6 ounce) package semi-sweet
      chocolate chips

6   tablespoons butter

Yield: 4 dozen

The Cake Layer:
- Preheat oven to 350°. Grease 9″ × 13″ pan.

- Cream together butter and sugar. Beat in eggs. Add dry ingredients a little at a time, mixing well after each addition. Add chocolate syrup and vanilla. Mix well.

- Pour into prepared pan and bake at 350° for 30 minutes. Remove from oven and cool thoroughly.

The Mint Layer:
- Cream together butter and 1 cup confectioners sugar. Blend in crème de menthe. Blend in remaining cup of confectioners sugar. (If too soft, add 1 or 2 tablespoons confectioners sugar.)

- Spread on cooled cake layer and chill 30 minutes.

The Frosting:
- Melt chocolate and butter in the top of a double boiler over hot, but not boiling water. Stir with a wooden spoon until smooth and well combined.

- Spread on top of chilled mint layer. Chill for 1 hour before cutting into 1 1/2″ squares. Serve chilled.

Rocky Road Fudge Bars

Very different, very rich, very chocolatey . . .

Bars:
1   ounce unsweetened chocolate
1/2   cup butter
1   cup sugar
1   cup flour
1/2   cup chopped pecans
1   teaspoon baking powder
1   teaspoon vanilla extract
2   eggs

Filling:
1   (8 ounce) package cream cheese, softened
1/4   cup butter, softened
1/2   cup sugar
2   tablespoons flour
1   egg
1/2   teaspoon vanilla extract
1/4   cup chopped pecans
1   cup semi-sweet chocolate chips
2   cups miniature marshmallows

Frosting:
1   ounce unsweetened chocolate
1/4   cup butter
2   ounces cream cheese (reserved from filling)
1/4   cup milk
1   (1 pound) box confectioners sugar
1   teaspoon vanilla extract

Yield: 3 dozen

The Bars:
- Preheat oven to 350°. Grease a 9″ × 13″ pan.

- Melt chocolate and butter in the top of a double boiler over hot, but not boiling water. Stir with a wooden spoon until smooth and well combined.

- Pour chocolate mixture into a medium size bowl and add remaining bar ingredients. Mix well. Spread evenly in prepared pan.

The Filling:
- In a small bowl, cream together 6 ounces cream cheese, butter, and sugar. Add flour, egg, and vanilla. Blend until smooth and fluffy. Stir in pecans. Spread over chocolate mixture. Sprinkle with chocolate chips.

- Bake at 350° for 25 – 35 minutes. Sprinkle with marshmallows and bake 2 minutes longer.

The Frosting:
- Prepare frosting while bars are baking.

- In a large saucepan, over low heat, melt chocolate with butter, 2 ounces of cream cheese, and milk.

- Remove from heat. Using a wooden spoon, stir in confectioners sugar and vanilla until mixture is smooth and well combined.

- As soon as you remove bars from oven, pour frosting over the bars and swirl together with marshmallows. Cool thoroughly. When cool, cut into bars.

Date Fingers

Just right for packing in a picnic basket or lunch box

1	cup butter
2	cups sugar
3	eggs
1	teaspoon baking soda
2	teaspoons water
1	(8 ounce) package pitted dates
3	cups flour, sifted
1	teaspoon cinnamon
1	teaspoon nutmeg
1	teaspoon pumpkin spice
1/4	teaspoon ground cloves
dash salt	
1	cup chopped walnuts
2	tablespoons sugar

Yield: 5 dozen

- Using an electric mixer, cream together butter and 2 cups sugar. Continue beating until mixture is light and fluffy. Add eggs one at a time, beating well after each addition.

- In a cup, combine baking soda and water. Mix well to break up any lumps. Pour into creamed mixture and beat.

- Snip the dates into small pieces with scissors. (Snipping with scissors is easier than chopping dates with a knife.) Add dates to creamed mixture and beat.

- Sift together flour, cinnamon, nutmeg, pumpkin spice, cloves, and salt. With the mixer beating, gradually add the flour mixture to the creamed mixture, being sure to combine well. Beat in nuts. Chill dough for 2 hours.

- Preheat oven to 350°.

- Divide dough into 6 equal parts. On a lightly floured board, form each piece of dough into a roll 10″ long by 3/4″ in diameter. Place 2 rolls on each ungreased cookie sheet. Flatten rolls to a 1/4″ thickness. Sprinkle with sugar.

- Bake at 350° for 15 minutes. Remove from oven and immediately make diagonal slices 1 1/2″ apart to form fingers. Remove date fingers from cookie sheet and cool on wax paper. When cool, store in an air tight container in a cool dry place.

Double Dutch Nut Clusters

Candy store perfection . . . so easy and yet so good!

1 cup semi-sweet chocolate chips
1 cup milk chocolate chips
2 cups unsalted dry roasted peanuts,
    cashews or almonds

Yield: 4 dozen

- Line 2 cookie sheets with wax paper.
- Melt chocolate in the top of double boiler over hot, not boiling, water. Stir with a wooden spoon until smooth.
- Cool for 5 minutes, *but do not refrigerate.*
- Stir in nuts. Be sure to coat nuts well with chocolate. Drop by teaspoons onto prepared cookie sheets. Refrigerate overnight. Store in an air tight container in a cool dry place.

Note: Do not prepare on a rainy day.

Buckeye Balls

Children love rolling and dipping these popular treats.

2 cups creamy peanut butter
1/2 cup unsalted butter, at room
    temperature
1 teaspoon vanilla extract
1 (1 pound) box confectioners sugar
1 (6 ounce) package semi-sweet
    chocolate chips
2 tablespoons solid all-vegetable
    shortening

Yield: 5 dozen

- Line 2 cookie sheets with wax paper.
- In a large bowl mix peanut butter, butter, vanilla, and confectioners sugar with hands to form a smooth dough. Make individual olive size balls by rolling the mixture in the palms of your hands.
- Place balls on cookie sheets and chill one hour.
- Melt chocolate and shortening in the top of a double boiler over hot, not boiling water. Stir with a wooden spoon until smooth. Pour chocolate mixture into a small bowl.
- Remove balls from refrigerator. Insert wooden toothpicks and dip halfway into chocolate. Place coated balls back on the prepared cookie sheets and chill for 30 minutes or until chocolate coating is firm. Store in a plastic container in the refrigerator. Serve chilled.

Easy Caramel Corn

A family room snack for your armchair quarterback!

1 cup popcorn kernels
1/2 cup margarine
1/2 cup light brown sugar
1/4 cup light corn syrup
1/4 teaspoon salt
1/4 teaspoon baking soda
1 teaspoon vanilla extract

Yield: 1 big bowl

- Pop kernels in two batches, using 1/2 cup kernels for each batch.

- In a medium size glass or ceramic bowl place margarine, sugar, syrup, and salt. Cook 4 minutes on high in microwave. Add baking soda and vanilla and stir to combine.

- Pour popcorn into a large brown paper grocery bag. Pour syrup mixture over popcorn while shaking bag. Fold bag closed. Shake well.

- Put bag in microwave and cook 1 1/2 minutes on high. Remove and shake well. Return to microwave and cook 1 minute on high. Remove and shake well. Return to microwave and cook for 30 seconds on high. Remove and shake well.

- Put into a large bowl. Let cool and eat.

Honeynutters

A no-bake snack made and enjoyed by children of all ages!

1 (8 ounce) package cream cheese, at room temperature
1 tablespoon honey
1/3 cup chopped raisins
2 tablespoons chopped walnuts
3/4 cup graham cracker crumbs

Yield: 2 1/2 dozen

- Line a cookie sheet with wax paper.

- Mix together cream cheese, honey, raisins, and nuts.

- Make individual olive size balls. Roll each ball in graham cracker crumbs.

- Place on prepared cookie sheet and chill until firm. Serve chilled.

Mocha Truffles

Serve with after dinner coffee . . . they're sinfully divine.

12   *ounces semi-sweet chocolate*
4   *tablespoons unsalted butter, softened*
1/2   cup coffee flavored liqueur
unsweetened cocoa powder
sweetened chocolate drink mix powder
confectioners sugar

Yield: 2 1/2 dozen

- Melt chocolate in the top of a double boiler over simmering water. Remove from heat. With a wooden spoon, beat in the butter. Add liqueur and continue beating.

- Pour chocolate mixture into a small bowl. Cover and refrigerate until firm, about 2 hours.

- Roll into balls using a teaspoonful of the mixture for each ball. Roll one third of the balls in cocoa powder. Roll one third of the balls in chocolate drink mix powder. Roll one third of the balls in confectioners sugar. Refrigerate until serving time.

Note: These can be frozen up to 4 months.

Chocolate–Macadamia Brittle

Out of this world!

1   *cup unsalted macadamia nuts,*
        coarsely chopped
1/2   cup unsalted butter, at room
        temperature
1/2   cup sugar
1   *tablespoon light corn syrup*
3/4   cup chopped sweet chocolate.

Yield: 1 1/2 dozen

- Line bottom and sides of a 9″ round cake pan with aluminum foil. Butter foil.

- Mix nuts, butter, sugar, and corn syrup in a medium size saucepan. Cook over low heat until sugar dissolves. Increase heat. Cook and stir the syrup to the soft-crack stage (280°).

- Pour into prepared pan. Sprinkle with chocolate. As chocolate melts, spread evenly over brittle.

- Cool 15 minutes. Remove candy from pan and peel off foil. When completely cooled, break into bite size pieces.

Note: Do not prepare on a rainy day.

Cookbook Committee

CO-CHAIRMEN 1989–90:
Marylea Schmidt   Sharon Quaintance

CO-CHAIRMEN 1987–89:
Thelma Negley   Victoria Chane

CHAIRMAN 1986–87:
Linda Parker

COMMITTEE 1986–90:

Phyliss Anderson
Liz Atkinson
Nancy Barone
Susan Belka
Gay Borchert
Karen Holly Brown
Julia Buteaux
Joann Cameron
Nancy Carle
Debra Chambliss
Isabel Chason
Liz Clothier
Marnie Coates
Sandy Codd
Alice Cutler
Diane D'Alconzo
Patti Daly
Julie Farris
Heidi Gammon
Susan Graham
Brenda Grant
Ellen Griswold
Susan Gross

Marla Gusmer
Julia Hanson
Laura Hardin
Missy Howard
Jennifer Hyde
Marianne Jason
Jennifer Jeffrey
Ruth Kollmer
C. Merry LeBlond
Kathleen Mastracchio
Stacey McHugh
June Meehan
Betsy Merclean
Susan Morris
Jennifer Farris Moss
Carolyn Mulligan
Kerry O'Brien
Amy Peters
Pat Pollara
Nancy Pope
Nancy Puglio
Sharon Quaintance
Susan Raphel

Cathyann Ray
Dana Rich
Barbara Sandelands
Diane Schaffrath
Marylea Schmidt
Catherine Smith
Nancy Stewart
Betsy Szlasa
Lisa Taylor
Lisa Thebault
Kori Theis
Jean Thomas
Susan Thomas
Hally Toia
Kay Vallario
Nancy Vandenberg
Nancy Walsh
Livia Waters
Blair Wilson
Kirstie Wilson
Annette Worthington
Jean Zinngrabe

Contributors

The Cookbook Committee expresses its grateful appreciation to League members and friends who shared their ideas and recipes and gave unselfishly of their time and talents. Each recipe has been tested for accuracy and excellence. We regret that we were unable to include many recipes which were submitted, due to similarity or availability of space.

A special thank you to our families who have been so patient and supportive during the past 3 years.

Ande Albright
Nancy Alexander
Janet D. Allocca
Kristin Altar
Amy Altenburger
Carol Anderson
Phyllis S. Anderson
Lori Anthony
Daralyn Gordon Arata
Kathleen Badcock
Maureen Badcock
Dale K. Badenoch
Astri Baille
Linda Baines
Linda Baker
Sheri Ball
Terri Barker
Ruth Barney
Nancy Ruth Barone
Tina Barsh
Deb Bates
Lillie Bayless
Mary Ann Belka
Susan Elliott Belka
Roberta Bennett
Bob Beran
Lynn Beran
Ann Bernhard
Judy Bickel
Melissa Bilger
Alsion Bippart
Sissy Bolcar
Phyllis L. Bonanno
Gay Borchert
Sue Bosland
Jinx Boutwell
Katie Bradford
Joan Brady
Suzanne Brask
Catherine Brawner
Judith Browne
Karen Brownell
Susan Bruen
Helen H. Bryant
Sherry Burke
Vivian Burk
Bruce Burns
Carrie McCoy Bush
George Cadwallader

Nancy Cadwallader
June Caffrey
Carol Camerino
Joann Cameron
Susie Carlman
Marilyn Case
Debi Cass
Christine Catanzaro
Pamela Chamberlain
Debra Chambliss
Victoria P. Chane
Isabel Scott Chason
Patricia B. Chobrda
Esther Christensen
Barbara C. Cifelli
Ellen Thomas Clapp
Derbigny Clark
Garrett Ross Clark
Maryjo Clendenny
Jennifer Clow
Marnie Coates
Paul Coates
Jackie Connelly
Mrs. William Connelly
Nancy Rieman Cook
Elizabeth Cooke
Helen Cornell
Debi Smith Corrigan
Debbie Crane
Kyle Cunningham
Alice D. Cutler
Diane D'Alconzo
Kathleen Daly
Patricia Daly
Cathleen Dayton
Cathy DeBovis
Allen deCastro
Janet Del Chiaro
Jewel S. Dennis
Holly Denton
Judith Dickinson
Mary Ellen Dill
Anne N. Dodd
Helen Donald
Jill Dunn
V. Dawn L. Dupak
Mary Egan
Ann Emery
Julieanne Ennis

June G. Enos
Mrs. David H. Eshman
Amanda C. Evans
Annabelle Evans
Barbara Evans
Karen A. Evans
Pamela Fairley
Julia A. Farley
Jill E. Farris
Joan E. Farris
Julie E. Farris
Barbara Feinour
Dana Ferrell
Mrs. Thomas E. Ferrell
Mary Flavin
Jennifer Fleischer
Susan Fleming
Billie Flynn
Sally Forester
Leslie Forman
Nancy P. Fox
Lynda Franklin
Claire Gabelli
Camille Gaines
Elizabeth Gainis
Jill M. Gates
Mrs. James S. Geiringer
Judy Geller
Gayle Gildermann
Melinda A. Gilligan
Mariben S. Glasscock
Stacy Golding
Elizabeth Ann Graham
Brenda Grant
Marcia Grafton
Roberta Greer
Karen Y. Grobert
Cheryl Gross
Laura Gruber
Suzy Gumm
Jan Gurgel
Anne Marie Hague
Terri Haley
Carmelita Hall
Catherine Hall
Julia Hanson
Laura Hardin
Pamela B. Harding
Chris Harrill

Kathleen Hastings
Sandra Hawrylo
Carol Head
Marty Herlong
Karen Hilker
Polly Hill
Jennifer Hiser
Kent Hiser
Betsy Holdsworth
Betsy Flynn Hollo
George P. Hollo
Katherine R. Holt
Marin (Missy) Howard
Joanne L. Howell
Eunice Huettner
Carolyn Hughes
Nancy Hults-Rubin
Jennifer Hyde
Joan Hyde
Mrs. Walter Ismael
Jennifer Jeffrey
Laura N. Jennings
Mrs. Erik Johnson
Marguerite C. Johnson
Mary Beth Johnson
Nan Johnson
Tina Johnson
Nancy Jones
Patricia Shears Jones
Claudia Kane
Jo Anne Karns
Bonnie Kauffman
Elizabeth Kay
Abby Kean
Patti Kendrick
Andy Kerr
Bill Kerr
Doug Kerr
Nan Kerr
Pamela Snite Kerr
Audrey Kimball
Dorliss King
Marianne King
Mindy Kirby
Betsy Klausing
Helen Cornell Koenig
Candace Kurlak
Dee LaForte
Deborah Lambert

Mrs. Donald Lamobell
Lee Anne Lan
Mary Ann Langdon
Elaine Lawrason
Syril T. Lebbad
C. Merry Le Blond
Rita Lee
Jean Leimert
Ann P. Lewis
Betsy Lewis
Eileen Lindeman
Susan Little
Susan Livera
Julie Lowe
Kay Ludecke
Patricia Ludlam
Janet Lynch
Elizabeth Lyons
Bobbie MacGregor
Ann MacLeod
Kay Malone
Lucy Frye Marston
Sally Martin
Kathy McAdoo
Judy McClellan
Nan Tull McDaniel
Megan McEnroe
Joan McFarland
Mrs. James J. McIntosh
Betsy McKeever
Carol A. McKinney
Alison M. McMahon
Janet McMillan
Merrie McNair
Linda Shehan McNeer
June C. Meehan
Lisa Seals Meek
Joan Meier
Susan Meier
Claire Thompson Meister
Mrs. G. Jeff Mennen
Betsy MerClean
Penelope Merrill
Lynn Meyer
Perla Meyer
Alfred Meyers
Diane Meyers
Helen W. Meyers
Pamela Meyers
Amie Michel
Jane Mignarelli
Kathleen Miller
Susan Miller
Ginger Miller-Jones
Pam Misiewicz
Wendy Mitchell
Marcia W. Mix
Jean Montgomery
Patricia Moody

Susan Morris
Nancy Morrow
Irene Mortko
Dennis Moser
Susan Thomas Moser
Jennifer Farris Moss
Mary Lou Moss
Patricia Muchmore
Rita Muldoon
Carolyn Mulligan
Eloise Mulvihill
Christine E. Murphy
Yvonne Murphy
Joan Murray
Nancy Murray
Amanda Myers
Pamela W. Myers
Barbara Malia Narus
June A. Nash
Melanie Naumann
Ina Nechita
Mike Negley
Thelma Negley
Mae Neupert
Mrs. Gary A. Neuser
Mrs. John Nice
Margaret D. Nicholas
Nance Nixon
Judith Nussbaum
Peggy Oakes
Jill M. Oates
Norrie Oelkers
Ruthee Oelschlager
Susan Oldendorp
Cheryl Outlaw
Linda Cardillo Pacchiano
Linda Adams Parker
Joan P. Partridge
Bernice Paton
Carolyn Peters
Sandra Petrell
Bobbi Phillips
Ruth K. Phillips
Anne Pierce
Lisa D. Pierson
Annette Pone
Nancy Pope
Christina Carroll-Porczynski
Nancy Puglio
Sharon S. Quaintance
Elizabeth R. Ramee
Carole Ramsey
Marianne Rapps
Cathy Ann Ray
Joan D. Ray
Lisa Reed
Cathy Reilly
Elizabeth Reiss
Nancy Reynolds

Mary Rianhard
Dana Rich
Susan H. Richardson
Suzanne Ringwood
Mandy Rogers
Judy Roman
Susan Root
Diane Seutter Rose
Susan Rost
Karen Rovick
Joann Ruffing
Catherine Ruhl
Mariann Ruth
Paula Ruth
Ruth M. Ryan
Margaret Sabo
Barbara Sandelands
Maria K. Sapol
Beth Saradarian
J.D. Sawyer
Mary G. Sawyer
Augusta Scattergood
Valerie E. Schafer
Diane Schaffrath
Linda Scheutze
Jean Schilllings
Kay Schlough
Marylea O'Reilly Schmidt
Joan Schneider
Susan Schneider
Hank Schuyers
Dale Scolnick
Darby Scott
Ann Seals
Peggy Segalas
Dona Talbot Seutter
Suzanne Shearer
Sherry Sheehan
Katherine H. Sheeleigh
Cathryn Shiver
Jean Shunk
Helen Sinnis
Ashley Skurla
Catherine T. Smith
Mel Somina
Debra Snyder
Alice Sparks
Mary Spencer
Madeleine Spies
Evelyn Spinner
Lynne Stagi
Jane Steinkopf
Mrs. W.B. Stevenson
Nancy J. Stewart
Nancy Strathearn
Marina Striggles
Debby Strong
Jimmy Sutton

Judy Sutton
Betsy Szlasa
Carolyn Szlasa
John Szlasa
Marilyn Sztuk
Ann Tannen
Heather Tannen
Lisa D. Taylor
Lisa L. Thebault
Jane B. Thomas
Susan Thomas
Janet W. Thompson
Joan Titus
Teri Tobler
Hally Toia
Carole S. Tomlinson
Clark Tomlinson
Jack Tomlinson
Sarah Tower
Susan Trimble
Mary G. Tucker
Irene & Robert Upton
Nancy Upton
Kathryn Urban
Nancy VandenBerg
Mrs. Robert Van
    Valkenburg
Cathleen Vermylen
Amy Walling
Mary Ellen Walsh
Nancy Walsh
Suzanne Walters
Carolyn T. Ward
Lorraine Ward
Mary Ward
Brian Waters
Susan Heidenwolf Weaver
Martha Weaver
Carolyn Wehner
Ann B. Westerlund
Peg Whitney
Bonnie Jones Wicks
Pam Wildrick
Suzanne Wille
Louise Monte Williams
Kirstie Wilson
Lynne Wilson
Shelly Winter
Mary Witunshi
Leigh L. Wohlfarth
Annette Worthington
Nancy Wynant
Christine Yundt
Lee Zackrison
JoAnn Zagari
Claude Zinngrabe
Danny Zinngrabe
Jean Zinngrabe

Index

The Junior League of Morristown, Inc. • 7 Kings Place • Morristown, NJ 07960 • 973-605-5386

Please send me ____ copies of *A MATTER OF TASTE* at $21.95 each $ _____

Plus postage and handling: first book at $3.00 $ _____

                     additional books at $2.00 each $ _____

      New Jersey residents please add sales tax of $1.32 per book $ _____

                                     TOTAL $ _____

Please make checks payable to *A MATTER OF TASTE* or charge to:

❏ Visa   or   ❏ MasterCard   Card Number _____

Expiration date _____   Signature _____

Mail to: NAME _____

           ADDRESS _____

           CITY _____ STATE _____ ZIP _____

Proceeds from the sale of A MATTER OF TASTE will benefit the community through the many worthwhile projects of The Junior League of Morristown, Inc.

....

Please send me ____ copies of *A MATTER OF TASTE* at $21.95 each $ _____

Plus postage and handling: first book at $3.00 $ _____

                     additional books at $2.00 each $ _____

      New Jersey residents please add sales tax of $1.32 per book $ _____

                                     TOTAL $ _____

Please make checks payable to *A MATTER OF TASTE* or charge to:

❏ Visa   or   ❏ MasterCard   Card Number _____

Expiration date _____   Signature _____

Mail to: NAME _____

           ADDRESS _____

           CITY _____ STATE _____ ZIP _____

Proceeds from the sale of A MATTER OF TASTE will benefit the community through the many worthwhile projects of The Junior League of Morristown, Inc.